MAKE A FRESH START

MAKE A FRESH START

Margaret Korving

First published in 1988 by
Kogan Page Ltd, 120 Pentonville Road, London N1 9JN

Typeset from author's disks by Saxon Printing Ltd., Derby.

Printed and bound in Great Britain by Biddles Limited of Guildford.

British Library Cataloguing in Publication Data
Korving, Margaret
Make a fresh start : a careers guide for adults.
1. Great Britain. Vocational education
I. Title
370.11'3'0941

ISBN 1-85091-659-4

Contents

Preface

If you have picked up this book, you probably feel your life could be better in some way. You may wish to improve your work or home life, your leisure time or your prospects. The ideas, profiles and lists of courses in Make a Fresh Start can help you change your life a little, or a lot.

Robin, a former secretary, decided to train as an aerobics teacher through an evening course, so that she could start her own exercise studio. Peter, after 18 years as a manager in the construction industry, took a full–time course to qualify as a social worker. Andrew, an industrial chemist, used redundancy money to pay for a retraining course to teach English as a foreign language. (He flew off to a job in Japan five days after qualifying.) June retrained in the evenings as a Tour Manager. Hugo studied motorcycle repair full–time –he used to work in horticulture. Eddy is learning musical instrument technology after 15 years as a cabinet–maker. *You too could change.*

Many students whom I met through my BBC Radio series 'Back on Course' in the mid–1980's contributed ideas for this book. Other contributions came from colleges that I visited to do research for careers features that I was writing for the *Daily Telegraph, She* and *Home and Freezer Digest*. Many listeners and readers also shared their ideas with me for Make a Fresh Start. I thank them all. A special thank-you to the colleges who responded so swiftly to me request for confirmation that courses on which I had gathered information in 1987 were still running in 1988. Many have not only continued their special provision for mature students, but have put on additional courses to suit the growing number of people who want to make a fresh start.

Margaret Korving

Examine Your Life

Why do you want to Change?

YOU NEED A NEW JOB

Redundancy is nothing unusual these days, but you may have to retrain, or move to where the work is, or employ yourself (using redundancy pay to set up in business), or organise a mix of part–time, voluntary and self–employed work. Or you might keep your right to state benefits by studying part–time under the Employment Training Scheme or the 21–hour rule (details in 'Costs and Grants' section later).

YOU NEED MORE MONEY

Get it by improving your qualifications or retraining for something that pays better or lets you earn in your spare time because you have acquired a new freelance skill. You can reduce your outgoings by moving into a new social circle with other students, by starting up in a home–based business or by getting a job with extras – subsidised accommodation or a company car.

YOU'D LIKE MORE FRIENDS

Find these by training for work that is more companionable, or by switching to a work/study area that attracts mainly men or mainly women if you want to meet the opposite sex. Give up your job to study at college, where you'll have the chance to make friends who share your interests. Or start on a spare–time course that lets you meet new people.

YOU'RE BORED WITH YOUR JOB

Well, you may not need to change your work as such – just the place where you do it (by moving from the country to the town, for instance). Or, if you have transferable skills, you could change employers – say, from being a secretary in a commercial firm to being secretary to a novelist or on a farm. You can retrain for a new lifestyle, go self–employed, add spare–time or voluntary work, or take an evening course that's so demanding, that you'll need your boring job for a rest!

YOU'RE AT A LOOSE END

All of a sudden, the family is grown up and you're free to please yourself. Or you've finally paid that mortgage and can take early retirement – to do what? You can get help with decision–making through a New Opportunities course, follow that lifelong dream to go to university (there are often lower entry requirements for mature students), or move to the seaside/country/city where you've always fancied living, and build up a new set of interests and friends through your personal choice of courses.

YOU WANT BETTER PROSPECTS

You may be unqualified, or, have out–dated skills, or no skills at all: then you really need to restart and retrain. Perhaps you are in a job with a top–heavy management structure, so you need to learn how to find new employers. Maybe you need extra knowledge – computer know–how, for instance – so that you can divert into a more promising job area or take exams you didn't pass at school. On the other hand, you may have paper qualifications but no practical skills or, conversely, want to retire from practical jobs to catch up on subjects like art or music or literature that you've never had time to think about. Or you could benefit from 'add–on' courses to extend your prospects and brighten your future.

YOU NEED SOMEWHERE TO LIVE

Unemployment often equals homelessness. You can look for jobs which traditionally have residential perks and train for them as a mature student. Then again, some educational courses will give you a roof over your head while you learn (some universities and polytechnics offer accommodation on campus for most of their students; so do some schools of nursing). And, once you have a steady job, getting rooms and flats will be easier. Organisations like banks and building societies which provide home loans and housing groups are often more sympathetic to people who have clearly tried to help themselves.

YOU'RE RESPONSIBLE FOR OTHERS – BUT NEED A CHANGE

If you have to look after children or an elderly or disabled person, the answer may be self–employment, unemployment plus home-based study, or finding a way to train for jobs with unsocial hours (so that others can 'home–sit' while you work evenings, nights or weekends). Job–sharing is another idea, once you have skills to offer. Or you can follow a home/study/work/leisure plan with other responsible relatives, or maybe people you meet through a single–parent group. If you live far from a bus route or are scared of late–night travel after evening classes, distance learning or short holiday courses (while a friend stands in for you at home) may widen your horizons. Once you start digging for information, you meet other people who have tackled the same kind of problem and may have solutions new to you. The Open University, Open College and Open Learning Federations are reaching out to people with home responsibilities to make it easier for them to improve their circumstances.

How about some examples? Check the self–assessment section, next, for illustrations of needs, problems, priorities – and solutions.

WHERE ARE YOU NOW?

This range of questions and answers illustrates familiar problems experienced by people who want to make a fresh start, and should help you assess what are the most important factors you personally need to take into account. The section headed 'What Are Your Needs?' pinpoints reasons for wanting to take a course to change your life. In 'What Are Your Problems?' ways are suggested of overcoming the difficulties that often prevent people doing what they want. And the section headed 'What Are Your Priorities?' shows how to pick out the kind of course that will meet your personal objectives.

This is done in question–and–answer forms, because when people write to newspaper, magazine and radio careers advisory services, the same sorts of questions crop up again and again. No two people have exactly the same needs, problems and priorities, but you can often identify ways to tackle your own situation from the answer to someone else's problem.

WHAT ARE YOUR NEEDS?

What is the main reason you have decided to make a fresh start?

INDEPENDENCE

'I need a skill, qualification or training that will mean I can earn something for myself, regardless of where I may move and my previous skills. I need to extend my abilities and add to my knowledge to feel secure.'

Take a look at skills you can take with you, maybe to let you set up in a small way at home – for instance, musical instrument technology or motorcycle maintenance, or a universally useful training such as selling or dressmaking or lorry driving that you could earn from in any part of the country.

STATUS

'I want to take a course with an end product tht shows I have worked hard and achieved a recognised target. I won't be really satisfied until I have a national qualification, or a job or business of my own that gives me a place in society.'

Check courses that lead to nationally recognised qualifications like the BTEC Higher National Diploma or Certificate, or to the awards of a professional institute. If you're thinking of a small business, learn the ropes first – the 'Small Business and Self–Employment' section of this book lists a range of possibilities from running a guest house to owning a shop. (People are more likely to invest in you if you can show you've trained for your business.)

COMPANIONSHIP

'I want to make contact with people who share my interests, so I can feel part of a group and have the pleasure of talking over subjects I find interesting, without feeling I might be boring people.'

Many universities, polytechnics and colleges offer this sort of opportunity – you might begin by reading the reports included in the 'Degree and Advanced Courses' section from students at Hatfield Polytechnic (Southern and Eastern region). Dotted through the book, though, you'll find examples of people who've met others like themselves as the result of taking a study course. It may not have been their primary reason for studying – often they had to retrain, or needed qualifications for promotion – but making new friends with the same interests was a bonus.

CREATIVITY

'I need to do something that develops the creative side of my nature. It's all very well being useful and capable, but I have ideas and imagination, and I won't be satisfied until I have tried my hand at creating something original.'

Throughout this book you'll find examples of 'creative courses', from working in silver to floristry and from studio ceramics to wrought ironwork. Opportunities are not simply on a leisure course basis. Mature students may be accepted on high–level art courses on the basis of work they have done in their own time. Check the 'Retraining and New Skills' as well as 'Degree and Advanced' course lists.

CONTRAST

'My life is dull and predictable. There's no variety in my job and my responsibilities involve doing the same thing at the same time, most days. I am looking for an interest or a new career that will be a complete contrast to everything else that I have done.'

How about book and archive conservation? Or training to be a tour manager? Or taking a part–time Registered Nurse training? Here are just three possibilities. Whatever your age, you might find it helpful to skim through the 'New Directions for Late Starters' suggestions on p.OO.

SERVICE

'I want to get some skills that will let me be useful to people who need help. There's nothing basically wrong with the way I live at present except that I feel I could be contributing instead of just being sorry for people. You know what they say – 'if you're not part of the solution, you're part of the problem.'

Many of the colleges in this book have devised special courses for people who want to contribute to the community. The range is vast, from training for voluntary service at Rockingham College in Rotherham to postgraduate courses in art and drama therapy at Hertfordshire College of Art. Meanwhile, bear in mind that upper age limits for entry to nursing, remedial and social care professions are going up every year; not just because the supply of young entrants is running out, but because training authorities who have given a chance to mature people have discovered how valuable their 'life experience' can be.

WHAT ARE YOUR PROBLEMS?

What difficulties must you tackle before you can make a fresh start?

FEAR OF FAILING

'I disliked school and got out as soon as possible. Even though I have to get qualifications to get a job (or to get out of a boring one),I dread going back to the classroom and making a fool of myself in a crowd of teenagers, just as I used to make a fool of myself at school.'

You can ensure that you will be with people who have to face similar problems if you choose a 'Fresh Start' or 'Return to Learn' course, or if you begin at home, using a 'Distance Learning' route (this is the up–market term for postal courses).

POOR SCHOOL RECORD

'I didn't dislike school, but I didn't get much out of it, either. I did well in a few subjects that I liked, but there aren't many opportunities for people without English and Maths, which I failed. And it's hardly likely I'll pass them after all these years if I couldn't do it when I was young.'

'Open College' and 'Access' schemes are examples of courses meant for you. Many colleges offer special provision for people who need basic exam passes in subjects like English and Maths. For Maths, you can look also at Polymaths, which goes from beginner to degree entry standard. Incidentally, teachers who advertise in the paper that they coach children for reading, writing and arithmetic will also often take adults for private lessons. Sometimes they'll even visit your home to teach you.

CAN'T KEEP UP

'I've tried taking evening classes but I can't seem to keep up because I keep missing classes, owing to overtime and shift work. What I need is something adaptable. A 'plan–it–yourself' course would be ideal, but I don't know that I have the staying power to work away at a postal course all on my own. Any ideas?'

You're the sort of person for whom flexible study courses have been devised. 'FlexiStudy' courses were evolved by the National Extension College, but there are now a number of adaptations of this system, in which you learn mostly at home but with access to a local tutor for help and encouragement. NEC can give a list of colleges using their system; your own college may have its own flexible learning system too. The word 'Open' attached to a university or college usually means flexible learning methods, as well as flexible entry requirements.

LEFT SCHOOL WITH NO QUALIFICATIONS

'My daughter showed me some of the things she had to learn for GCSE and it would be quite beyond me. Finding out how little I know has made me even keener to catch up (because coping at work has shown me I'm not incapable of learning). But I do need to start from scratch. There weren't GCSEs or O–levels in my day! Is there any kind of preparatory course for people in my situation?'

No problem. 'Basic Skills' courses start from the beginning with English and Maths – or maybe the course will be called Literacy and Numeracy. Colleges tend to use their own titles for the same course but you can easily see which are designed for beginners. There are also some special courses for new immigrants (or old immigrants who have never quite got to grips with the language of their adopted country). 'Open College' schemes are another possibility, and often let you learn mostly at home. Look at the range of 'Pre–Entry' courses listed in this book for examples, and ask your student daughter or son to collect prospectuses or leaflets from local colleges, which will have the latest ideas for people who are restarting.

FAILED A-LEVELS

'I gave up after two attempts at A–levels. Now I'm stuck, with no hope of ever getting to university, which was always my dream. Yet I'm not a fool and I find it easy to pick up theory related to my job. Is there any way in which I can offer my job qualifications, instead of A–levels, for entry to a degree course, because I do still want to go to university?'

Universities, polytechnics and colleges are ahead of you! They've discovered that people with work–related qualifications (many of which involved studying in the evening as well as holding down a day job) are a very good bet when it comes to degree course study. Warwick University's research shows they do better than conventional A–level entrants. You can offer BTEC (or the old ONC/D or HNC/D) or many professional course qualifications instead of A–levels, and there is a range of specially designed 'Access' courses for mature students to take instead of A–levels, to prepare them for degree level work. The ECCTIS Handbook (see the 'Information' section in this book) shows you which universities, polytechnics and colleges will accept job–related qualifications for entry. Check the sections headed 'Sample and Access Courses', 'Pre–Entry' and 'Degree and Advanced Courses' for more ideas.

EXAM NERVES

'I don't want to take exams. They always made me sick with nerves at school, and I never did myself credit. But I do find certain subjects interesting, and I'd like to pick up where I left off in some areas, if only I can avoid tests. Any chance of colleges taking people who *don't* want to pass exams and get qualifications?'

University Extra–Mural courses are primarily for people who study for pleasure and interest. But you can also pick out single courses from degrees at many polytechnics. This is usually called being an 'Associate' student, or in some cases a 'Visiting' or 'Listening' student. City of Birmingham Polytechnic and Hatfield Polytechnic are two examples of polytechnics with this sort of scheme. You do not have to take an exam at the end of such a course (though you may find you want to do so, in which case you can apply). Many Open University courses are designed for non–examation candidates – people who want to learn for the pleasure of studying. And there are plenty of short courses, open to non–examination candidates, including one–day courses (University of Kent), evening courses, Saturday study days and summer schools (Middlesex Polytechnic, for example). NB: it's worth remembering that you can also take an exam course without applying to take an exam. In other words, if you want to do GCE A–level English Literature, you can go on the course, but won't be forced to fill in the exam entry form and pay your fee!

WHAT ARE YOUR PRIORITIES?

GUARANTEED JOB PROSPECTS

'I need to qualify for a new job. I'm prepared to learn full–time and work hard, but there must be a genuine chance of a job at the end of it, and I must stand a chance of getting that job. How can I pick a course with real prospects of employment?'

Look first for employer–based training. Examples: for off–licence or service station management; for health service jobs like nurse or operating theatre technician; for social service careers, like fireman or police officer. Look out too for courses sponsored by the Manpower Services Commission. (As this book goes to press, it is being proposed that the MSC should be retitled the 'Training Commission', but, because this change won't be reflected in college prospectuses, look out for the initials 'MSC' in front of a course title.) When a course is funded by the MSC, it's usually a clear indication that the job prospects have been checked out, since the money to support the course comes from government retraining funds. Again, the European Social Fund provides money to support some courses which improve people's employment prospects, so the initials 'ESF' also suggest that demand for people with the skills concerned has been investigated and found satisfactory. If ever you're not sure about prospects, get advice from trade unions, professional associations or employers' federations – it's in their interest to encourage new trainees in skill shortage areas (and not to encourage people to enter already crowded fields of work).

CHANGES OF PROMOTION

'I have a job, but my prospects are poor and I want to study to improve my future. Any course I take must be a recognised one that employers will approve, and it will have to fit in with my work, because I can't afford to give up – I might not be able to get back into a job again. Can I make sure of choosing the right course?'

No–one is likely to give you an unconditional guarantee, but trade unions and professional associations (see above) will advise on recognised courses and areas where particular skills are in short supply. For example, the Royal College of Nursing has drawn attention to the shortage of specially trained Intensive Care Nurses: a trained nurse who takes a post–registration ITU course should find plenty of job opportunities. The Department of Education and Science's 'Teaching as a Career'

Unit has advertised widely for people to train for shortage areas – in early 1988, these were: maths; physics; business studies; craft, design and technology. Training allowances, bursaries and/or grants are usually provided for people taking extra courses in 'shortage' skills areas.

There's also been a huge expansion in Open Learning facilities (see page OO) which means you can learn when it suits you. And in many jobs there are opportunities to go on short updating courses, either arranged by your firm (look on the company noticeboard and in the organisation's magazine) and conducted during working hours, or by some outside body in the evenings. Don't overlook the value of an Open University degree, or an Open Business School qualification or a London University external degree. Employers are generally impressed by people who demonstrate that they care enough about improving their prospects by studying in their spare time, even if the subject doesn't directly relate to their present job. (Having a degree can also open up a range of second career possibilities.)

I WANT A SAFETY NET

'My job is quite a good one, but these days, you never know what's round the corner. I'd like to add a second string to my bow. Then, if I should be hit by redundancy, I'd have something else I could turn to for a living. But the course will have to be in my own time – evenings, weekends, holidays – and, of course, something that welcomes mature students. What are the choices?'

Dozens. You could take a part–time degree or an open learning course, or spend part of your holiday time and money on an intensive private course in some special skill – anything from lorry–driving to word–processing. Or you could take evening classes in a creative skill like cake–icing or upholstery–making, or in a maintenance skill such as carpentry or tree–pruning or tiling, which would give you scope for spare–time, home–based employment. Check the course lists for your region and also the 'Information Sources' list in this book for more ideas.

I CAN ONLY STUDY DURING SCHOOL HOURS

'I want to prepare to go back to work when my children are old enough for school. I can study part of the day or take an evening class, and my priority is to find something that will demonstrate I have a brain and haven't let it go rusty while I've been at home. What are the choices?'

This depends on where you live. Some places have courses from 10 a.m. to 3 p.m., designed especially for people like you. Any course under the 21–hour rule (see 'Costs and Grants' section) might be organised in such a way that it fits into school hours. The European Social Fund (mentioned earlier) puts up some money for courses to suit 'women returners', especially for those who want to train for jobs that are not traditionally women's work, such as building or engineering. If you're not sure what might be best for you, look out for daytime courses with titles like 'New Opportunities for Women', or 'Wider Opportunities' (likely to be listed in the 'Pre–Entry, Sample and Access Courses' section).

I DON'T KNOW HOW TO CHOOSE

'I've spent a lifetime in the wrong job. Now I want to make a complete change. Quite what to do I'm not sure, but if I could find a list of all the possible jobs and courses, I dare say I could find something for myself. Is there anywhere that lists all the choices and entry requirements?'

I don't know of one single directory that covers all you want to know, but to begin with ideas for careers that you might research, any good careers guide kept in public libraries, such as like The Daily Telegraph Careers A–Z, Equal Opportunities *or the* Careers Encyclopedia, *will be helpful. Colleges often put on courses that let you sample a range of skills and study areas – look for titles like 'New Directions', 'Wider Opportunities', 'Multi–Skills'. On* *p.OO* *I've listed examples of careers where maturity is often an asset. Remember that Jobcentres and commercially run employment agencies can usually tell you what kind of people are in demand in your area. Having located the range of likely jobs, you can trace courses through the local Educational Guidance Service (see 'Information Sources' section), by asking the librarian in the public library reference room (they often stock a range of college prospectuses), or by writing to the Head of Adult/Continuing Education at your local college.*

EDUCATION IN RETIREMENT

'All my life I've gone out to work to earn the money to go to work and earn the money. Now (as I'm taking early retirement/have had a windfall/have discovered I can get a mature student's grant) I want to study for my own satisfaction. Exactly how do I begin?'

The whole wide world of learning – academic, creative, practical, inventive – is out there, waiting for you. Sandwell College in Liverpool told me about one 82–year–old who did well in signwriting. Hatfield Polytechnic introduced me to a number of 7O–year–olds enjoying a degree course in Contemporary Studies. So how about beginning by leafing through the regional lists of courses in each section of this book, to get an idea of choices within easy travelling range? Then get free prospectuses, and if you have a dream that you want to follow up but which doesn't seem to be covered, track down a professional institute/trade body concerned with it, and ask them about training. *(See the 'Information Sources' section, p.OO, for further details.)* *Never hesitate to write to a college's Adult/Continuing Education Department; as the percentage of young people in the country declines, colleges of all kinds are setting out to attract mature students, and that means anyone from 21 upwards. Some colleges will gladly introduce you to other 'late starters' who'll tell you what it's like to enjoy learning for its own sake, and how they started. Polytechnics are particularly good in this respect.*

I CAN'T AFFORD A COURSE THAT COSTS MONEY

'I am unemployed and it's as much as I can do to survive on benefits, without paying for classes. People tell me there are 'special courses for the unemployed'. What are they about, and how do I find out about them?'

First get a leaflet from your local DHSS office about the 21–hour rule, whereby you can retain your right to benefits while you study, as long as you keep to certain basic rules about when you take classes (explained more fully in this book's 'Costs and Grants' section). Look through the other sections for ideas for courses. Many are for unemployed people, and often the 'unwaged' are also eligible: this lets in people who can't actually look for work outside the home because they have a child to care for – colleges may have creches for which children of single parents or of anyone else with special problems get priority. Courses specially devised for unemployed/unwaged people may be free or at a fraction of the usual cost. Some courses, also, attract special MSC or ESF training benefits – check these out. In industries where there have been large-scale redundancies, there may be special retraining schemes with extra financial benefits. Ask your trade union if you think this could be a possibility.

ANY IDEAS FOR COPING WITHOUT A GRANT?

'I started out on a course and was given a grant, but I gave it up halfway. Now my LEA says I'm not eligible for another grant. All the careers I look at require a degree, like the one I first tried for. How can I get a degree without a grant?'

Take your degree part-time, by day or in the evening, or take an Open University degree. It will be worth the same as any conventional, full-time degree – in some employers' eyes, it will be worth more, because everyone knows how much work is involved in studying in your spare time, after working. Part-time postgraduate courses are also widely available if you have 'graduate status' but need to upgrade your knowledge, or add a vocational slant to your education. Incidentally, degree study hours often make it possible to hold down a part-time or evening or weekend job as well as study. Many people manage to combine study for an evening or OU degree with full-time work.

I CAN PAY FOR TRAINING, BUT IS IT SAFE TO GO TO A 'PRIVATE' COLLEGE?

'I have redundancy money which I could invest in a course of training or study, but I must make sure I'm spending it wisely; when it's gone, it's gone. How can I discover which courses are recognised, and also what demand there might be for people with particular qualifications which can be obtained quite quickly through a 'crash' course?'

In the case of a job-related course, check it out with the appropriate professional or trade body: for instance, the Hotel, Catering and Institutional Management Association, the British Antique Dealers' Association and so on. In the case of an educational course, ask the local Education Authority, the Educational Guidance Centre (see 'Information Sources', p.OO) or the Jobcentre. Special-interest magazines, with titles like 'The Grocer', 'The Bookseller', 'Construction News', have articles about labour demand in the areas they serve. You can usually look at them in the library reading room, though you may have to ask the librarian if they're not displayed for readers.

GRANTS – HOW MUCH, WHERE, FROM WHOM?

'There's no question of my being able to finance a course. Though I need to make a change, it's either got to be through getting a job with a firm that trains me, or by doing a course that attracts a grant. How does anyone find out which courses get grants?'

The section of this book headed 'Costs and Grants' lists addresses you can contact about grants. Colleges themselves also sometimes know of sources of finance. For instance,there might be one scholarship in memory of a past student that they administer, or a local fund they can tap into, or they may know of a loans scheme (you pay back when you're qualified and start work). On p.OO, among the careers in which maturity can be an asset, you'll find some which offer paid training, too.

WHERE CAN I FIND LISTS OF INTENSIVE COURSES?

Because of my job (teacher, actor, nurse, sales representative) I can only manage short, intensive 'crammer' courses, or maybe summer holiday/ weekend courses. How do you find these?'

There's a nationally recognised guide called the Directory of Independent Training and Tutorial Organisations, *published by Career Consultants and available in public libraries. Summer schools get advertised in the Sunday papers such as the 'Sunday Telegraph',* Sunday Times *and* Observer. *Weekend and other short courses are listed in the* Residential Short Courses Guide *(£1.15 by post from the National Institute of Adult and Continuing Education, 19b de Montfort Street, Leicester LE1 7GE).*

IS THERE SUCH A THING AS A MOBILE COURSE?

'My husband is in the services, and we move every two years or so. What courses can I take, moving from college to college? I can't leave my family to study, even if I did get a grant.'

It's never easy to move between colleges, but it's getting easier thanks to ECCTIS. This stands for the Educational, Counselling and Credit Transfer Information Service. It records, on computer, facilities to transfer between courses in the same subject in different parts of the country. Any college should be able to find out whether credit transfer facilities are available for a course you are taking. Also, any college with an 'Open Learning' facility is likely to take you, whatever level you've reached. Open University courses and Open College courses are marvellous in this respect (see 'Open and Distance Learning Courses', p. OO). You can stop when you have to move, and then begin again as soon as you have the time, so even if you are posted abroad, you can pick up your course when you get home.

YOUR NEXT MOVE

The sections that follow list courses in five main groups:

Pre–Entry, Sample and Access Courses
Retraining and New Skills Courses
Small Business and Self–Employment Courses
Open and Distance Learning Courses
Degree and Advanced Courses

Each is divided into regions – London and Middlesex, Southern and Eastern England, Central England, Northern England, Wales and Western England,

Scotland and Northern Ireland. You should find a selection of choices within range of your home. If you don't have home responsibilities that mean you have to choose from courses within a bus or car ride from your base, your options are even wider and you can scan the whole book for courses that may appeal to you. In local authority colleges, you usually pay the same fees whether you're a resident or from another county,though concessionary fees may be for locals only.

New Directions for Late Starters

For this section of Make A Fresh Start, you can thank or blame a gentleman who wrote to me following the publication of one of my careers articles on part-time degrees. He said – it's an exact quote – 'I am a failed civil servant of 30. Can you suggest any kind of career where I would not be too old to begin again?'

If you're one of the lively 40-or 50-year-olds choosing a university degree, or tackling a retraining course, or trying to decide on the best sort of small business to begin, no doubt that reader's attitude sounds very odd. You could be a 24-year-old without qualifications, in a boring job without prospects, who knows exactly what the writer feels like. For it's far from unusual to have people in their mid-twenties, let alone thirties, very uncertain about how and where to change direction. With every five years you add, it can be more difficult.

Like that reader, people who land up in the wrong career often see themselves as having 'failed'. It's a great pity because, ten years on when they're in a different career, they'll probably look back and realise that the only failure was in sticking out something that made them so miserable for so long.

You're certainly not too old at 30 to begin something quite new. There are quite a few occupations where 'maturity' is deemed to be a real advantage. They are jobs where you have to take responsibility ... where you need to be tolerant ... where you need self-control ... where you need self-discipline (all qualities people are likely to develop as they grow older). And while there are many occupations where mature people are *acceptable* as an entrant, there are some where they are *positively welcomed*. I'm not just talking about 30-year-olds. Depending on the job, the usual upper age limit for entry to training can be 40 or 45 or 50. And 'usual' itself is a pretty flexible term. For instance, someone with a long career in, say, community nursing, who may have been forced by ill-health to do something less physically strenuous, could well be accepted for training in a counselling job, or in administrative work with a charity, or as an appointments clerk in a hospital.

Here are some ideas to look through for jobs where maturity can be a plus factor:

LICENSED PREMISES

Managing a pub, managing an off-licence, barman/barmaid in pub, club, hotel. Managing a works social club. Managing a wine bar. Managing the bar in a golf or other sports club. Working for an outside catering firm, responsible for drinks and hire of glasses.

COMMUNITY WORK

Social worker (for local authority, charity, voluntary unit, in residential home). Warden of old people's home or sheltered accommodation. Caretaker of private residential development for the elderly. Care assistant in state/private old people's home, nursing home. Counsellor (paid or unpaid work – the latter can give you the experience to be accepted for training for paid work), in marriage guidance – now called 'Relate' by the way – with teenagers, with cancer or AIDS patients, drug/alcohol-dependent people, depressed or anxious people, those suffering from under/overeating problems, the suicidal, the bereaved. Working as a play leader, in a playgroup, or sometimes in a children's hospital. Running a youth club, helping at a day centre for handicapped or elderly or lonely people. Home helping (involves welfare work as well as domestic aid – clients of all age groups). Training as, or working with, a funeral director.

TEACHING

In areas that are in short supply in schools – Maths; Physics; Business Studies; Craft; Design and Technology – where it can be valuable to have come from industry and be able to show teenagers where your subject fits into the employment scene. And similarly at college, passing on your work skills, whether teaching Welding or Word-Processing. Local colleges often invite people to write to them with details of any subject they can offer. They may be prepared to try offering a course like Making Silk Flowers or Tax Tips for the Self-Employed if they know they have a suitable instructor available. Teaching basic Literacy and Numeracy to adults – perhaps beginning as a volunteer tutor, then getting the offer of paid work at a college. Teaching English as a Foreign or Second Language – in colleges or by private coaching. Acting as a correspondence course tutor, marking work and advising students by letter or phone. Teaching your hobby – swimming, dressmaking, public speaking. Driving Instruction (for those who can pass Department of Transport exams).

SELLING

Direct sales – to friends and neighbours by party-plan or mail-order catalogue. Telephone sales – promoting insurance and savings schemes, or perhaps something like a building modernisation service. Industrial sales: using previous career knowledge, e.g. as a nurse or engineer or chef, to obtain sales training from a manufacturer so that you can sell scientific or technical or material products to business users. People who've worked in retail selling (anything from china and glass to food and drink) can often use their product knowledge as the foundation for training with pay with a manufacturer, too. Moving on from being an industrial or commercial sales person, you might become a manufacturer's agent at any age, using contacts made during your career. Companies looking for agents advertise in national newspapers and special-interest magazines.

THERAPIES

Not all the therapies in the following list are practised in NHS hospitals or can be obtained in the community through the NHS – where one may be given a particular therapy under the Health Service, I have used the symbol 'NHS': Acupuncture, Alexander Technique, *Art Therapy (NHS), Bach Flower Therapy, Chiropractic, *Diet Therapy (NHS) and alternatives, *Drama therapy (NHS), Herbalism, Homoeopathy (NHS), *Horticultural Therapy (NHS), Hypnotherapy, *Industrial Therapy (NHS), Massage (not to be confused with *Physiotherapy (NHS)) *Music Therapy (NHS), Naturopathy, *Occupational Therapy (NHS), Osteopathy, *Psychotherapy (NHS) and alternatives, *Radiotherapy (NHS).

* means that an NHS-recognised training is available.

These are examples of therapies in which a mature approach can be welcome. Some, though have demanding entrance requirements. Adults taking GCSE/A-level courses to meet these should check that they won't have reached the upper age limit for entry to training before they qualify. (See *'Equal Opportunities'* mentioned in Information Sources, p.OO).

CARING OCCUPATIONS

Apart from those mentioned under 'Social Work' above you can train as a Registered Nurse or Enrolled Nurse up to the age of 45 in many health authorities and up to 50 in some. The original part-time RGN course at Portsmouth mentioned in the 'Retraining and New Skills' section has prompted others; details from the Nursing Careers Information Centre, 26 Margaret Street, London, W1N 7LB. Medical Reception work (Appointments Clerk in hospital, working for a clinic or health centre, Medical Secretarial Work, Practice Administration for a health centre) is often very suitable for mature people and a modest part-time job can develop into a full-time career. Beauty Therapy and some of its specialities – Epilation or Cosmetic Camouflage, for example – are good mature-entrant areas (see also the ''Small Business and Self-Employment section).

SERVICES

Many an engineer turns Technical Illustrator or Technical Author. Building Craft skills can lead to Site Supervision, or individual skills can be redirected, e.g. carpenter and joiner to Shopfitter. Automobile engineering/ bodywork skills can convert to Car Restoration services. Green-fingered gardeners with artistic and sales interests can retrain in Floristry. Experienced campers and caravanners can do seasonal work as Campsite Couriers or Caravan Site Wardens. Much-travelled people can train as Tour Guides. Find yourself a chance to work on an exhibition stand as a demonstrator of something you know a lot about – and lo! you have experience as a demonstrator, and can try agencies to get more of the same work with different products or services.

OFFICE SKILLS

The more you have, the better your job chances, but remember to *select* from your range when you apply for jobs that ask for specific abilities. Let's see – there's Typing, Audiotyping, Shorthand typing, Word Processing, Bookkeeping, Costing, Computerised accounts, Filing, Computerised Information Storage, Ordering and Re-ordering, Stock Checking, Telephone and Reception skills, Telex, Fax, Photocopier Operation, VAT Records, PAYE Calculations, DHSS Deductions, Mailing List Operating, Progress Chasing (orders, debts), Official Returns (e.g. farm, tax, health), Statistics Collection, Transport Booking and Timing (planes, traines, car-hire, route-planning and estimating), Dispatch by Red Star, Courier Service at home or abroad, including Insurance, Customs Declaration ... still think you know all about office work? Job specialities include: Accounts Technician, Legal Executive, Services Manager, Personnel Office Assistant (diversification – Employment Agency Interviewer), Conference Executive, Hotel Receptionist, Information Clerk (e.g. at an Airport), Advertisement Sales Clerk, Freight Forwarding Assistant, ...etc., etc. Your age may limit where you start but, as we all know, 'It's not where you start but where you finish' that matters. Get the skill, get the job – and you can then get going.

See also 'Small Business and Self-Employment Courses': there are ideas there too.

PRE-ENTRY, SAMPLE AND ACCESS COURSES

The 'toe-in-the-water' approach to changing your life

Introduction

Many people are apprehensive about changing direction, particularly when it means committing themselves to a course of study or training. Even for those who have already developed an interest in a particular subject or skill, there's often the hurdle to overcome of fearing that college might be rather like school. Not everyone has had the happiest of schooldays.

Then there's the financial aspect. Grants, training awards and bursaries are not easily come by. Redundancy money can be used up quickly. It's small wonder that a lot of people hesitate about deciding on a new direction. After all, if they get it wrong, they could lose their one chance of affording to retrain.

It's wise too, to make sure you start your new interest or retraining course at the right level. You don't want to feel you are falling behind the rest – or that you are so far ahead of the majority that you're bored.

SO MANY CHOICES

For a large number of people, the problem is too many choices. There are great thick prospectuses, full of courses that might be suitable, and whole ranges of skills or subjects that could be in demand, so that you find it hard to sort through them. The temptation can be to pick out something you've tried at home – plumbing, catering, painting, computing, writing – without realising that the professional approach is different from that of the enthusiastic amateur. You may well be able to adjust, of course, but you could be overlooking something else that you would enjoy even more, starting from scratch.

Getting into higher education – for degrees, higher diplomas or professional qualification courses – needs even more careful selection, if only because the courses take so long. It's rather like investing a lot of money in a new car. If you are going to invest a lot of time in higher education, a 'running in' period makes sense, to help you get into the swing of things.

This section of the book suggests a solution to the problems of choice, in the form of 'toe–in–the–water' courses. You may well find that colleges have different names for these. One of the big problems for adults who want to make a fresh start is to sort out what all the different course names and initials mean. 'Restart' is obvious enough, but what about 'Alternative

Admissions'? Then there are 'Gateway', 'Pathway' and 'Polyprep'. All of these have been popular with individual colleges. You could well be offered 'New Directions' or 'Wider Opportunities' to say nothing of 'Return to Learn', 'Fresh Start' and 'Second Start'.

'Access' courses are widespread and usually offer an alternative to A–level entry for mature students who want to satisfy entry requirements for a degree or higher diploma. 'Open' used in conjunction with a course title can *either* mean that the course is open to any student, regardless of his or her preliminary qualifications (or lack of qualifications), *or* it can mean 'out in the open', i.e. you mostly work at home with correspondence lessons, but have access to a college lecturer by phone, or for face–to–face advice when you need it. Details of how these various systems work, and of the national initiatives – the Open College, the Open Tech and the Open University – are to be found in the 'Open and Distance Learning Courses' section of this book.

DIFFERENT WAYS OF BEGINNING

To help you sort through the maze, this first section of *Make A Fresh Start* concentrates on courses I have picked out from the selections sent to me by colleges, which the organisers clearly intend to be for 'beginners' or 'returners'.

They may be *sampling* courses, whereby adults can go to a college and try out half a dozen different skills or subjects, with advice on how to choose among them to make the most of their talents and opportunities.

They may be *foundation* courses to lead unqualified people into higher education by providing an introduction to new subjects, where you can go along like a steam train in the things you are good at, while getting special help with any problem areas. This kind of course also teaches you how to use libraries, take notes and write essays or reports.

They may be *higher education preparation* courses (anything with the 'Access' label is likely to be designed for this), which will usually cover the study of several subjects and general study skills, so that if you complete the course successfully, you'll be quite ready to start a degree or higher diploma on equal terms with school–leavers.

Some colleges also welcome mature students, on what is called an *infill* basis, to the courses that they offer to school–leavers (A–levels, say, or City and Guilds), wherever they have space in a class. If you choose to share classes with teenagers, bear in mind that you won't be taking a pre–designed course for late starters, so you'll have to keep up to the average pace. Sometimes colleges put on special 'Mature Students GCSE/A–level' courses – it's always worth asking.

Anything with the words 'Sample' or 'Foundation' in the title is usually a course designed to take people from all kinds of backgrounds with no previous qualifications or experience. For this sort of course it would be unusual to be asked for any special entry requirement, other than your willingness to try.

THESE LISTS ARE JUST A SAMPLE, TOO ...

Having watched this book grow, it's clear that had I aimed at listing every possible course available, we could have ended up with a directory the size of the *Encyclopaedia Britannica*. So perhaps it is just as well that not every one of the 500 or so colleges I contacted in my nationwide survey responded. Some of those which did answer felt that giving national publicity to local courses might not be a good idea – they already had a job to squeeze in all the people in their own community who wanted to take part. You may have to book early for a popular course, but it's worth knowing that when there is a big demand, colleges will often take 20 or so people off the waiting list and put on an extra course for them. They have to make an income, just like the rest of us, and won't want to turn eager customers away.

The 'Pre–Entry, Sample and Access Courses' list doesn't include every course available, therefore, but should give you an idea of what sort of courses are likely to be offered in your region. If your own town doesn't appear to offer anything to suit you, first check that they haven't established a course since I did my research (new courses are cropping up all the time; sometimes colleges have to wait for education department or MSC approval to provide them). If you're unlucky, look at the region as a whole, and see if there's anywhere within travelling distance that has a suitable course.

Also check the *'Information Sources'* list at the end of this book for other national course guides you can consult. With the best will in the world, no–one can guarantee to include every course. Some will be announced after a book has gone to press. Others may still exist, but have had a change of title or location, to make a better use of a region's study facilities. New courses are always being 'piloted' to sample the response in a particular area.

Remember, too, that college principals are often very responsive to demand. If you find a course that sounds right for you, even if it's not in your area, ask your local college if they can put on something similar. The key factor usually is to have enough mature students to make a course economic. Group action – a letter to the college from a club or trade union, a petition with a lot of signatures, or an approach from a Job Club or Community Relations Officer – can be very effective.

COSTS AND GRANTS

There's a special section on this at the end of the book. Just for now, you need to know that courses which are 'MSC–funded' or 'MSC–sponsored' are usually free, and may be offered part–time to take advantage of the 21–hour rule. This DHSS rule means that people on unemployment or supplementary benefit can study for up to 21 hours a week without losing benefits. You have to satisfy certain requirements – details are in the 'Costs and Grants' section of the book.

For certain full–time courses, you may get a discretionary grant from your local education authority, or a grant from EEC funds (anything that's 'ESF–sponsored' could be covered). And courses at the special Adult Residential Colleges attract mandatory grant: see the 'Costs and Grants' section again. You'll find these adult preparatory courses for higher education spread out between this section and the 'Degree and Advanced Courses' section; I've classified them as requested by the colleges concerned, so check both sections. Finally, some adults get grants or loans from trade unions, charities or banks. (I met one chap who'd built up his credit card limit when he was in work so that when he was at art school, he could manage with evening work and dollops from Access. He worked flat out in vacations to pay off his credit card and thus have funds for next term. This arrangement is from ideal and I don't recommend it, but it did work out for him.)

STUDENT AND COLLEGE VIEWPOINTS

To show you what a wide range of people take pre–entry courses and what they feel about them, I've collected some 'consumer reports' from students, and from the people who teach them. Unless I've been specifically asked by colleges to use the description 'College spokesman/woman', I've used 'College spokesperson' as a shorthand term for male and female college principals, senior lecturers, tutors, counsellors and others on the tutorial side who offer helpful advice to people considering retraining. Contributions come from the following:

Access: City and East London College
Adult Training Strategy: Croydon College
Continuing Education: University of Kent at Canterbury
Drop–In Workshops: Percival Whitley College, Halifax
Second Start and New Directions: Somerset College of Art and Technology
Open Study: Thames Polytechnic
Polyprep: Hatfield Polytchnic
Returning to Work/Study: Shipley College
Student Education: Newry
Summer School: Middlesex Polytechnic
Visiting Student: City of Birmingham Polytechnic
Wider Opportunities for Women: New College, Durham

The courses listed are from colleges responding to a questionnaire sent to all universities, polytechnics and colleges of higher and further education in 1987, re–checked and updated by a further survey in February 1988. Some independent colleges have provided information and this has been incorporated.

NB: Don't overlook the possibility of a pre–entry course in the 'Open and Distance Learning' section of this book, if you'd prefer to start learning at home. Check the 'Degree and Advanced Courses' section, too, for an outline of the 'Associate Student' way of sampling degree course study.

THE COURSE LISTS

Courses are listed in order of town name within region. The full address of each college is given in the regional address lists at the back of the book. You may wonder why I've chosen this layout. It's because, quite often, a college name doesn't indicate where it is. For instance, Cassio College is in Watford, and the Hertfordshire College of Building is not in Hertford but in St Albans. Grouping colleges together in regions makes it possible for you to see what might be on offer within reasonable travelling distance of your home base (or maybe your job).

If you contact your local college, you may well find more courses on offer – courses that were not confirmed when we went to press or that have been newly introduced to satisfy demand. I am always glad to know about new pre–entry and sampling courses – and to have your views of them, perhaps for inclusion in the next edition. Please write to me through the publisher, Kogan Page, whose address is at the front of this book.

THE REGIONS

Colleges and other training sources with entries in this book are grouped into six regions:

London and Middlesex	London area, including Middlesex. Many Colleges in Southern and Eastern England may also be accessible from London.
Southern and Eastern England	Kent, Sussex, Surrey, Hampshire, Berkshire, Buckinghamshire, Hertfordshire, Bedfordshire. Essex, Cambridgeshire, Suffolk, Norfolk.
Central England	Oxfordshire, Hereford and Worcester, Northants., Leicestershire, West Midlands, Shropshire, Staffordshire, Derbyshire, Lincolnshire, Nottinghamshire.
Northern England	Cheshire, Lancashire, Merseyside, Humberside, West Yorkshire, South Yorkshire, North Yorkshire, Cumbria, Durham, Tyne and Wear, Northumberland.
Wales and Western England	Avon, Gloucestershire, Wiltshire, Dorset, Devon, Cornwall, Gwent, South Glamorgan, Mid Glamorgan, West Glamorgan, Dyfed, Powys, Gwynedd, Clwyd.

Scotland and Northern Ireland	Dumfries and Galloway, Borders, Strathclyde, Lothian, Central, Fife, Tayside, Grampians, Highlands, Co. Antrim, Co. Armagh, Co. Down, Co. Fermanagh, Co. Londonderry, Co. Tyrone.

London and Middlesex

Colleges appearing in this section are listed below by district, except where the location of the college is obvious from its name. This should help you to discover the most accessible college offering the course that you want.

Avery Hill, Dartford, Mile End, Woolwich	Thames Polytechnic
Barnet, Enfield, Haringey	Middlesex Polytechnic
Barking, West Ham	North East London Polytechnic
Bloomsbury	Birkbeck College, University of London
Camden, Islington	North London Polytechnic
Clerkenwell	City University
Deptford	South East London College
Elephant and Castle	Polytechnic of the South Bank
Euston, Holborn, Oxford Circus	Central London Polytechnic
Hackney	Cordwainers Technical College
Holborn	Central London Adult Education Insititute
Isleworth	West London Institute of Higher Education
Leicester Square	College for the Distributive Trades
Moorgate	City and East London College
Tooting	South West London College
Waterloo	Morley College, Vauxhall College of Building and Further Education
West Norwood	South London College

London – General

A guide to Access courses 1988–89 in the London area is published by the Inner London Education Authority. It lists Access courses which provide guaranteed places on a linked course at a university, polytechnic or other institution of higher education to students who complete their courses successfully. Academic entry qualifications are not usually needed. Ask in your public library for the guide to *Cross-ILEA Access Courses 1988–89*.

Birbeck College
Access course. Open Routes. Provisional First Year entry scheme (see 'Degree and Advanced Courses'). University of London Preparatory Course in Mathematics, 1 year, part time. (For language preparatory courses, see City and East London College.)

Camden Training Centre
Returners (for women), part time. Open Door English as a Second Language, part time.

Central London Adult Education Institute (formerly City Lit)
Fresh Horizons, with range of subjects, plus study skills and tutorials to catch up on missed opportunities, full time or part time, day or evening: Breakthrough, to build up confidence in reading, writing and discussion skills, part time day or evening. Study Sessions, part time day or evening. Open Study, part time evening study skills, plus own choice of subjects.

Central London Polytechnic
Accepts Access course students from Kingsway College. Modern Engineering Foundation course for students with Arts/Humanities A-levels who wish to pursue a technological career, full time. Certificate of Continuing Education for mature students thinking of returning to education (mode not specified).

City and East London College
Access to Social Work Foundation course (students from ethnic minorities), full time, linked to Diploma in Social Work of Polytechnic of North London. Access Preparatory BEd course (students from Caribbean community), full time, linked to Polytechnic of North London degree. Similar part time course available for all candidates, also linked to PNL. Access Preparatory BEd course (students from the Bangladeshi community and other bilingual applicants who wish to become primary school teachers) linked to course at Thames Polytechnic. Access to HND and BA Business Studies at Polytechnic of North London (for people from ethnic minorities, especially black women),full time. Access to Modular BA Humanities at Polytechnic of North London, part time. Access to Nursing at Princess Alexandra School of Nursing, The London Hospital, (for students bilingual in English and a language such as Bengali, Somali or Chinese, resident in Tower Hamlets or Hackney), part time. Preparatory courses in languages for students preparing to enter Birkbeck College, University of London to read Classics, French, German or Spanish,full time. University preparation course for those aiming to take Arts or Social Science degree courses, linked to Essex University (other universities and polytechnics also possible), full time or

part time. Access preparatory course in physical and social sciences, linked to modular degree at City of London Polytechnic, designed primarily for mature women returners, part time. Access to Modular BSc Social Sciences degree at North London Polytechnic (including Librarianship), part time. Access to Speech Therapy training (for bilingual students), linked to City University, Central London Polytechnic or University College, London, part time.

Access: viewpoints

'During the Access course, we've studied English Literature, which has taken up a main section, Communications – developing our skills of verbal and oral communication – Study Skills, which everybody on the course needed, and Maths, which played quite an important part. We've also touched on Psychology, Philosophy and some Sociology, and for the last term, we've been going to the Polytechnic where we will be doing our degree, for an introduction to our specialist subject.'

[Access student, City and East London College]

'For a long time, higher education establishments have been aware that A-levels are not very good predictors of performance on degree courses, and that there was scope for a one-year course that concentrated on the skills needed for an autonomous student to take a degree course. Access courses are an attempt to give a second chance to people who, through no fault of their own, haven't got to where they ought to be.They provide an alternative to A-levels which is less broad in content but equally deep, and therefore more suited to adult students.'

[Spokesperson, City and East London College]

City Lit

– see Central London Adult Education Institute, above.

City University

Open Study, part time,day or evening, for adults wishing to return to higher education.

College for the Distributive Trades

Access to Higher National Diploma in Distribution course, part time,under 21-hour rule.

Cordwainers Technical College

BTEC, First Diploma in Footwear and Leathergoods Studies, full time (1988 or 1989 start, depending on validation). Primarily designed as foundation course for 16-year-olds but may also be suitable for adults.

London University
Does not provide Access courses, but does accept a large number as satisfying General Entrance Requirement. (See 'Degree and Advanced Courses').

Middlesex Polytechnic
Return to Study courses in subjects like psychology, economics, social work, geography for mature students considering full time or part time degree or other higher education courses. Also Pre-degree course for mature students returning to study; Return to Learning course for older people. Certificate course, part of Modular Certificate/Diploma/Degree scheme (see Degree and Advanced courses). All-ages Summer School, many options and chance to earn credits for a degree.

Summer School: viewpoints
'I came last year to the Summer School because I thought it sounded interesting, and the year before that I'd been on another course run by Middlesex Poly, which was called "Return to Learning" to see if I would like the atmosphere – and I did like it. I live in Brighton, and managed my first Summer School by commuting up and down. That year I did the Foundation of English Literature, and this year I did one of the courses that lead from that – "The Short Story". The course is three afternoons a week and you have to leave quite an amount of time for reading and writing essays. Apart from that, the grounds are very beautiful and you can reach the underground fairly easily to get to London. At last year's Summer School, I took the course exam and got a credit. Then I went for an interview at Sussex University, which is near where I live, and they were very interested in the fact that I'd spent my summer getting this credit, in fact they have accepted me unconditionally for next term to take a degree – presumably based on attending two Summer Schools.'

[Summer School student, Middlesex Polytechnic]

'The actual tuition that a student receives comprises perhaps 10 or 12 hours a week for five weeks, but students are also entitled to have a free run of the campus, which is sited so that they have easy access to London, while they're also located in a glorious country park setting. We have all sorts of sports and leisure facilities and have laid on a wide social programme for students. There's a well stocked library, special facilities for art and music, and the Summer School students are free to take advantage of any of these aspects of the campus.'

[Spokesperson, Middlesex Polytechnic]

Morley College
English and Maths workshops, part time or evening. Second Chance

English, Second Chance Maths and Second Chance French, part time. Study Skills, part time. Fresh Start in Social and Community Studies, Fresh Start in Science, Fresh Start in the Humanities, Fresh Start in Languages, daytime or evening classes, all available under 21-hour rule for unemployed people. (See 'Costs and Grants'.) Open University Preparatory Course (Saturday mornings). University of London External Degree Preparatory Course in English, evenings. Wide range of introductory courses in subjects as diverse as Basic Art and elementary Arabic. Part of Open College of South London (see 'Open and Distance Learning Courses'). Studies/Humanities, part time.

Newham Community College

Access by Independent Learning, part time day or evenings: leads to Diploma of Higher Education courses at North East London Polytechnic, or to other courses (e.g. BEd, Certificate of Qualification in Social Work) at North East London Polytechnic and other higher education centres. Return to Learning, part time day; to improve basic education, help progress to employment or to other college courses, e.g. BTEC vocational courses or Access. College says: 'Late start for parents – some creche places available.'

North East London Polytechnic

Accepts Access students on a wide range of degree courses from the following colleges: Newham Community College, Waltham Forest College, Hackney College, Redbridge Technical College, Havering Technical College, *all* colleges in Essex LEA, Luton College of Higher Education, Tottenham College of Technology, Kilburn Polytechnic, Peterborough Technical College, West Suffolk College of Further Education. Also conversion course for candidates with Arts/Humanities A-levels who wish to study Engineering.

North London Polytechnic

Wide choice of Access courses through City and East London College, Haringey College, Kingsway College, South London College and Southwark College. Also 'Women into Architecture and Building' part time course, satisfying entry requirements for PNL degrees in Architecture and Interior Design. Women's 'Scope'course, part time, 10 a.m–3 p.m., includes work experience in fields as diverse as Computing and Social Work. Foundation course in Women's Studies (may be a pathway into evening degree), evenings. A letter from a Polytechnic spokesperson says: 'Whatever unique identity belongs to this Poly, it concerns our commitment to mature students, second-career trainers and 'second chancers' ...over 60% of our population is over 21 at entry, and in some faculties (e.g. Social Studies) 90% of students are in this category.'

Paddington College

Access courses, all taking place between 10 a.m. and 3 p.m. during term, duration one year: Computing Access, linked to degree or HND at Central London Polytechnic; Science Access, linked to degree or HND in various sciences and associated subjects (e.g. life sciences, environmental science at Central London Polytechnic or HND Food Technology at Polytechnic of the South Bank – can also lead to courses in Chiropody, Physiotherapy, Osteopathy, etc.). Engineering Access, linked to degree or HND at Central London Polytechnic. Teaching Access (for students with an intimate knowledge of the Caribbean or Asian communities) linked to BEd degree at Middlesex Polytechnic. Threshold courses, same hours and duration as Access, roughly equivalent to A-levels, for adults who did not complete their education when younger, leading to degrees in Arts and Sciences. Threshold courses also available part time, day or evening. Pre-Access preparatory course part time, may lead to any Access course. English and Study Skills, for students whose first language is not English, afternoons only. Also one-year courses, normally 10 a.m.–3 p.m. in English, Study Skills and Fresh Opportunities, with substantial education and careers advice, for adults wishing to return to education or re-train. Special provision for students whose first language is not English. Introduction to Business for Bilingual students (20 hours per week).

Richmond Adult College

Fresh Start part time, modular daytime course in Humanities and Social Sciences. Art Access, part time, options include Design, Drawing, Painting, 3-D Computer Graphics – students make up their own College Portfolio. Both Fresh Start and Art Access can provide access to higher education courses or re-entry to work.

South Bank Polytechnic

Involved in 16 Access courses run by local FE colleges. Access courses with links into: Law; Built Environment; Business Studies, Maths, Science and Computing; Physical Sciences, Electrical and Electronic Engineering; Mechanical Engineering; Environmental Engineering; Health, Biotechnology and Environment; Languages; Social Sciences; Teaching; Food Technology; Home Economics; Hotel, Catering and Institutional Management; and Nutrition with Biology. The last-named leads to eligibility for registration as a State Registered Dietician.

South East London College

Preparatory BEd course (students from ethnic minorities) in conjunction with Goldsmiths' College, full time. Prparatory BEd course (Design and Technology) in conjunction with Thames Polytechnic, full time. Special GCSE/GCE and A-level courses for adults (housewives, shift workers, etc.) between 10 a.m. and 3 p.m. invarious subjects. Foundation course for

Information Technology users, part time, day and evening. Electronics for Women (no previous knowledge or particular mathematics standard required),part time 9.30 am–3.15 pm. ESF-funded one-year full time (school hours and terms) preparatory course for women wishing to become Engineering Technicians, probably leading to City and Guilds awards. Preparatory courses for the new City and Guilds 726 Information Technology award, full time, part time or evenings.

South London College
Access courses in: Business Studies; Food Studies; Engineering; Geology; Health, Biology and Environment; for Pharmacy Technicians; in Social Administration. Adult Foundation courses in: Business Studies; Food Studies; Social and Community Work. Mode not specified, but all the courses listed above are organised in association with the Open College of South London, so it's reasonable to expect that flexible study arrangements will be available.

South West London College
Return to Study, full time. Access into Professional Accountancy, leads into Chartered Association of Certified Accountants' course, full time. Second Careers (three days). Foundation course in Counselling full time. Part of Open College of South London. Directed Private Study section (see 'Open and Distance Learning').

Thames Polytechnic
Avery Hill Campus: Access courses in association with City and East London College, Hackney College, South East London College, Woolwich College. 'Open' course in conjunction with South Greenwich Adult Education Institute,at Eltham Campus. Students attend up to six hours a week, between 10 a.m. and 3 p.m. Courses to suit individual needs and wishes, with a choice of subjects and the chance to study English and Maths. No entry requirements.

Open Study: viewpoint
'When the children were very young, I needed to get away from home responsibilities a bit and broaden my horizons. I see now that I wasn't sure at the time whether to try sociology or yoga! Then I saw a part-time course advertised at what was then 'Avery Hill College' (it's now part of Thames Polytechnic). It sounded ideal. It was two evenings a week, with about six hours of work to do at home – a bit of everything, Sociology, English, History, Maths. Mostly there were women in my age group [thirties] but some men too. During the course we were also introduced to the idea of higher education and I ended up at North East London Polytechnic, where

I eventually gained a first-class honours degree in the School of Independent Study.'

[Former Open Study student, Avery Hill Campus, Thames Polytechnic]

WOOLWICH CAMPUS:
Polystudy – unit-based courses, part time. New Opportunities for Women, part time. Making Experience Count – self-assessment course for the unqualified, part time. Participates in the 'Greenwich Education and Training Advice' Education Shop at Woolwich – free advice,on the spot. (See also 'Degree and Advanced Courses'.)

Uxbridge College
Open Access, part time. MSC-sponsored 'Women Towards Management', part time. MSC-sponsored New Opportunities for Women, part time.

Vauxhall College of Building and Further Education
Access to Diploma in Office Administration, part time. Access to Law, full time. Alternative Entry (preparation for entry to courses in Social Science and Youth and Community Work), part time. Black Culture Hair and Beauty, full time or part time. Return to Study (basic education), full time or part time. Introduction to Journalism from a Black Perspective, part time. Access to Certificate of Qualification in Social Work, part time. Construction Technician Sampling course for Women, full time. Access to the Built Environment, full time. Access to Recreation and Leisure Management, part time. Computers at Work, full time or part time. Newstart – General (Return to Learning), full time or part time. Newstart – Art and Design, full time or part time. Newstart – Media Studies, full time or part time. Newstart – Science, Electronics and Computing, full time or part time. Adult Foundation – English as a Second Language, full time or part time. Painting and Decorating for Women, part time. Plumbing for Women, part time. Information Technology for Women, part time. Drop-In Programme – Skills Sampling in Construction, full time. Introduction to Computers for Women, part time. MSC-sponsored Work Preparation – English as a Second Language, full time.

West London Institute of Higher Education
Fresh Start, part time (evenings) can lead to entry to degree courses. Options in American Studies, Beliefs and Values in World Religions, English, History, Understanding Britain.

Westminster College
Access to BA Home Economics and Teacher's Certificate at South Bank Polytechnic, full time. Access to BEd Primary Education at South Bank Polytechnic.

Willesden College of Technology
Access to Science, full time. Gateway to Study, full time (17-hour course). Preparatory courses for Open University (Maths, Science, Social Science, Humanities), evenings.

In addition to the above, a number of other London colleges offer pre-entry courses, but did not supply any information. A useful free leaflet has been prepared by the Central and West London Open College, 35 Marylebone Road, London, NWl 5LS, which could help you track down a centre or course that matches your personal needs.

The following colleges in London supplied information in 1987 about their pre-entry courses, but no response was received to 1988 enquiries. Readers may nevertheless wish to make individual contacts:

Brixton College
City of London Polytechnic
Goldsmiths College
Hackney College
Hammersmith and West London College
Kingsway College
Tottenham College of Technology

Southern and Eastern England

Basildon College of Further Education
Return to Study, Access course (to higher education and employment), GCSE/A-levels, Foreign Languages – all with hours to suit mature students.

Basingstoke Technical College
Access – Pre-Degree course,part time and under 21-hour rule. Pre-degree Foundation Course in Art and Design part time. University Preparatory course, evenings. GCSE/A-levels for mature students, part time, day and evening. Basic Literacy/Numeracy, part time evening. MSC Restart, one week full time.

Bedford College of Higher Education
Access to BEd Primary Education full time. Also, subject to CNAA approval: Access to BEd (Hons) Secondary – Physical Education or Indian Dance, full time; Access to BA (Hons) Combined Studies, full time.

Boreham Wood:
De Havilland College – see under Welwyn Garden City

Bracknell College
Return to Work, part time.

Brighton Polytechnic
MSC-sponsored HITECC conversion course for people of A-level standard but without A-level Maths and Physics (or similar qualifications) wishing to prepare for entry to advanced courses in engineering or technology. Well motivated mature candidates are welcome and may be able to offer work experience in lieu of A-levels. Certificate in Art, Craft and Society scheme, part time, provides opportunity for 'second chance' education and may support entry to more advanced courses.

Bromley College of Technology
Return to Study, part time.

Cambridge: Cambridgeshire College of Arts and Technology
Return to Study, part time. Open University preparatory course, evenings. Adults welcome on part time day and evening A-level courses. MSC-sponsored HITECC conversion course for people of A-level standard but without A-level Maths and Physics (or similar qualifications) wishing to prepare for entry to advanced courses in engineering or technology. Well motivated mature candidates are welcome and may be able to offer work experience in lieu of A-levels. Access Certificate Course (being organised – ask college for details).

Cambridge College of Further Education
Pre-School Playgroups Association Foundation course, part time.

Canterbury College of Art
Foundation Course in Art, full time. Mature students welcome.

Canterbury College of Technology
GCSE/A-levels for mature students, selected academic subjects, full time and part time. MSC-sponsored Job/Career Change programme, part time including Business Studies, Computing, Electronics and Information Technology. Open University Pre-Foundation course, part time. Access courses, full time and part time. Open College courses and other Open Learning courses. British Coal JACCS courses, full time. Women into Technology, part time.

Canterbury: University of Kent at Canterbury
New Opportunities for Women, part time. Access courses: Humanities; Social Sciences; Maths; Natural Sciences (the last two are currently being planned). Study Day; Study Evening; Gateway courses. All these are part-time. Also a range of general education courses (not leading to a qualification) is available.

Continuing Education at Kent: viewpoint
'The students on our courses come from all walks of life: housewives, train drivers, unemployed and retired people, school teachers and manual labourers; adults of all ages and previous educational histories. Some come just for the pleasure of study; some with the definite intention of proceeding to further studies.

Students of our Access courses have identified several unexpected gains: most mentioned new confidence, supportive friendships and intense mental stimulation. They gained 'encouragement and an appetite for learning'... 'a restoration of confidence in one's ability to write' ... 'a sense of achievement in learning' ... 'the enjoyable company of the other students on the course also provided an unexpected bonus' ... 'the group discussions stimulated my tired little grey cells beyond recognition.'

[Spokesperson, School of Continuing Education, University of Kent]

Chichester College of Technology
Access to Science and Technology degrees at University of Surrey, details from college.

Colechester Institute
Access course, part time, under 21-hour rule. Open University preparatory course, part time. GCSE/A-level for mature students, full time, part time, under 21-hour rule. Basic Literacy/Numeracy, full time, part time, under 21-hour rule. Multi-Skills, full time, part time, under 21-hour rule. Open Learning scheme (see 'Open and Distance Learning').

Croydon College
Wide range of courses in Adult Training Strategy programme for people from a Community Programme/Unemployed background, including Basic Numeracy and Literacy and Wider Opportunities for Women as well as Jobsearch training schemes. (See also 'Retraining' section – many courses 'start from scratch' in teaching employment skills.)

Adult Training Strategy at Croydon: viewpoint
'For people making a 'fresh start', it is vitally important that if they are going to become confident in an education and training area, they must feel welcome at the site and on the particular course. On the Adult Training Strategy at Croydon College, our team of specialists emphasise the welcoming environment and maintain this throughout a level of high-quality training. In our fourth year now, we are training approximately 240 people a week, of which 40% can expect to go on to further employment, 40% will go on to further education and training, and many of the others will continue to get help and counselling.'
[Spokesperson, Adult Training Strategy Provision, Croydon College]

Eastleigh College of Further Education
Access courses in Humanities and Technology, full time and part time.

North East Surrey College of Technology
A-levels for mature students, part time, between 10 a.m. and 2.15 p.m. Flexilearning (see 'Open and Distance Learning'). Back to Study – short course. Basic Numeracy, evenings. Access course preparing adults for degree in Sciences at Brunel University or Kingston Polytechnic.

Guildford College of Technology
Access to BEd degree at Kingston Polytechnic, part time. Return to Study, part time. GCSE part time provision.

Hatfield Polytechnic
New Opportunities for Women, part time. Polyprep, part time (leads to a Certificate in Preparatory Studies). Associate Student scheme, part time (see 'Degree and Advanced courses'). Learning in Later Life, part time. Polyphysics, part time. MSC-sponsored HITECC conversion course for people of A-level standard but without A-level Maths and Physics (or similar qualifications) wishing to prepare for entry to advanced courses in engineering or technology. Well motivated mature candidates are welcome and may be able to offer work experience instead of A-levels. This college is very sympathetic to mature students.

Polyprep: viewpoints
'On the Polyprep I course, they give you four or five different subjects. Study Skills; English; we did a little bit of Anthropology, which was very exciting, knowing how it all started, a little bit of Biology; then we had Numeracy – which I failed dismally. But the lecturers taking us seemed to be specially picked, they let you down very lightly. There was no embarrassment in front of other students. Nobody knows what marks you get, except between you and the lecturers. It's done very tactfully. At the end of the course, you'd have to be very very bad, you'd have to flounder in all the subjects, not to find at least one thing to do that's interesting. At the end, the lecturer said to me, 'If you really wanted to, and you've got the gumption to try, you could do a degree course.' Well, for a retired person looking for a new role, this was absolutely marvellous.'

[Polyprep (now undergraduate) student, Hatfield Polytechnic]

'We have been in the business of designing routes back for mature students since about 1970, and we have quite a variety of routes back. We tend to design a route for a target group. For instance, we pioneered the New Opportunities for Women courses. Polyprep is for men and women who want to come back into higher education. They use the course to re-acquaint themselves, or perhaps acquaint themselves for the first time, with how to study. It's quite tough. They come in for two days a week and it's an 18-week course. They have to read and de-gut a book, present written work, do all the things all students have to do and most of them get turned on by this, even if they're petrified at first. It's a tool of analysis for the student, and a measure of their potential ability.'

[Spokesperson, Hatfield Polytechnic]

Hemel Hempstead: Dacorum College
Fresh Horizons for Women, part time Return to Learn, part time, enables adults to get a first qualification in English and Maths. (See also 'Open and Distance Learning'). MSC-sponsored Training Link Course, 10 a.m.–3 p.m., to help people who want to train under the MSC Job Training Scheme to decide what they would like to do and assess their skills. Job-seeking and

self-presentation are included as well as basic skills and skill-sampling opportunities.

High Wycombe: Buckinghamshire College of Higher Education
MSC-sponsored HITECC conversion course for people of A-level standard but without A-level Maths and Physics (or similar qualifications) wishing to prepare for entry to advanced courses in engineering or technology. Well motivated mature candidates are welcome and may be able to offer work experience in lieu of A-levels.

Hornchurch: Havering Technical College
Access course, linked to chosen degree subject(s) and college/polytechnic/ university, part time. Fresh Start, part time. Open Leaning (see 'Open and Distance Learning').

Kingston Polytechnic
MSC-sponsored HITECC conversion course for people of A-level standard but without A-level Maths and Physics (or similar qualifications) wishing to prepare for entry to advanced courses in engineering or technology. Well motivated mature candidates are welcome and may be able to offer work experience in lieu of A-levels. (See also 'Degree and Advanced courses'.)

King's Lynn: Norfolk College of Arts and Technology
Open Access course (English Literature, History, History of Art, Social Science) linked to University of East Anglia – school hours, Tuesday, Wednesday,Thursday. Access to Nurse Training, linked to Queen Elizabeth Hospital, King's Lynn – Thursday mornings (creche available) or evenings. MSC-sponsored Training Link Course full time, basic skills and vocational training, preparing for MSC Job Training Scheme.

Luton College of Higher Education
Access to Further Education (for multi-ethnic students), part time under 21-hour rule. New Horizons for Women, part time. MSC-sponsored Restart full time. Open University preparatory course, part time. GCSE/A-level for Mature Students, part time.

Merton College
Access to higher education (Law, Business Studies or Accountancy), full time or part time. Access to degree in Information Systems Design at Kingston Polytechnic, full time. Access to Arts and Social Science degrees at Kingston Polytechnic, full time. Return to Study, part time or evenings.

Merton Institute of Adult Education
Access, Fresh Start, New Directions, Extra-Mural University and Workers Educational Association classes. Saturday schools.

Newbury College
Return to Study scheme to suit individuals; can include GCSE, A-levels, BTEC National awards, various technical courses. Also evening course in Study Skills. MSC-sponsored Restart full time and other MSC-sponsored courses for unemployed people.

Norwich City College of Further and Higher Education
Access courses to University of East Anglia, full time or part time. 'Options': Return to Study, part time summer course; 'Way-in' – GCSE Return to Study for Adults, part time; New Opportunities for Women, part time; Open Learning (see 'Open and Distance Learning Courses'); College Certificate in Community and Welfare Studies, full time or part time.

Portsmouth College of Art, Design and Further Education
Return to Study and GCSE/A-level courses through Portsmouth Open Learning Programme (see 'Open and Distance Learning').

Portsmouth: Highbury College of Technology
Adults' Pre-Degree full time and part time, leads to degrees at West Sussex Institute of Higher Education (and elsewhere). Wider Opportunities for Women, part time. MSC Restart courses,full time. Flexistudy and Open Learning courses (see 'Open and Distance Learning').

St Albans College
Mature students welcomed on infill basis on any part time GCSE/A-level course. Access full time but hours mainly 9.30 a.m. to 3 p.m. Leads to university and polytechnic entrance.

Slough: Langley College of Further Education
Return to Study, part time.

Southampton Technical College
Access to La Sainte Union College of Higher Education degrees in English, Modern Languages, European Studies or Theology, and will assist Access to BEd. P/t. Wider Opportunities for Women, part time. GCSE/A-level/AS levels/BTEC courses, full time or part time; some GCSE courses with special 'mature student' syllabuses. Flexistudy courses (see 'Open and Distance Learning').

University of Southend
Return to Study, part time, through Adult Education Department.

Southend College of Technology
Access course (to suit individual aims and directions), full time or part time. MSC-sponsored New Opportunities for Women, part time. Return to Study, part time, 10 a.m.–3 p.m. to suit parents. Also Open Learning (see 'Open and Distance Learning'). This college is very sympathetic to mature students.

Stevenage College
Pre GCSE, GCSE/A-level for mature students, Basic Literacy/Numeracy, all full time or part time.

Surbiton: Hillcroft Adult College
Residential. Women Only. CNAA Modular Certificate, can lead to higher education, training or employment. No entry requirements, students receive mandatory grants. Also part time Return to Learning and Linked Learning, short residential follow-up, during Easter or Summer. (See 'Degree and Advanced Courses' for more details.)

Sutton College of Liberal Arts
Return to Study, part time. Open University preparatory course, part time. Women Back at Work, evenings (for intending returners). GCSE part time day and evenings.

Watford: Cassio College
New Opportunities for Women, part time. Introduction to Counselling, part time and evenings (can lead to advanced courses at Stevenage or Hatfield). GCSE and A-level courses, full time, part time and evenings. Improve your Maths/English (suitable as pre-entry to GCSE). Pre-Nursing (with provision to take GCSEs), full time or part time. City and Guilds part time day courses in Cookery, Fashion, Embroidery and Flower Arranging, all classified by college as suitable pre-entry courses.

Watford College
MSC-sponsored HITECC conversion course for people of A-level standard but without A-level Maths and Physics (or similar qualifications) wishing to prepare for entry to advanced courses in engineering and technology. Well motivated mature candidates are welcome and may be able to offer work experience in lieu of A-levels. Pre-Higher Education Course, full time for those wishing to enter teaching or social sciences. GCSE/A-levels for mature students, full time and part time. Open Access to New Technology, part time (Multi-Skills). Wider Horizons courses by arrangement for those preparing for Open University or similar. (See also 'Open and Distance Learning'.)

Welwyn Garden City: De Havilland College – (also Borehamwood, Hatfield)

Access to Further and Higher Education, part time (modular), programmes from nine to twenty hours per week. Return to Study, part time. Social Studies for adults, part time, European Studies, part time. GCSE/A-levels for mature students, part time and special evening course in English. MSC-sponsored Restart, one week full time. Spectrum – courses for adults with special learning needs, full time and part time: part-time help on one-to-one basis with reading, writing, spelling and basic maths (can be in student's or tutor's home). Artprep (for young students, but mature candidates also welcome), full time, part time by arrangement. Open Learning (see 'Open and Distance Learning').

Wimbledon School of Art

The school says: 'Significant mature student entry to Art Foundation course', full time.

The following colleges in this region supplied information in 1987 about their pre-entry courses, but no response was received to 1988 enquiries. Readers may nevertheless wish to make individual contact:

Chelmsford: Essex Institute of Higher Education
Farnborough College of Technology
Folkestone: South Kent College of Technology
Luton: Barnfield College
Reading College of Technology

Central England

Abingdon College
Access courses designed to meet entry requirements for Oxford Polytechnic degree courses, full time or part time. Return to Study GCSE/A-levels for adult students, part time or on infill basis. Basic Education in English or Numeracy, on individual basis, evenings. Courses for students with special needs (physical or educational), part time. Open Learning scheme (see 'Open and Distance Learning').

Birmingham: City of Birmingham Polytechnic
Associate Student Programme (see 'Degree and Advanced Courses'). Listening and Visiting Student Programme – range of about 200 subjects from Media Studies to Maths, Accountancy to Fine Art, part time about two hours per week per subject. May lead to degree entry.

Student Programme: viewpoint
'I was a clerical worker with absolutely no opportunity for promotion, so I started going to night school. I did an O-level first of all, and went on and passed that, and did an A-level – by which time I'd got so engrossed in the education system, I really wanted to become a full-time student. But then the disaster came. I failed an A-level. I'd already applied to come to the Polytechnic, so I rang up, praying I could get on still, and received an awful lot of sympathy. The Visiting Student Counsellor was contacted about me. He then contacted me and said would I like to join the Visiting Students, so I jumped at the chance. They told me that if I worked hard, I'd be able to get on to the full-time degree course. I'm unemployed at the moment, so the course only costs me £6. for the year – that's two hours a week, and I think millions of other people ought to take up this opportunity and do this.'

[Visiting Student, City of Birmingham Polytechnic]

'Visiting and Listening students attend lectures and seminars we are running for our existing students. Visiting students are eligible to take the assessment or examination in the unit or course they are studying. Listening students may or may not be eligible to take the assessment, but if attendance is satisfactory, the student gets a transcript to show this. Most Listening students are sitting in on the courses in order to update their professional knowledge and skills.'

[Spokesperson, City of Birmingham Polytechnic]

Birmingham: Matthew Boulton College
Mature students' Alternative Admissions schemes, part time to BEd and BA courses at Birmingham Polytechnic (no qualifications required). Alternative Admissions study skills course, part time for mature students wishing to apply to various universities/polytechnics. GCSE, part time and evenings. New Opportunities for Women, part time. Preparatory Studies, part time, for those who need an introduction to study skills before starting other courses. Open University Preparatory Course, part time.

Bridgenorth and South Shropshire College of Further Education
Return to Work Programme for women, part time, school hours only. New Horizons (Caring, Business Studies or GCSE/A-levels), full time, part time or under 21-hour rule.

Chesterfield College of Technology and Arts
Access (Social Studies, Creative Design, Science and Technology,Environmental Studies), part time under 21-hour rule. GCSE/A-level mature students course, part time under 21-hour rule. Basic Literacy/ Numeracy, part time under 21-hour rule. MSC Restart, part time under 21-hour rule.Open Learning (see 'Open and Distance Learning').

Coventry: Henley College
Adult Literacy/Numeracy. Pre-GCSE Maths. How to Study Effectively. Taking Stock – course covers Life Patterns and General Health Care. Modes unspecified, ask college. 'Gateway' for all Open College courses, they say.

Coventry Polytechnic
New Opportunities for Women, part time, school hours only. Return to Learn (afternoon or Saturday morning). Associate Student scheme and 21-hour rule courses (see Degree and Advanced courses). MSC-sponsored HITECC conversion courses for people of A-level standard but without A-level Maths and Physics (or similar qualifications) wishing to prepare for entry to advanced courses in engineering or technology. Well motivated mature candidates are welcome and may be able to offer work experience in lieu of A-levels.

Derby: Derbyshire College of Higher Education
Gateway course, part time between 10 a.m. and 3 p.m. for mature students to explore their capabilities and options. Pathway I, follow-up course, same attendance pattern, introducing Contemporary English Literature and

Human Studies, with Study Skills and Numeracy. Pathway II, same attendance pattern, extends knowledge through a selection of several subjects. Certificate awarded on successful completion of the two Pathway courses can be used as alternative Access to degrees taught by the college (see 'Degree and Advanced Courses').

Dudley College of Technology
Access to Polytechnic Higher Education in Humanities, Social Sciences, Business Studies, Information Technology, Social Work, Science and Technology under 21-hour rule. Access course to Afro-Caribbean/Asian hairstyling, under 21-hour rule. Return to Study, part time. Pre-GCSE (Preliminary year in English Language: Mathematics) evenings. GCSE/ A-levels, all age groups, full time, part time or evenings. Basic Literacy/ Numeracy – wide range of courses, including English and Communication Workshop. MSC-sponsored Restart one week and Drop-In facility. Women's Access course and a General Entry course for Craft, Design and Technology, full time or under 21-hour rule.

Hinckley College of Further Education
'Alternative Programme' for unemployed people under 21-hour rule. Wide range of skills and subjects, from Antique Restoration to Access course; all ability levels are catered for; can lead on to other college courses.

Keele University
Foundation Year (an introduction to the three-year Honours degree programme) is an excellent basis for mature students, or for students not completely decided about their course requirements, according to the university. (See also 'Degree and Advanced Courses'.) Extra-mural courses in association with Lichfield College, part time.

Kettering: Tresham College
General Education Workshop, part time, courses designed for individual students. Adult Basic Education, evenings, English and Maths Workshop for mature students, times to suit individuals. Gateway Workshop for mature students, half-day units, choices to suit individuals (includes Information Technology, Word Processing, Shorthand, Typewriting, Office Systems etc.) GCSE for mature students (two centres). Infill opportunities on wide range of GCSE and A-level courses. Open University Preparatory Course. Open Learning Courses. Multi-Skills Workshop (see also Retraining, Small Business, Distance Learning). This college has clearly made a special effort to welcome and cater for adults. Access course began September 1987.

Kidderminster College
Replan courses for unemployed people, part time under 21-hour

rule:options are: Introduction to Welding, Photography, Word-Processing and Music Keyboard. Return to Learning, part time. Open Access programmes, part time. 'Open Office', part time. Flexistudy (see 'Open and Distance Learning'). Adult Basic Education (including English as a second language), part time.

Leamington Spa: Mid Warwickshire College of Further Education
Open Access (Life Sciences) leading to degree entry requirements of Coventry (Lanchester) Polytechnic, part time, school hours. Open Access (Business Studies) leading to higher education, part time, school hours. Fresh Start, part time, school hours or evenings – introduction to study and range of courses. GCE A-levels for mature students, part time school hours only. English as a Second Language for Workseekers, part time, school hours only. GCSE/A-levels, part time on infill basis. New Opportunities for Women, part time, mornings only. Second Chance to Learn (in association with Workers Educational Association) part time. Many part time introductory and specific skills courses for unemployed adults (see 'Retraining and New Skills Courses'). Open Learning provision (see 'Open and Distance Learning').

Lichfield College
This college is in the process of expanding its adult and community education facilities. At present it offers Basic Literacy/Numeracy on an individual basis, GCSE/A-level courses on an infill basis and many art and special-interest courses (see 'Retraining and New Skills Courses').

Loughborough: Co-operative College
Residential adult college owned by British Co-operative Movement, which provides full-time education for mature people as well as management courses for staff from Co-operative shops and Co-operative banks. Offers full time Diploma in Policy Studies for people aged 23 and over without any prior qualifications (course covers social, business, historical and political issues, including community development, economics trends, national policies, political institutions and commercial and voluntary organisations). Selection by interview; experience in voluntary or community activities is a distinct advantage. Grants available to cover fees, course expenses, maintenance, allowances for dependents and personal expenses.

Loughborough Technical College
Access part time or under 21-hour rule. Return to Learn, full time and part time. Gateway, part time. Open University Preparatory Courses, part time. Mature students' GCSE/A-level, full time and part time. Basic Literacy and Numeracy, full time and part time. MSC-sponsored Restart, full time, short course. Basic Skills Workshop – Reading/Writing/Numeracy. Open Learning (see 'Open and Distance Learning'). This college shows extra consideration for students with special needs – disabilities or learning difficulties –

and has equipment that can be loaned to students for the period of their course (e.g. Microwriters, braille writers, etc.)

Newcastle-Under-Lyme College

Intensive GCSE and GCE 'block-timetabled' courses for adults. Replan provision as part of general Staffordshire scheme, details from college.

Newark Technical College

Return to Study/Return to Learn, full time, part time, and under 21-hour rule. Mature Matriculation, full time, part time and under 21-hour rule. Open University Preparatory Course, part time. GCSE/A-level mature students course, full time, part time and under 21-hour rule. Basic Literacy/ Numeracy, full time, part time and under 21-hour rule. MSC Restart, part time. Drop-In scheme.

Nottingham: South Nottinghamshire College of Further Education

Return to Study. Open University Preparatory Courses. GCSE and A-level mature students courses. Basic Literacy/Numeracy. Second Chance/Wider Opportunities. Drop-in scheme for Literacy and Numeracy. Modes not specified – ask college.

Oxford Polytechnic

Local resident adults can prepare for higher education on a 20th-Century Studies Course run by the North and West Oxford Community Education Commitee, The Ferry Centre, Summertown, Oxford. Other Access courses are run by Oxford College of Further Education and Abingdon College of Further Education. MSC-sponsored HITECC conversion course for people of A-level standard but without A-level Maths and Physics (or similar qualifications) wishing to prepare for entry to advanced courses in engineering or technology. Well motivated mature candidates are welcome and may be able to offer work experience in lieu of A-levels.

Redditch College

GCSE courses for mature students, full time. GCE A-level courses for mature students, full time. Pre-Nursing and Pre-Social Work courses for mature students, full time. Basic Skills (Literacy and Numeracy), part time under 21-hour rule. Adult Preparation Training, part time, for long-term unemployed,includes skill sampling. Open Learning scheme (see 'Open and Distance Learning'). Flexistudy (see 'Open and Distance Learning'). MSC-sponsored Restart, full time, short course. NB: It is proposed that this college should merge with North Worcestershire College to become North East Worcestershire College in September 1988, so the range of courses may be affected then.

Retford: Eaton Hall International
Certificate in Teaching English to Speakers of Other Languages – preliminary course; combines distance learning and residential block (see 'Open and Distance Learning'). Entered here at college's request as it is seen as a preparatory course for Teaching English as a Foreign Language (see also 'Retraining and New Skills Courses').

Shrewsbury College of Arts and Technology
Access course leading to entry to degrees at North Staffordshire Polytechnic, full time.

Solihull College of Technology
GCSE/A-level courses for mature students including adult unemployed – Flexistudy. Also Open College facilities (see 'Open and Distance Learning').

Stafford College of Further Education
Open Access course in 20th-century life, evenings, can lead to a degree course at North Staffordshire Polytechnic. Open Learning Access courses are available in a variety of GCSE, GCE and Business Studies subjects. Also Introductory Course in Catering, leading to City and Guilds certification, for people currently employed in the hotel, catering and tourist industries who wish to improve their career prospects.

Stoke-on-Trent: Cauldon College of Further and Higher Education
Access course in English, Sociology, History, Psychology, Study Skills, part time, day or evening, leading to degree courses at North Staffordshire Polytechnic and other higher education institutions.

Stoke-on-Trent: North Staffordshire Poloytechnic
'Sampler' courses, part time, day or evening – choose from Computing, Politics, Law, Sociology, Economics, Business and Management Studies, History. Also Associate Student scheme (see 'Degree and Advanced Courses' section). Study Experience Course in Economics; degree preparation for unqualified candidates who want to 'test the water' – evenings or afternoon and evening. Open College course, part time in association with Stafford College of Further Education and Telford College of Arts and Technology. MSC-sponsored HITECC conversion course for people of A-level standard but without A-level Maths and Physics (or similar qualifications) wishing to prepare for entry to advanced courses in engineering or technology. Well motivated mature candidates are welcome and may be able to offer work experience in lieu of A-levels.

Stourbridge College of Technology and Art
GCSE, full time and part time. NB: College says: 'Mature students

particularly welcome and do not always have to conform to (standard) entry requirements.'

Stratford-upon-Avon: South Warwickshire College of Further Education
Access to Higher Education (times to suit family commitments or part-time employment) in association with Coventry Polytechnic and the University of Warwick – various course options. Twentieth Century Studies, full time for mature students,moderated by university and polytechnic representatives; Open Access to Science, between 10 a.m. and 3 p.m., can lead to courses in subjects as diverse as Biotechnology and Primary Teaching. Open Access to Engineering, between 10 a.m. and 3 p.m. can lead to various courses, including Engineering Science, Systems Engineering (involving Computerisation); Return to Learn (includes counselling sessions), part time.

Sutton Coldfield College of Further Education
Access course, part time. Alternative Admissions scheme, part time. Open University Preparatory Course, part time, Pre-GCSE, part time. GCE A-level Mature Students course, part time. Basic Literacy/Numeracy, part time. MSC Restart, full time short course. New Opportunities for Women, part time.

Tamworth College of Further Education
Access course, full time, an alternative to the traditional A-level route for mature students who want to acquire the skills to study in higher education. MSC-sponsored Adult Preparation Training, part time, under 21-hour rule.

Walsall: West Midlands College of Higher Education
Access to BEd degree, full time, in association with former Warley College of Technology (now part of Sandwell College).

Warley/West Bromwich: Sandwell College
(Amalgamation of Warley College of Technology and West Bromwich College of Commerce and Technology.) Access to BEd degree at West Midlands College of Higher Education, Walsall, full time, applicants from ethnic minorities particularly welcomed. MSC-sponsored Adult Preparation Training for unemployed people, part time under 21-hour rule (option for women to sample engineering and computer studies). MSC Restart programme, full time. Basic English, English as a Second Language, English for Immigrants, all part time. Women in the Community (confidence building, women's rights and history), part time. Assertiveness Training (women and ethnic minorities), part time.

Warwick University
The Open Studies Programme offers day and evening courses in a variety of

subjects: no entry qualifications are required. Certificate courses, based on the Open Studies Programme, are offered part time in Women's Studies, and are planned in Archaeology, Local History and Counselling. Certificate-level study can be a stepping stone to a part time degree course. (See also 'Degree and Advanced Courses'.)

Wellingborough College
GCSE for mature students, part time under 21-hour rule. GCE A-level, same conditions. City and Guilds Information Technology, BTEC First Certificate and BTEC National Certificate in Caring Services, part time under 21-hour rule, during school hours. Return to Study, Access and Open University Preparatory courses are also available, modes not specified - ask college.

West Bromwich: see Warley/West Bromwich: Sandwell College

Wolverhampton: Bilston Community College
Access to higher education, part time, under 21-hour rule. Wide choice of specialisations including Art and Design, Business/Computer Studies, Race Relations, Engineering, Sciences (Biology, Physics), Library and Information Studies, Psychology etc. Can lead to degree/HND entry or professional course. Adult Skills course, part time under 21-hour rule – wide choice of skills from car body repair to computer programming (see 'Retraining'). City and Guilds Background to Technology Project, part time under 21-hour rule (application of new technology to science, engineering and commerce). Pathway I – part time under 21-hour rule; general education with emphasis on English and Maths for mature students; may be preparation for higher education. Basic Education, for adults who have not studied for many years and need help with speaking and writing English – could be particularly useful for ethnic minority students – part time under 21-hour rule. Also Women-Only courses, funded by European Social Fund, all 20 hours per week for 32 weeks; e.g: Women Re-Entrants; Vocational and Language Training for Women (may be very helpful for those Asian women who have a poor command of English); Women and New Technology; Women in Science and Engineering; Women in Supervision and Management; Women and Self-Employment; Women and Craft Design Technology. NB: This college appears to be particularly sympathetic to the needs of unemployed adults and anyone with a problem to overcome, whether it's lack of former education, disability or language difficulties.

Wolverhampton: Wulfrun College of Further Education
Access. Return to Learn. Mature Matriculation. Open University. GCSE/A-Opportunities. Multi-Skills. Basic Literacy/Numeracy courses. Mode unspecified – ask college. (See also 'Open and Distance Learning'.)

The following colleges in the Central region supplied information in 1987 about their pre-entry courses, but no response was received to 1988 enquiries. Readers may nevertheless wish to make individual contact:

Banbury: North Oxfordshire Technical College and School of Art
Buxton: High Peak College
Derby College of Further Education
Henley-on-Thames: King James's College of Henley
Hereford: Herefordshire Technical CollegeHinkley: North Warwickshire College of Technology and Art
Leicester: Coalville Technical College
Lincoln: Lincolnshire College of Art and Design
Nottingham: Basford Hall College
Nottingham: Trent Polytechnic
Stoke-on-Trent Technical College
Telford College of Arts and Technology
Witney: West Oxfordshire Technical College

Northern England

Altrincham: South Trafford College of Further Education
Access to Higher Education, part time, under 21-hour rule. Return to Study, part time, under 21-hour rule. GCSE/A-level for mature students, full time, part time, under 21-hour rule. Basic Literacy/Numeracy, part time, under 21-hour rule. English as a Second Language, part time. Flexistudy (see 'Open and Distance Learning Courses').

Ashton-under-Lyme: Tameside College of Technology
Threshold, full time or part time under 21-hour rule – aimed at access to degree/higher diploma courses at universities, polytechnics and colleges, via Manchester Open College Federation.

Barrow-in-Furness College of Further Education
Mature students' full time, part time and evening courses to suit individual needs for GCSE/A-level courses: also 'Drop-In' facilities. (See 'Open and Distance Learning Courses').

Blackburn College
Return to Learning, part time or full time, individually planned. Basic Skills to Pre-GCSE level, part time or full time,individually planned. English Language support courses for bilingual students; Communicating Across Cultures (groups or individuals from minority ethnic groups). Also Open College (see 'Open and Distance Learning Courses').

Bolton Institute of Higher Education
Associate Student scheme (see 'Degree and Advanced Courses').Polymaths, which can lead to degree course, part time, evenings.

Bradford and Ilkley Community College
Preliminary Course in Art and Design, part time for mature/unemployed students. Electronics for women, part time Foundation course, school hours and terms only. Basic technology courses for Women, including Motor Vehicle Craft Studies, Vehicle Body Repair and Refinishing, and Electronics. Return to Learn, part time. Certificate for Mature Students (Humanities and

Social Sciences), full time or part time, to prepare for entry to higher education or professional training. Certificate for Mature Students (Business Studies), part time, – successful students are eligible for the HND or HNC course in Business Studies. Access course to BEd or Postgraduate Certificate in Education, part time, for people from the Indian subcontinent who are fluent in more than one language and with an overseas qualification, such as MA or BA. Access to Bilingual Employment (ABLE), full time, for people who speak Urdu, Punjabi or Bengali together with English, and want to improve their chances of finding a bilingual job; may also open doors into further education.

Bradford University

According to the university: 'The University has just approved the introduction of a Foundation Year enabling candidates without conventional qualifications for entrance to Engineering (degree) courses to convert to engineering. Candidates could include holders of 'inappropriate' A-levels, BTEC Computer Studies/Business Studies qualifications, Irish School Leaving Certificate, Scottish 'highers', mature students, or anybody who in the judgement of the University has proven himself/herself in a field other than engineering and would benefit from following a degree course in engineering. The one-year course would enable candidates to continue to a conventional degree course in Chemical Engineering, Civil Engineering, Electrical and Electronic Engineering or Mechanical Engineering. The first intake is planned for October 1988.'

Bridlington: East Yorkshire College of Further Education

Access to Higher Education, part time. Return to Study, part time. Pre-GCSE part time. GCSE/A-levels for mature students, part time.Basic Literacy/Numeracy, part time. MSC-sponsored Restart, in one-week blocks. New Opportunities for Women/Wider Opportunities, part time. Drop-In Scheme. MSC Adult Preparation Training, Multi-Skills, part time. Also Open Learning (see 'Open and Distance Learning Courses').

Burnley College

Gateway for Women (introduction to further education and vocational retraining). Access (counselling and advice for adults returning to further education – does not appear to be a substitute for A-levels). Open College (adult entry into higher education – ask for details). Open College (Maths and Numeracy Workshop). NB:modes unspecified – ask at the college.

Consett: Derwentside Tertiary College

Higher Education Foundation Certificate, part time, can lead to a range of degree/diploma courses at polytechnics in North East England. Open University Preparatory Course, part time. GCSE/A-level for mature students, part time under 21-hour rule. Basic Literacy/Numeracy, part time under 21-hour rule. Restart, part time under 21-hour rule. New Opportunities for Women/Wider Opportunities, part time under 21-hour rule. Scope (employment workshop), three-day course. Adult Basic Education Course, part time, individually planned. Open Learning (part of Durham Access Centre of North East Open Learning Network).

Dewsbury College

Access course for ethnic minority students, full time linked to social sciences courses at Leeds Polytechnic, Sheffield Polytechnic, Bretton Hall College, Wakefield, Bradford and Ilkley Community College. Fresh Start (Continuing Opportunities Programme) for unemployed people, under 21-hour rule. Gateway course, for ethnic minority students, part time under 21-hour rule – can lead to Access or other courses. Breakthrough course for all adults, part time under 21-hour rule, can lead to Access or other courses. New Opportunities for Women, part time, school hours, one day a week. Basic Skills Workshop, part time under 21-hour rule. Study from home (see 'Open and Distance Learning Courses').

Durham: New College Durham

New Beginnings – basic numeracy and literacy course, part time. Wider Opportunities for Women, part time. Scope – skill-sampling course for unemployed people, part time. Open University Preparatory Course, evenings. Open Learning and Flexistudy (see 'Open and Distance Learning Courses').

Wider Opportunities for Women: viewpoint

'Nearly 100% success has been achieved in helping students proceed to work or further training and education. One student does it all – she works part-time in a kitchen shop, has taken a training course to qualify as a Citizens Advice Bureau volunteer worker, passed her Marine Navigation certificate and started her own business on a part-time basis. That's exceptional, but we find that coming on the course shows women that there *are* many openings for them, even in times such as these, if they can present themselves well and are willing to tackle new activities. Women have the chance to sample Computing, Catering, Office Technology, Sport, Art and Design, Music and Drama, Welding, Carpentry, Car Maintenance, Painting and Decorating, Bricklaying and Electrical Engineering. Sessions are also held on job search skills and self-presentation.'

[Spokesperson, New College Durham]

Gateshead Technical College

Higher Education Foundation Course (in association with Newcastle College of Arts and Technology), part time over one, two or three years – can lead to degree/diploma courses at Newcastle-upon-Tyne Polytechnic.

Replan for Women, 10 a.m. to 3 p.m., one day a week. Adult Literacy/ Numeracy, part time, day and evening. Open Learning and Flexistudy (see 'Open and Distance Learning Courses').

Halifax: Percival Whitley College of Further Education
Access to Higher Education, under 21-hour rule. Pathways (for students for whom English is a second language) in Computing and Science, Business and Secretarial work, Social and Welfare Services, Service Industries, full time and part time. Alternative Admissions course, full time and part time. Open University Preparatory Course, part time. GCSE/A-level course for mature students, full time and part time. Scope programme (with language support) includes Multi-Skills provision, part time.Drop-In Communications Workshop. Drop-In Mathematics Workshop. Community Drama course for mature students under 21-hour rule.

Workshops with a Difference: viewpoint
'The Communications Workshop houses all the resource materials a student of English and Communications could wish for, with a cheerful, vigorous and helpful staff .... The drop-in nature of attendance is bound to suit everyone, whether coming to consult a tutor, use the audio equipment, cameras, word-processors and so on, or simply to practise some of the many communications exercises on file' ... 'A wellequipped, expertly staffed Mathematics Workshop is available to all. More than 100 students a day pass through ... you can work at your own pace, with a teacher at your elbow to provide guidance and support when needed. The workshop is designed to suit all kinds of students, from 'starters' to 'returners'.
[Spokesperson, Percival Whitley College of Further Education]

Huddersfield Polytechnic
MSC-sponsored HITECC conversion course for people of A-level standard but without A-level Maths and Physics (or similar qualifications) in engineering or technology. Well motivated mature candidates are welcome and may be able to offer work experience in lieu of A-levels. ESF-sponsored Women into Technology course, full time, school hours and terms only.

Lancaster College of Adult Education
Participates in Open College of the North West: part time courses, wide range of subjects. GCSE Mature Students, part time (four subjects only). Basic Literacy and Numeracy, part time. NB: This college can send you a free leaflet about the Open College of the North West with contacts in all the participating colleges.

Leeds: Park Lane College of Further Education
Mature Matriculation Preparation course, full time or part time. Pre-Degree

Study Skills, Open University Preparatory Course, part time. 'Start Afresh', part time for people away from education for some years: includes career planning. Practical Study Skills, part time, to be taken before or during a study course. Assessment Programme for anyone who thinks he/she may have difficulty following the Start Afresh course. Individual Programme, to tackle weaknesses or to allow people to start at times between course start dates. (See also 'Retraining and New Skills Courses' for wide range of 21-hour courses.) Pre-degree Law Access course, part time. MSC-sponsored Job Club. NB: College is particularly welcoming to mature students.

Leeds Polytechnic
Skills Training and Career Development Programme, 10 weeks, part time. Course can lead into a wide range of vocational courses (see 'Retraining and New Skills Courses').

Liverpool: South Mersey College
Access course leading to degree and Certificate of Qualification in Social Work (CQSW) entry at universities, polytechnics and institutes/colleges of higher education. Second Chance course, including Open Learning Workshop in Maths and English for adults of all ages without qualifications, wishing to improve basic skills and develop new areas of interest in order to progress to such courses as GCSE, A-level or Access.

Manchester Polytechnic
Polymaths, part time, can lead into degree in mathematics. Certificate in Environmental Studies, part time, can lead into Diploma of Higher Education or degree in Environmental Studies. MSC-sponsored HITECC conversion course for people of A-level standard, but without A-level Maths and Physics (or similar qualifications),wishing to prepare for entry to advanced courses in engineering or technology. Well motivated mature candidates are welcome and may be able to offer work experience in lieu of A-levels. NB:Excellent free 'Mature Students' Handbook' available, from Manchester Polytechnic, All Saints, Manchester M15 6BH.

Manchester: South Manchester Community College
'Gateway': general access course for mature students, full time, part time and under 21-hour rule, for those who are not certain which subjects they would like to study in higher education: mainly leading to the Diploma in Higher Education at Manchester Polytechnic. 'Pathway' access course under 21-hour rule, includes Local History, Sociology, English Language and Literature, Maths, Study Skills, Computing. Operates during school hours only. 'Threshold' access course, full time, part time and under 21-hour rule, for those who wish to do degrees in Humanities and Social Sciences. 'Vocational' access course, for those who wish to do degrees or diplomas in Social Work or Youth Work and Community Work, and people

who need to develop confidence and skills because they have had little academic success at school or since. Courses are widely accepted by universities, polytechnics and colleges of higher education. Playgroup for students' children. Courses lead to qualifications from the Manchester Open College Federation (see 'Open and Distance Learning Courses'). Mature students are warmly welcomed at this college.

Manchester University
New Horizons, part time – a 'taster' course across a wide range of subjects plus study skills; available October-March. Wider Horizons, part time – extends New Horizons course, but individual units may be taken. Return to Study – distance-learning version of New Horizons (see 'Open and Distance Learning Courses'). Career Studies programme, flexible hours, for people looking for a change.

Manchester: UMIST University of Manchester Institute of Science and Technology
Mature Matriculation Scheme (see 'Degree and Advanced Courses'). Also 'Conversion Course' for people with qualifications that are good (e.g. Arts A-levels, grades BBC or better) but inappropriate for the Integrated Engineering degree course. After the first year, the subsequent three years are common with UMIST's existing engineering degree courses.

Manchester: Withington Centre for Community Education
Fresh Start, part time. Return to Study, under 21-hour rule. Open College courses through Manchester Open College Federation, various subjects and levels. Pre-GCSE, part time. GCSE/A-levels for mature students, part time. Basic Literacy/Numeracy, part time. Open Workshops in Modern Office Skills, Maths, English, Book-Keeping, Basic Skills, Business English, English as a Second Language.

Middlesbrough: Longlands College of Further Education
GCSE. Introduction to Computing. Access courses. Women's 'Taster' and Access courses (various vocational areas). Basic Skills (Literacy and Numeracy). Personal Counselling. Scope-type infill provision, for adults seeking to update skills in vocational areas. Prepare for Engineering, Electrical Engineering, Electronic Engineering, Computer Engineering, Information Technology – all these for people without qualifications. Pre-entry 'top-up' units for people with qualifications, e.g. Bridging Courses from Electrical craft level to BTEC Higher Award entry; Access to Higher Education Course, range of modules available.

Middlesbrough: Teesside Polytechnic
Access to Humanities, Social Studies, Information Technology, Computer-Aided Engineering, Mathematics, via part time Access/Gateway programmes. MSC-sponsored HITECC conversion course for people of A-level

standard but without A-level Maths and Physics (or similar qualification), wishing to prepare for entry to advanced courses in engineering or technology. Alternative admissions: well motivated mature candidates are welcome and their work and life experience may be accepted in lieu of formal qualifications.

Newcastle-upon-Tyne Polytechnic
Higher Education Foundation course,in association with Newcastle upon Tyne College of Arts and Technology, Gateshead Technical College, Derwentside College, Peterlee College and North Tyneside College: 14 subject modules are available, each one designed to take a year to complete, with the student attending college for half a day per week per module. Well motivated mature candidates are welcome and may be able to offer work experience in lieu of A-levels. Also Associate Student scheme (see 'Degree and Advanced Courses').

Ormskirk: Edge Hill College of Higher Education
Return to Study, part time. Associate Student, part time (see 'Degree and Advanced Courses'). Open College scheme (see 'Open and Distance Learning Courses').

Peterlee College
MSC-sponsored full time one week Restart and Scope, under 21-hour rule for unemployed adults; includes 'taster' experience of college courses. Replan scheme for unemployed adults under 21-hour rule,comprising Drop-In workshops to develop basic skills:e.g. Maths, Letter-Writing, Interview Techniques. New Opportunities for Women/Wider Opportunities, part time. Multi-Skills (Engineering), part time. Access to Higher Education course for adults, mode not specified – ask college. Adult Literacy Workshop, part time, drop-in basis. Adult Literacy, evenings. Flexistudy (see 'Open and Distance Learning Courses').

Preston: Lancashire Polytechnic
Foundation Studies course, part time, to help students assess their suitability for higher education. New Opportunities for Women, specially timed between 10 a.m. and 3 p.m. LEA-sponsored Access course for students from ethnic minorities, part time, leading to entry to a degree course. Assessment of Prior Learning, full time. Foundation Course in Science and Technology for Women, full time. MSC-sponsored HITECC conversion course for people of A-level standard, but without A-level Maths and Physics (or similar qualifications), wishing to prepare for entry to advanced courses in engineering or technology. Well motivated mature candidates are welcome and are able to offer work experience and prior learning, certificated or not, in lieu of A-levels. Associate Student Scheme (see 'Degree and Advanced Courses'). Part of Open College of North West.

Detailed advisory interview available for mature students considering return to education.

Rochdale College of Adult Education
Preparation for Employment, under 21-hour rule: Job-Search Skills and New Technology.

Rotherham College of Arts and Technology
Access to higher education, full time and part time, leading to Certificate of the South Yorkshire Open College. Women's Access to Information Technology, full time and part time. New Opportunities for Women, part time. Women's Studies, part time. Women's Studies, part time (in Multi-Skills workshop). Access to Employment and Training, under 21-hour rule (for people over 25 who have been unemployed for 12 months or more). Return to Learning, part time (roll-on roll-off entry) under 21-hour rule, and Return to Study, under 21-hour rule, leading to Certificate of South Yorkshire Open College. Communications for Employment and Training (for students from ethnic minorities who need help with English), under 21-hour rule. PHIT (Physically Handicapped into Information Technology), under 21-hour rule. Multi-Skills Workshop, part time. Special Workshops, including Multi-Skills and English language support, primarily for those whose first spoken language is Mirpur Punjabi, part time.

Rotherham: Rockingham College of Further Education
Broader Opportunities for Women, part time. Open College scheme to prepare for higher education, part time, credit-based – acceptable for entry to various universities, polytechnics, colleges. Flexistudy (see 'Open and Distance Learning Courses') and Preparation for Nurse Training.

Sheffield Polytechnic
The Polytechnic and other colleges in the region have developed a number of preparatory Access courses which can lead to many of Sheffield City Polytechnic's degree-level programmes. There is also an Associate Student scheme, part time. (See 'Degree and Advanced Courses'). The South Yorkshire Open College may be contacted through Sheffield City Polytechnic, 36 Collegiate Crescent, Sheffield S10 2BP.

Sheffield: Rother Valley College of Further Education
Access to Higher Education, full time and part time. Return to Learn, part time. Mature Matriculation, full time and part time. GCSE/A-level for mature students, part time. Basic Literacy/Numeracy, part time. New Opportunities for Women/Wider Opportunities, part time. Drop-In scheme, part time. 3-D Studies (Pre-Polytechnic Art and Design degree courses), part time.

Sheffield: Shirecliffe College
A-level Alternative course, to prepare adults for higher education, part time. Access course for Asian students, part time and full time, including help with mother tongue.

Shipley College
Return to Study, part time – can lead into higher education, BTEC, City and Guilds or O-levels. New Start for Women, part time. Returning to Work/Study, part time (see below). GCSE/A-level – mature students welcome on infill basis. English for Home Crafts, part time, for students for whom English is a second language. Drop-In New Skills scheme (see 'Retraining and New Skills Courses').

Returning to Work/Study: viewpoint
'It's a first step in helping adults decide in which direction they will proceed – further study and training, or directly securing employment. This course is specially designed for people without educational qualifications. They may have left school early, recently become unemployed or have been out of the job market for several years... As well as participating in a practical Job Search exercise, the course will include a very basic introduction to the computer's role in the workplace, with guidance in 'hands-on' experience ... a chance to improve communcation skills ... individual counselling and plenty of opportunities for discussion in a friendly, relaxed atmosphere with like-minded adults and skilled staff. Attendance is on Mondays between 9.30 and 3 p.m., and no attendance is required during school holidays and half-term breaks. Crèche facilities are available.'

[Spokesperson, Shipley College]

Southport College of Arts and Technology
Lancashire Open College evening courses, various levels and subjects, for unqualified adults who want to improve job prospects or work towards higher education. Return to Study – GCSE/A-levels, part time, day and evening. Basic English for adults, evenings. English as a Foreign Language, evenings.

South Yorkshire Open College – see under Sheffield Polytechnic

Sunderland Polytechnic
Informal Learning Scheme for Science students (units or parts of units from degree and higher diploma courses). MSC-sponsored HITECC conversion course for people of A-level standard, but without A-level Maths and Physics (or similar qualifications) wishing to prepare for entry to advanced courses in engineering or technology. Well motivated mature candidates are welcome and may be able to offer work experience in lieu of A-levels.

Polytechnic Certificate in Art and Design Foundation Studies. Modes not specified – ask college.

Wakefield: Bretton Hall College
Mature student courses, part time, for those preparing to return to education, prepare for university matriculation, take Open University Foundation Courses. (See also 'Open and Distance Learning Courses').

Warrington: North Cheshire College
New Opportunities for Women, part time. Return to Study, part time (self-selected modules). Access courses part time: many subjects at various levels (level 4 courses can lead into degree studies). 'Jigsaw' Programme, part time, includes study skills, personal evaluation, educational counselling. NB: the Dean of Studies says: 'The college is particularly geared to the needs of those adults who wish to 'Make a Fresh Start'. A variety of course structures enable adult men and women to take advantage of the University of Manchester 'Mature Matriculation' provision. All our full-time courses are open to mature students.'

The following colleges in this region supplied information in 1987 about their pre-entry courses, but no response was received to 1988 enquiries. Readers may nevertheless wish to make individual contacts:

Barnsley: Barnsley College of Technology
Barnsley: East Barnsley Community Education Service
Blackpool and Fylde College of Further and Higher Education
Darlington College of Technology
Doncaster Metropolitan Institute of Higher Education
Grimsby College of Technology
Leeds: Kitson College of Technology
Liverpool Polytechnic
Liverpool: Sandown College
Nelson and Colne College
Newcastle College of Arts and Technology
Sheffield: Granville College
South Shields: South Tyneside College
Wakefield District College
York University

Wales and Western England

Aberystwyth: Ceredigion College of Further Education (Aberystwyth, Cardigan, Felinfach)
GCSE A-level for mature students, part time, under 21-hour rule (no specific entry qualifications required). Agriculture, preliminary, part time. Horticulture, preliminary, part time. (See also 'Retraining and New Skills Courses' for short courses with vocational application that can be taken without prior qualifications.)

Barnstaple: North Devon College
Access to further education for unemployed people (e.g. to Business Studies, Caring Skills, Catering). Return to Study, part time. GCSE/A-levels – mature students welcome on standard courses. MSC-sponsored Restart one-week, full time and 'Drop In' facility.

Bath: Norton Radstock Technical College
Start Courses, part time. Second Step for Women, part time. Adult Basic Education, evenings. Access to Information Technology, mainly evenings.

Bridgewater College
MSC-sponsored Fresh Start. Women into Work (for women 25 and over exploring non-traditional areas of work). Access course: Humanities and Social Science, linked chiefly to Bristol Polytechnic. Access course: Science (starts 1988) – to higher education, various establishments. Details of times from college. Open Learning (see 'Open and Distance Learning Courses').

Bristol: Brunel Technical College
Access to Science, part time, under 21-hour rule, timetabled to suit people with domestic commitments. Designed to meet Bristol Polytechnic entrance reauirements for one of: HND Applied Physical Sciences, HND Applied Biological Sciences, BSc Hons. and BSc Scientific Instrumentation, BSc Applied Chemical Sciences (subject to CNAA approval). 'Freeway' Open Learning (see 'Open and Distance Learning Courses').

Bristol: Filton Technical College
Access to Social Science, Humanities, Education and Social Work, part time, currently under 21-hour rule, may lead to degrees of Bristol University and Bristol Polytechnic. Proposed Access to Craft, Design and Technology in conjunction with Bristol Polytechnic, for women and for people from ethnic minorities. GCSE/A-level courses open to mature students, full time and part time. Adult Literacy – tuition for new readers who may join the evening class at any time. Flexistudy courses (see 'Open and Distance Learning Courses').

Bristol Polytechnic
MSC-sponsored HITECC conversion course for people of A-level standard, but without A-level Maths and Physics (or similar qualifications), wishing to prepare for entry to advanced courses in engineering or technology. Well motivated mature candidates are welcome and may be able to offer work experience in lieu of A-levels.

Cardiff: South Glamorgan Institute of Higher Education
Diploma in Social and Industrial Studies, full time (grants available); no formal qualifications required. Successful completion of this course may lead to the student's acceptance on vocational courses within the Institute, or on degree courses in the areas of history, social sciences and law, at university or polytechnic.

Cardigan – see Aberystwyth: Ceredigion College

Cheltenham: College of St Paul and St Mary
Access to BEd, full time, mainly for students from ethnic minorities. Preparing for Higher Education, part time and full time.

Chippenham Technical College
GCSE open to students of all ages, full time and part time. Access to Nurse training for mature students. Job Applications Techniques, evenings. New Opportunities for Women, part time. Adult Literacy/Numeracy, various part time. Progressive Literacy, evenings. Flexistudy (see 'Open and Distance Learning Courses'). All full time courses at this college are open to adults.

Dolgellau: Coleg Meirionnydd
Open Learning (see 'Open and Distance Learning Courses').

Exeter College
Access to Higher Education, details from college.

Exeter University
Runs a programme of Access to Higher Education courses (Arts and Social Sciences), part time in school hours only, at a range of colleges in Devon and Cornwall. From September 1988 it is hoped to offer Access to Science and Technology courses.

Felinfach- see Aberystwyth: Ceredigion College

Haverfordwest: Pembrokeshire College of Further Education
GCSE/A-level mature students, full time. MSC-sponsored Restart, full time. Drop-In Scheme, part time. Pre-Nursing – mature students taken on infill basis. MSC-funded Access to Information Technology, part time.

Llanelli: Carmarthenshire College of Technology and Art
Access to Higher Education. New Opportunities for Women/Wider Opportunities: details from college.

Pontypridd: Polytechnic of Wales
Access course – Industrial Society and Culture, part time, can satisfy entry to Polytechnic's Humanities degree course, full time or part time. Conversion course for entry to Engineering degrees, details from college.

Salisbury College of Technology
Basic Literacy/Numeracy, part time. MSC-sponsored Restart course, full time and part time. 'Drop In' facility. MSC-sponsored Women Returners course, part time. MSC-sponsored full time and part time JTS courses. MSC-sponsored Women Returners Secretarial and Clerical course. Adult Education Foundation, part time and evenings. Adult Education Extension (about A-level standard), part time and evenings. How to Study (return to study course), evenings, suitable for Open University preparation. Words and Ideas – Spoken Skills, part time, may lead to RSA Spoken English: it can improve interview technique, sales skills. Introduction to Social Sciences, part time. Access course to Higher Education. Open Learning (see 'Open and Distance Learning Courses').

Street: Strode College
Return to Study, part time. GCSE/A-level mature students, part time. Basic Literacy/Numeracy, part time. New Opportunities for Women/Wider Opportunities. Open Learning (see 'Open and Distance Learning Courses').

Swansea: Gorseinon College
Return to Learn, part time. Projected Open University Preparatory Course. Projected Job Training Scheme Induction week.

Swansea: University College of Swansea
Preparatory courses in History, Politics, Philosophy, English and Sociology for mature students, full time.

Taunton: Somerset College of Arts and Technology
Access to Higher Educastion, under 21-hour rule. New Directions for Men, part time and New Directions for Women, part time, both incorporating Second Start. Return to Learn, part time. GCSE/A-level for mature students, part time. Basic Literacy/Numeracy, part time. MSC-sponsored Restart, full time. New Opportunities for Women/Wider Opportunities, part time and under 21-hour rule. New Directions (Multi-Skills course) under 21-hour rule.

Second Start and New Directions: viewpoints
'There were some of us who desperately needed legal advice, facts about social security benefits, Inland Revenue information. We all had different needs. On the Second Start course, there was always something for you, maybe not every week, but if you weren't actually needing what was provided that week by the person who was coming to give us advice, you could always see why the advice that was being given to other people was important; you were learning indirectly from what they were being given.'

'One of the things that was very interesting involved the self-analytical exercises they gave us. You had to actually draw, in illustrative form, how you saw your life, and it was really interesting. One lady, I remember, did her life looking as if it was a road map and she had roundabouts where she didn't know which of the turnings to take, and they were all marked as different options for her, which I thought was a very clever way of doing it. It's really then that you realise life is full of choices and it's nice to know the options that are open to you.'

'When you've been through a divorce or a bereavement or something of that sort, I think initially you always feel inadquate. Probably it's unjustified, but I think there's always a certain feeling of inadequacy and going into a college means you've got to sort yourself out and say 'I can do it. I'm just as good. I might even be better than some of the people who are here' – but you've got to make yourself go.'

[Students, Somerset College of Art and Technology]

'The classic opportunity that we can give people is to identify needs that they have got and get something done about them, but I think much more important than that is that if you do manage to get over the threshold and join a course, then you have this marvellous experience of finding out that other people have been through precisely the same experience that you have. You've got something to offer not only yourself in that way but other people as well.'

[Spokesperson, Somerset College of Art and Technology]

Tiverton: East Devon College of Further Education
Return to Learn, part time.

Weymouth College
Open Access service with Teach Yourself units; Learning Resource centre (see 'Open and Distance Learning'). Also free short and block courses in Building, Electronics, Modern Office Skills and Computing.

The following colleges in Wales and the West supplied information in 1987 about their pre-entry courses, but no response was received to 1988 enquiries. Readers may nevertheless wish to make individual contacts:

Cardiff: Rumney College of Technology
Cheltenham: Gloucestershire College of Arts and Technology
Deeside: North East Wales Institute of Higher Education
Llandridnod Wells: Radnor College of Further Education
Totnes: Dartington College of Arts
Weston-super-Mare Technical College and School of Art

Scotland and Northern Ireland

Belfast College of Technology
No pre–entry but many courses for unemployed adults (see "Retraining and New Skills Courses").

Clydebank College
SCE/GCE for mature students. Return to Study. Modular scheme for National Certificate. Details from college. Open Learning Unit (see "Open and Distance Learning Courses").

Dundee: Duncan of Jordanstone College of Art
First Year General Course in Art and Design accepts up to 10% of students without formal qualifications but with good portfolio of work.

Dundee University
New Opportunities for Men and Women, part time (especially relevant for entry to Arts and Social Sciences courses at this university). Wider Opportunities for Women: New Technology course, part time, in association with Dundee College of Further Education.

Edinburgh: Napier College
Open Learning courses (see "Open and Distance Learning Courses").

Edinburgh University
New Horizons. Wider Opportunities for Women – details from university.

Glasgow University
Department of Adult and Continuing Education. Introduction to Study for mature students, mainly evenings, but part time day possible. Successful completion of the course may lead to entry to the Faculties of Arts, Divinity, Law and Financial Studies (with respect to the Law degree) and Social Sciences.

Glasgow: Strathclyde University
Return to Study, evenings. Pre–Entry course, may lead to entry to degrees in

Arts Social Studies, evenings. Continuing Education Certificates, may lead to entry to part time degrees (see "Degree and Advanced Courses").

Inverness College of Further and Higher Education
Modular programme, part time, allowing individuals to plan own Return to Learning, Open University Preparatory Course part time or 21–hour rule. Open Learning (see "Open and Distance Learning Courses").

Newry: the Continuing Education Programme (Southern Education and Library Board)
Time for Women, part time, Women in Mind, part time, Women on the Move, part time – these three offered at Crossmaglen, Newry and Kilkeel. Choices for Women, evenings, offered at Warrenpoint/Newry. Other courses at Newry include: Rural Action Project, part time, Courses for 50–plus, Courses for Volunteer Bureaux, Return to Study, Unemployed Action Group, Job Search Course, Certificate in Foundation Studies for Mature Students, and many others, as may be seen from the college response to enquiries:

Student–Led Courses: viewpoints
"We would like to stress our approach of meeting the needs of people on an ongoing basis. Sometimes this means one–day courses or short block courses, etc. The type of course also changes depending on certain groups and we find ourselves in a facilitating position regularly, regarding the needs of individuals and groups."
[Spokesperson, Newry/Kilkeel Further Education Area]

Newry: Newcastle College of Further Education
GCSE/A–level for mature students, part time, day and evening. Basic Literacy/Numeracy, part time, day and evening. Pre–School Playgroups, part time, for City and Guilds Certificate.

The following colleges in this region supplied information in 1987 about their pre–entry courses, but no response was received to 1988 enquiries. Readers may nevertheless wish to make individual contacts:

Aberdeen University
Aberdeen College of Commerce
Armagh College of Further Education
Ayr College
Glasgow: Cumbernauld College
Glasgow: Springburn College
Hamilton: Bell College of Technology
Larne College of Further Education
Limavady Technical College
Newtownabbey: Ulster University
Stirling University

RETRAINING AND NEW SKILLS COURSES

For people who want to make a complete change or gain new skills to enhance their prospects

Introduction

Just as I was checking the final entries in this section of the book, the Government announced a new initiative, 'Training for Employment', starting in September 1988. 'It is the most important and ambitious training programme for the adult unemployed ever brought forward in this country', they say. Although it is a very new scheme, I can pass on the essentials here, just in case you're one of the people who could be affected.

The main points are that the scheme is designed to give the greatest priority to longer-term unemployed people (though it will be open to all people who have been unemployed for more than six months). At first, it will cater for people aged 18-24, but (says the official press notice) 'within the lifetime of this Parliament, the Government will aim to offer help back into work for all those aged 18-50 who have remained unemployed for two years or more'.

It will provide up to 12 months training (some people won't need that long when it's a question of updating skills), and all trainees will be paid – not a lot, but more than they'd otherwise get on benefits. Anyone who has to train away from home may get extra money – for travel, lodgings, child care, etc. (See the 'Costs and Grants' section of this book for more details.)

The new training programme, which is to be called ''Employment Training', could well be a boon to people who've been unemployed a long time, and who have difficulty in persuading employers to take them on – or perhaps are so out of touch with the jobs market that they don't know what to retrain for. It's also offered to people who want to start their own business, so ask about it if you follow up any of the courses in the 'Small Business and Self-Employment Courses' section of this book. And it'll make use of all sources of retraining – employers, community projects, further education colleges, skill centres, etc. Knowing that this was coming, quite a few of the college authorities who sent in courses for this book added a rider to their letters, saying 'course method and content may change to suit the new scheme'. As I said in the Introduction to the previous section about pre-entry courses, opportunities change all the time. *You,* the user can have an effect on what's offered with the help of your Jobcentre or Job Club.

But having given a welcome to this new government scheme, let's remember that you don't necessarily have to take a government course to retrain. Or even a college course – you can train in employment. For example, nurses are accepted for training up to the age of about 45. The ideal age for trainee sales representatives is 25-35, though people do train when they're younger and older than this. You can go into retailing and catering at almost any age and work your way up to a position of special responsibility – whether it's to do with managing people (department supervisor or floor housekeeper), or using special skills (e.g. running the photocopying bureau in an office supplies shop or silver-service waiting at city banquets).

WHERE MATURITY IS AN ASSET

At the beginning of this book I've given a list of jobs where 'mature entrants' are welcomed (pp. 21-4). Individual employers may vary in their attitude to what is 'mature', but all the jobs are in areas where it's a specific advantage to have had some life experience. Other careers, for which courses are listed in this section, welcome candidates across a wide age range.

Quite a few of the jobs on that list *do* involve retraining, in one way or another. Sometimes you get in via a degree course (see the 'Degree and Advanced Courses' section). Sometimes it's possible to train by home study (see 'Open and Distance Learning Courses'). In other cases, a vocational training is essential.

FULL-TIME OR PART-TIME?

Retraining doesn't always have to be full-time. Indeed the current Job Training Scheme funded by government has many 21-hour courses. On these you keep your right to unemployment or supplementary benefit, since you study for less than 21 hours a week (see 'Costs and Grants' for the rules). In other cases, where a full-time course is needed, you may get an allowance from the MSC (Manpower Services Commission) or ESF (European Social Fund). Or you can try for a discretionary grant from your local education authority. Colleges are very knowledgeable about soures of grants, and it's always worth asking if former students have obtained any grant or award.

The list of courses in this section can only be seen as a sample of what's on offer. Although I contacted every university, polytechnic and college of higher or further education in the UK in 1987, asking for details of courses for adult job-changers, they didn't all reply. When I sent out copy for checking in February 1988, so that it could be as up to date as possible, some colleges didn't return it – even after a reminder. Who knows why this might be? There have been quite a few college amalgamations, which could affect the range of courses on offer. Some colleges don't want to attract outsiders to courses already filled with their own local 'mature returners'. But it does seem that some colleges are not as interested in mature students as others – certainly those who returned 1987 questionnaires that just said 'no' to any question about courses for adults.

ALL STUDENTS WELCOME

In contrast, there were colleges which clearly always go out of their way to cater for the more mature students. They responded quickly, and where they couldn't give exact details of courses, because they were waiting to see if they'd obtained funding, they said so. Others sent prospectuses with friendly, handwritten notes, inviting me to select any courses I felt specially suited to people restarting, and emphasising they welcomed adult students on all courses.

Studying on an 'infill' basis is worth explaining. It means that if there are vacancies in a class for young students, adults can take them up. This can be a very cheap way for colleges to train and for late starters to get a specific skill. It's sometimes possible to join a course that's already started as an infill student, if you have some experience of the subject, and a student has dropped out during the first term.

PERHAPS YOU WANT AN ADVANCED QUALIFICATION?

If you are planning a change of direction, check both this section and the 'Degree and Advanced Courses' section. Some major providers of second chances, such as the Polytechnic of North East London, concentrate their efforts at degree and higher diploma level, welcoming students without A-levels. They've had some remarkable about-turns in the 'second careers' area:- midwife to bereavement counsellor, florist to journalist, window-cleaner to tax officer, and so on. Those new careers gew out of taking a break from work and discovering new abilities through higher education.

HNDS AND HNCS ARE 'ADVANCED' TOO

'HND' stands for 'Higher National Diploma' of the Business and Technician Education Council. There's the HNC too- a Certificate version (usually shorter in duration, though by adding extra modules or units of work, you can convert it into a Diploma if you so choose). Many colleges wanted me to put their HND/HNC courses in the 'Degree and Advanced Courses' section, saying, quite rightly, that they are advanced courses of about pass degree level.

But there's something else about HNDs and HNCs that makes me think they are more suited to being in the 'Retraining' section. They are all *vocational* courses, concentrating on skills and knowledge related to jobs. If you take the HND or HNC, or the Scottish version, which is called the SCOTVEC qualification (SCOTVEC = Scottish Vocational Educational Council), you should have had sufficient training to start a new job straight away.

Degree courses, on the other hand, are not often seen as a form of training (obviously there are exceptions like medicine and dentistry). Having acquired a high level of education, graduates are usually expected to be able to pick up new skills and knowledge very quickly – which is why companies take on people with the most unlikely-sounding higher education qualifications to train in unrelated jobs (I came across one Performance Arts graduate training as a social worker).

But it's in this section that you'll find those advanced courses, because it is about courses and skills that match jobs.

A FEW INDEPENDENT COLLEGES

In this selection of retraining courses, you'll also find one or two run by private training colleges or individuals. Some were discovered during the making of the BBC Radio series 'Back on Course' for adult job-changers, with which I was involved for several years. Others have been recommended by people who have tried them. If there is a silver lining to redundancy, it's that it may be the only time that people have access to a large sum of money with which to pay for a training they've longed to take. In this context, I've listed a good book that lists private training courses in the 'Information Sources' section of this book. It covers everything from beauty therapy to flying.

TRAINING IN YOUR OWN TIME

Not everyone wanting to retrain is unemployed. One of the purposes of *Make A Fresh Start* is to suggest ways in which people can extend their horizons by getting some additional training, qualifications or practical skills on a spare-time basis. For many people, the idea of 'Open' or 'Distance' learningis both an attractive and a realistic way to study. They can keep on working in their jobs, or looking after dependents, yet still forge ahead getting areas of new expertise. If this applies to you, remember to check the 'Open and Distance Learning Courses' section of this book.

MORE COURSES TO COME

I'm happy to say that new courses are always being put on by colleges. In view of the new training programme starting in September 1988 with government support, you can bet that colleges nationwide are looking down their course lists and considering what they have to offer that might be just the thing for local sponsored trainees. Often this sort of opportunity is not advertised in the local paper until the last minute, because the college concerned is waiting for approval from the MSC (soon to become the Training Agency) or the European Social Fund. The moment approval arrives, they advertise.

But in these circumstances, if you've expressed an interest, they'll often tell you in advance what they hope they might be able to do. They may even be prepared to put your name on a waiting list for a place.

OTHER SOURCES OF ADVICE

Given that you know what you'd like to retrain for, a good way of finding out about ways to retrain and where courses are offered is to ask the appropriate trade or professional association. Many have lists of approved courses. Some will indicate courses suitable for mature people, or colleges that they have found sympathetic to the needs of older students in the past. The list of information sources at the end of the book will help you track down these organisations.

Jobcentres are also knowledgeable about retraining courses, especially free ones for unemployed people, and those which attract a retraining allowance. At present, for executives and professionally qualified people, there is a similar free advice service through PER – Professional and Executive Recruitment – which also publicises retraining courses. It seems possible that the PER service may be privatised (though they could still offer the same sort of service to jobhunters seeking retraining).

Educational Guidance Centres, where available (see the 'Information Sources' section), have advisers to consult and reference books to look in, but as yet not every town has such a service. The careers staff at local colleges are often willing to advise potential students. And there are independent careers guidance agencies (my personal recommendation is Career Analysts, 90 Gloucester Place, London W1), which charge a fee for testing your aptitudes and abilities and advising you both on new careers and ways of training to suit your circumstances.

When all is said and done, the one source of information that is accessible to everybody is the public library service. It may be a huge building in a city centre or just a travelling library in a van, but librarians can track down elusive information regardless of difficulties, given a few days for their research. Incidentally, you can telephone libraries with questions, and the person on duty to deal with queries will look up information or addresses for you.

STUDENT AND COLLEGE VIEWPOINTS

I have included contributions from individual students about the courses they have taken and in some cases, comments from college staff. 'College spokesperson' is a shorthand term for male and female college principals, senior lecturers, tutors, counsellors and others on the tutorial side who offer helpful advice to people considering retraining. You'll find personal contributions as follows:

Adult Training Strategy: Croydon College
Aerobics Teaching: West London Institute of Higher Education
Aeronautical Engineering: Brunel Technical College, Bristol
Antique/Ceramics Restoration: West Dean College, Chichester
Art and Drama Therapy: Hertfordshire College of Art and Design

Book Conservation: Colchester Institute
Community Service: Rockingham College, Rotherham
Electronics Conversion Course: Polytechnic of Wales, Pontypridd
Graphic Art and Design: Somerset College of Art and Technology
Independent Study: North East London Polytechnic
Hospital Play Therapy: Bilston Community College, Wolverhampton
Languages for Business: Solihull College of Technology
Medical Laboratory Technology: Manchester Polytechnic
Microelectronics: Rockingham College, Rotherham
Modelmaking: Hertfordshire College of Art and Design
Motorcycle Engineering: Merton College
Musical Instrument Repair: Merton College
Nursery Nursing: Camden Training Centre
Nursing: Queen Alexandra Hospital, Portsmouth
Residential Social Work: Suffolk College, Ipswich
Science Laboratory Technology: Manchester Polytechnic
Secretarial Work: Pitman Central College, London
Silverworking: West Dean College, Chichester
Social Work: Suffolk College, Ipswich, and Stevenage College
Teaching English as a Foreign Language: Eaton Hall, Retford
Tour Management: British Isles Study Programme
Vehicle Restoration: Colchester Institute
Working with Precious Metals: West Dean College, Chichester

Remember – these are only those subjects on which I have been given personal reports. The lists that follow contain many other retraining opportunities for adults, from taking a City and Guilds Certificate in Media Techniques (Press and Radio Skills) with Urdu or Gujurati or Arabic, full-time or part-time, to tackling a Guest House Owner's course by Open Learning, with tutorial back-up on the student's own premises if required. Many courses that can lead to second careers are to be found in the 'Degree and Advanced Courses' section, the 'Small Business and Self-Employment Courses' section and the 'Open and Distance Learning' section. Check these too.

THE COURSE LISTS

Courses are listed in order of town name within each region. The full address of each college is given in the regional address lists at the back of the book. If you have opened the book at this section, you'll want to know why I've chosen this layout. It's because, quite often, a college name doesn't indicate where it is. For instance, Cassio College is in Watford, and West Dean College is in Chichester. Grouping colleges together in regions makes it possible for you to see what might be on offer within reasonable travelling distance of your home, or perhaps your place of work.

If you contact your local college, you may well find more courses on offer – those that were not confirmed when this book went to press, or that have been newly introduced to satisfy demand. I am always delighted to know about new retraining courses and readers' experiences of them. Please write to me through the publisher Kogan Page, whose address is at the front of this book.

London and Middlesex

Colleges appearing in this section are listed below by district, except where the location of the college is obvious from its name. This should help you to discover the most accessible college offering the course that you want.

Avery Hill, Dartford, Mile End, Woolwich	Thames Polytechnic
Barking, West Ham	North East London Polytechnic
Barnet, Enfield, Haringey	Middlesex Polytechnic
Camden and Islington	North London Polytechnic
Deptford	South East London College
Elephant and Castle	London College of Printing
Euston, Hoborn, Oxford Circus	Central London Polytechnic
Greenford	British Isles Study Programme
Hackney	Cordwainers Technical College
Holborn	Pitman Central College
Isleworth	West London Institute of Higher Education
Knightsbridge	Tour Management Training Centre
Leicester Square	College for the Distributive Trades
Oxford Circus	London College of Fashion
Tooting	South West London College
Waterloo	Morley College
West Norwood	South London College

British Isles Study Programme (Independent College)
Full time Tour Management training course (also available in Edinburgh). Applicants must be at least 25 and preference is given to people with foreign language qualifications. Course is approved by the Association of British Travel Agents and leads to City and Guilds Certificate in Tour Management.

Tour Management: viewpoints
'I am a tour manager working on a freelance basis. The tours that I conduct

are very varied, as the itineraries are those requested by overseas travel agents with many specialist interests, e.g. sports, history, cathedrals, agriculture, houses and industry. My next tour will take me to Stratford-upon-Avon, Chester, North Wales, Edinburgh, the Scottish Highlands and the Isle of Skye. After that I will spend a week in Ireland.'

In addition to the BISP Tour Manager's course, I have qualified as a York Minster Accredited Guide, and have taken the BISP Graduate Training Tours to Hadrian's Wall, Cumbria and Ireland. I speak English, French and German fluently, and find much of my work in these languages.'

[Former student, British Isles Study programme]

'The City and Guilds of London Institute specifies exactly what students must absorb to earn the National Certificate: the techniques, the documentation to be dealt with, booking into and out of a hotel, set procedures, what to do if a passport is lost, and so on. The second part of the examination deals with the history, topography and geography of Britain and Ireland. It can include questions on art, stately homes, architecture and general knowledge.

The British Isles Study Programme includes a seven-day tour of Britain, during which each student is expected to present a prepared subject to his fellow students over the public address system. Each student acts as the 'Duty Tour Manager' for one day. The organiser arranges for problems to arise, such as a coach breakdown, a passenger with a sudden illness, or hotel operational difficulties, to ensure the student can cope.

Prospects are good as the incoming travel industry expands year after year, though in the first year, newcomers may begin with only short engagements. Some people only want to work for a limited period each season. For example, one lady is a school teacher who can only accept work when she's not teaching. Another is a retired Royal Navy Officer, who only wants to work a few weeks each year. Others are actors, and only want to work while 'resting'. Others want to work the full season, which means from April to late October.'

[Spokesperson, British Isles Study Programme]

Camden Training Centre

(In association with Kingsway College, Hackney College, Southwark College, North London College, Working Men's College, Kilburn Polytechnic, Project Fullemploy, Co-ops Advisory Group.) MSC-sponsored courses: Building Maintenance, under 21-hour rule; Carpentry and Joinery, full time; Microelectronics, full time; Gardening, full time; Printing, full time; Camden-sponsored Industrial Clothing Machining, full time. Cookery for the Catering Industry, for City and Guilds 706/1, part time, under 21-hour rule. Call Order Catering, for City and Guilds 700/1, part time, under 21-hour rule. Nursery Nursing (men and women over 26) for NNEB Certificate, full time. ESF-sponsored courses: Business Technology for

Women, full time; Building for Women, part time under 21-hour rule; Plastering for Women, full time; Carpentry for Women, full time; Introductory Building for Women, part time, under 21-hour rule; Introduction to Computing, full time; Women's Introductory Microelectronics/Women's Microelectronics (mode unspecified).

Nursery Nursing: viewpoints

'I'd been unemployed for two years,during which time I'd been working voluntarily with children at weekends, handicapped children in an adventure playground. Prior to that I'd worked in homes and schools for handicapped children, and I had thought of going on a comprehensive nursing course, for children and general nursing. When I saw the nursery nurse course advertised, I thought it would be a very good preparation – or it might be entire in itself. We learn about the normal child from 0 to 7,covering child development, child care and education, spending four days at the training centre and one day a week out on placement (and the course is also preceded and followed by placements). My ambition is to get experience after qualifying and then to do voluntary work overseas in a Third World country.'

[Student nursery nurse, Camden Training Centre]

'All our students are over 25 and take a standard entry test and are interviewed before acceptance. As well as child care, health, development and education, their course includes first-aid training, social studies, communication and a creative studies component so that they develop interests they can share with children.'

[Spokesperson, Camden Training Centre]

Central London Polytechnic

Sites at Euston, Holborn and around Oxford Circus area. Comprehensive evening and part time day Languages Faculty (25 languages) with courses at several levels. Diploma in English as a Second or Foreign Language, full time but attendance arranged between 9.30 a.m. and 1.30 p.m. for those with home responsibilities. Diploma in Law, full time (for mature students who obtain a Certificate of Eligibility from the Council for Legal Education). Diploma in Applied Social Studies/Certificate of Qualification in Social Work, full time,for mature students over 30.

Chelsea School of Art

Certificate in Interior Decoration, full time, mature students welcome.

College for the Distributive Trades

College says you may be admitted to any course 'as an exceptional case – this usually depends on age and experience'. Options include Furnishing and Interior Design, full time, (trade experience or special aptitudes may be accepted in lieu of 0-levels/GCSE), BTEC National Diploma and COTAC Certificate course in Travel and Tourism, full time (no maximum age limit; candidates with four 0-levels or equivalent), Fresh Food Merchandising (older applicants welcome; CSE or similar in two or three subjects). Separate part time course prospectus.

Cordwainers Technical College
Leathergoods Diploma full time, for City and Guilds, GCSE and A-level. Rural Saddlery, full time, for City and Guilds, Saddlery Skills Test and Worshipful Company of Loriners Certificate. BTEC National Diploma in Design (Footwear), full time. BTEC National Diploma in Footwear Manufacture and Design, full time. (Both BTEC courses start Autumn 1988, subject to approval and validation.) BTEC Higher National Diploma in Design (Footwear), full time. BTEC Higher National Diploma in Footwear Manufacture, full time. (Both BTEC courses start Autumn 1988 or 1989 subject to approval and validation.)

London College of Fashion
Certificate in Clothing Production, full time, for those over 21 planning to enter the clothing industry at technician level. You need at least threeGCEs, including English Language, and the college says 'it is not uncommon for students to be graduates'. Clothing Skills, under 21-hour rule, may lead to City and Guilds awards in Garment Making and Wholesale Cutting. BTEC HND Theatre Studies, full time:candidates with at least two years' experience in the theatre considered without formal entry qualifications; options in Theatrical Costume or Specialist Make-Up. Evening courses in Theatrical Hair Skills; Theatrical Wigmaking; Theatrical Make-Up techniques, open to people who participate in amateur dramatics as well as professionals. Trichology, evenings (foundation course for those without science background).

London College of Printing
HND Business Studies with options in Printing and Publishing, Journalism, Publicity and Promotion, full time. Entry concessions possible for those over 21. NB Candidates who successfully complete the course with the journalism option will also be awarded a Periodical Training Trust Certificate. Certificate in Pre-Entry Periodical Journalism, full time, entry concessions possible for those who show promise as journalists. Foundation in Media Studies, full time, unqualified mature candidates considered if they show ability to undertake the course. Diploma in Photo-Journalism, full time, for practising photographers, writers and journalists, but applications invited from mature students, particularly from ethnic minorities. Diploma in Publishing Production, full time, open to mature students seeking a change of career as well as those with publishing experience. Diploma in Graphic Origination and Reproduction, full time,open to candidates with relevant

industrial experience and examples of their work. Diploma in Creative Screen Printing, full time, as above. Certificate in Printing Techniques, full time, for those who have prospects of employment or see career prospects in printing. Certificate in Craft Bookbinding, full time, no formal entry qualification (extended study also possible).

Middlesex Polytechnic

(Six sites in and around Barnet, Enfield and Haringey.) Certificate/Diploma in Higher Education; Modular course, subjects can be vocationally related – e.g. Law, Art and Design, Education, Information Technology. Entry concessions possible for those over 21, DipHE can lead to degrees (see 'Degree and Advanced Courses'). Certificate in Industrial Relations and Trade Union Studies, full time or part time for potential full-time trade union officers: mature students without qualifications and with trade union experience specifically invited to apply. Introduction to Information Technology, full time and part time. Certificate of Qualification in Social Work, full time, aimed primarily at people aged 25 or over with some experience in voluntary or paid social service. Diploma in Drama, part time, can lead to LRAM Speech and Drama(performer or teacher) – entrance audition and interview. Diploma in Dramatic Art, full time, entry concessions possible for over-21s who satisfy course selection team that they are suitable and also pass the audition/interview and diagnostic written tests. RSA Diploma in the Teaching of Community Languages, part time, for teachers of community languages in LEA or community schools. Candidates should either have an A-level in an appropriate language (Greek, Turkish, Urdu, Punjabi, Gujarati, Hindi or Bengali) or have reached the level of a full secondary education in the medium of the specified language. Diploma of the Market Research Society, part time – unqualified mature students currently employed in market research or marketing are considered. Short courses with earning potential include Interior Design, Calligraphy, Photography.

Morley College

Many leisure courses, some with earning potential. Examples, all part time: Photography, Calligraphy, Glass Engraving, Craft Bookbinding, Hand and Machine Knitting, Quilt-making and Patchwork, Dressmaking, Toymaking, Jewellery Making, Cookery, Cake-Decorating, Radio Production Skills, Television Training (includes scriptwriting), Creative Writing – Novels, Plays, Writing for Radio and TV – Woodwork and Picture Framing. Language-learning facilities include Dutch, Norwegian, Polish, Japanese, Chinese. Music courses include Recording Techniques and Popular Composing and Arranging for Instruments (if you want to start your own group). Foundation course for Pre-School Playgroup Leaders. Nominal fee and 21-hour rule arrangements for unemployed/benefit claimants.

North East London Polytechnic
(Sites at Barking and West Ham.) Polytechnic Diploma/Certificate of Qualification in Social Work, full time, for candidates over 25 with some relevant experience. Diploma in Careers Guidance, full time. Consideration given to those over 25 with valuable employment experience but no formal entry qualifications. Diploma of Higher Education (Multi-Subject), entry concessions possible for mature students. Options include Architecture, Business Studies, Information Technology, Electrical Engineering, Psychology. DipHE by Independent Study, full time or part time – see below. Polytechnic Postgraduate Diploma in Management (also open to non-graduates – students may be self-employed), part time by self-managed learning. This polytechnic also welcomes mature students with unconventional qualifications to Engineering and Business Studies courses. Mature students generally welcome; more than a third of students are over 25.

Independent Study: viewpoint
'The School for Independent Study was established to enable students to plan for themselves their own programmes to study in partnership with the specialist areas of the polytechnic. The main age range is from 25 to 40, though students include people aged from 21 to 70. It is very suitable for career change:previous students have included a fireman who became a social worker and a florist who became a journalist. Students have to agree their programme with tutors, establish that they can get adequate supervision and present work for assessment like any other students. But unqualified people are considered (on science and technology programmes as well as the arts and social sciences) and work schedules can be devised to suit an individual student's circumstances.'
[Spokesperson, School for Independent Study, North East London Polytechnic]

North London Polytechnic
(Sites in Camden and Islington.) Polytechnic Diploma/Certificate of Qualification in Social Work, full time, open to mature candidates without formal qualifications (under 25s should have five 0-levels or three A-levels, including English). Diploma in Purchasing and Supply, full time or part time, for graduates or entrants with HND/HNC in Business Studies, or mature students with relevant experience. Diploma in Recreation Management, full time, for graduates or those with HND/professional qualifications, or exceptionally for over-27s with HNC or at least four years of management experience. (A range of part time courses related to recreation is available – ask the polytechnic.) Other courses which mature entrants might consider as a way of retraining or developing career prospects include Accounting Foundation, full time; Postgraduate Conversion Diploma in Computing (see 'Degree and Advanced Courses'), Diploma in Labour Studies, full time, giving exemption from Stage 2 exams of the Institute of

Personnel Management. Also evening degrees (see 'Degree and Advanced Courses').

Paddington College

MSC-funded Work Preparation courses, introducing a range of employment fields. Medical Records and Computing/Information Technology courses, arranged between 10 a.m. and 3 p.m. for mature students, the latter course particularly for bilingual students. Association of Accounting Technicians' Certificate in Accounting. NNEB Nursery Nurse training, full time, for mature men and women with a broad general education. Bilingualism is an asset for this course. Office training for adults – flexible modular packages in office skills and information technology, duration varies.

Pitman Central College

Range of secretarial and business studies courses, including the 15-week intensive secretarial course described below:

Secretarial Work: viewpoint

'I had been managing a shop, but after a year the demands of working every Saturday and all through holiday periods (we even opened on Bank Holidays as we catered for the tourist trade) prompted me to change careers. Secretarial training looked like a good launch pad with dozens of possible work environments from hospitals to newspapers. I spent my savings on a 15-week intensive course at Pitman Central College, and believe me, it *was* intensive. For the first five weeks there were two hours of shorthand homework every night and we worked hard all day, with only short coffee and lunch breaks. It paid off: at the end of the 15 weeks, all 20 people on the course left with Pitman Certificates for speeds of 80 wpm (or more) shorthand and 40 wpm typewriting, plus word-processing experience. I left college on Friday and started as a secretary in a graphic design agency on Monday. Ater a year, and substantial salary increases, I'm now office administrator with a receptionist and a junior to help me.'

[Former student, Pitman Central College]

Richmond Adult and Community College

ESF-sponsored Back to Business course, full time, for women aged 25-plus who have had their careers interrupted; includes updating on Computing and New Business Technology, Wide range of Office Skills courses, part time, including Beginners' Office Technology, school hours only and Refreshers' Office Technology, school hours only. P/t and evening courses with earning potential include Glass Engraving, Car Bodywork Repairs, Painting and Paperhanging, Upholstery, Doll Repair, Picture Framing, Dressmaking, Pottery, Chair Seating and Basketry.

South East London College
For adult job-changers, the college suggests: MSC-funded 'Women Into Non-Traditional Areas of Work' (WINTAW), 11-week full time course, school hours: includes mechanical and electronic engineering, construction, painting and decorating. Electronic Servicing (TV and Audio Equipment and Industrial Equipment) for City and Guilds award, full time. Microcomputer Technology, for City and Guilds award, full time. Basic Craft Principles in Electrical/Electronics or Mechanical Engineering (under 21-hour rule) Welding Craft Practice, for City and Guilds award, part time. Welding or Basic Hydraulic Pneumatic Systems or Basic Robotics, evenings. Electronics for Women, school hours and terms (ESF sponsorship possible). NC/CNC Machine Tool Setting, part time or evenings, for City and Guilds award. NC/CNC Machine Tool Programming, part time or evenings for City and Guilds award. Refrigeration Mechanics Course (Installation and Service), full time, for City and Guilds Award. BTEC National Diploma in Business and Finance full time, entry concessions possible for over-19s National Examinations Board for Supervisory Studies (NEBSS) Certificate and Local Government Certificate, part time, for potential supervisors. Work Study, students over 20, part time, day or evening. BTEC National Diploma in Computer Studies, full time, over-19s selected by aptitude test and interview. MSC-sponsored Cobol Programming course (sandwich), selection by aptitude test and interview. Information Technology Users courses (various levels), part time. Software Workshops for Information Technology users (business, education, medical; various entry requirements, part time, day or evening. MSC-sponsored Retraining – Accounts/Book-Keeper or Secretarial, full time. Home Economics for Family and Community Care, for City and Guilds award, full time, possibility of 21-hour rule entry for mature students. Catering Supervision and Management for City and Guilds Award, for over-21s with relevant City and Guilds certificate. The Cookery Certificate, day or evening. Creative Studies (Fashion), part time, for mature students, includes design, cutting, construction, for City and Guilds award; good basis for dressmaking business.

South London College
MSC-sponsored Wider Opportunities for Women, full time. Women-only BTEC National Diploma in Engineering, full time. Women-only BTECNational Certificate in Engineering, part time.

South West London College
Association of Accounting Technicians' Certificate, full time, no formal entry requirements. Chartered Association of Certified Accountants Graduate Conversion course, full time. Office Skills for mature students, school hours only, no formal entry requirements. English as a Second Language/Office Skills, mornings only, no formal entry requirements. Adult Secretarial, school hours only, no formal entry requirements. Access to Professional Accountancy, full time, no formal entry requirements. BTEC

National/HND and Certificate/HNC Business Studies, full time, entry concessions possible for over-19s. Introductory/Certificate courses in Supervisory Studies, part time, for potential supervisors. Institute of Training and Development Certificate, part time, no formal entry requirements.

Thames Polytechnic

(Sites at Avery Hill, Mile End, Dartford (Kent) and Woolwich, also incorporating Garnett College.) ESF-sponsored courses for women under 25 – 'Women into Business'' and 'Women into Advice Work (Educational)'. Computer Studies, evenings. Landscape Architecture – Certificate/Diploma (graduates only), evenings or day and evening. Diploma in Management Services (Health Services), graduates, nurses, paramedical professionals and health service administrative staff, day and evening. Physics for teachers of other subjects, day and evening. HND Civil Engineering, full time or sandwich, applications welcome from mature students unable to satisfy normal entrance requirements. HND Computer Studies, full time, open to mature students with varying qualifications/experience but able to show suitability. HND Information Technology, full time, same entry specification. Mature students welcome to apply for all full time and part time courses; entrance requirements not always needed for over 21s.

Tour Management Training Centre

(Independent College – S Little, Course Manager.) Tour Management Training Programme, January-March, part time, leading to City and Guilds award in Tour Management (Europe) and Association of British Travel Agents' Seal of Approval. Knowledge of foreign languages is an advantage. Selection by interview each autumn.

Uxbridge College

MSC-sponsored 'Women and the Electronic Office', full time, 10 a.m.-3 p.m., including use of computers and word-processors. MSC-sponsored 'Applied Business Computing', full time, in aspects of computing for graduates and other mature candidates wanting to change direction. Flexiskill courses in Typewriting (Beginners and Refresher), Word-Processing, Book-keeping and Audio-Typing. Part-time, in modified form, at low cost. Flexible courses developed by women for women wishing to return to work.

West London Institute of Higher Education

Diploma in Social Work/Certificate of Qualification in Social Work; entry concessions possible for those over 25; preference may be given to those with some social work experience. Diploma in Occupational Therapy, full time, entry concessions possible for mature students. BTEC HND in Computer Studies, full time, entry route available for mature students with some computing experience. Short computer courses, including Introductory Programming, Worde-Processing: Wordstar and Word-11, use of spreadsheets and databases. P/t and evening courses, some devised to meet special needs, see below:

Aerobics Teaching Course: viewpoints
'I'd like to teach aerobics but I feel I have to improve my style first of all, and I plan to complete my course and get the Diploma so that I'll feel really qualified to teach. It's demanding: you attend for two hours of theory and two hours of practical work three nights a week, and they also wanted us to have 0-levels and some kind of background in fitness, either attending aerobics classes, or running for a certain period or some other kind of regular exercise programme.'

[Student, West London Institute of Higher Education]

'The course came about largely through the initiative of the Physical Education Association of Great Britain, who were interested in developing a course which would be acceptable in an area of study where there's been concern by PE educators about the level and competency of instructors in fitness and health centres. We had also been approached by commercial organisations to set up training courses for their instructors. The student response on this first course was out of all proportion to what we expected: several hundred applicants for 16 places! Hopefully, there will be an extension of the scheme on a national basis so students outside London can find approved centres by approaching the Physical Education Association.'

[Spokesperson, West London Institute of Higher Education]

The following colleges in this region supplied information in 1987 about their retraining courses, but no response was received to 1988 enquiries. Readers may nevertheless wish to make individual contact:

City of London Polytechnic
Ealing College of Higher Education
Goldsmiths' College
Hackney College
Tottenham College of Technology

Southern and Eastern England

Basingstoke Technical College
JTS Office Skills Refresher, part time, includes choice of skills training. Mature candidates accepted on full time Diploma for Personal Assistants, part time Secretarial/Office Skills, on short courses in Word-Processing Familiarisation, and on infill basis to part time Typewriting.

Brighton Polytechnic
BTEC HND Public Administration, full time, entry concessions possible for those aged 21-plus. NB: This policy may apply to other Brighton HNDs and also part time HNCs. Polytechnic Certificate scheme in Art, Craft and Society, part time, special options include Art, Bookbinding and Repair, Printmaking, Photography, Three-Dimensional Craft (Wood, Metal, Ceramics or Plastics), Printing and the Graphic Arts. Diploma of Higher Education (Business Studies) part time, open to wide range of candidates, including, for example, those with a teacher's certificate or diploma and, exceptionally, unqualified mature students with adequate business experience. Can lead to a degree (see 'Degree and Advanced Courses'). Polytechnic Certificate course in Computer Studies, part time. Computer Workshops, various levels, from beginner upwards. Postgraduate Diploma in Counselling, part time, for candidates with or without academic qualifications who have substantial experience in the counselling field. Polytechnic Diploma in Creative Embroidery, part time, mainly for teachers, but others who can demonstrate ability considered. Foreign languages, part time, various levels: French,German, Spanish, Greek, Italian, Russian, Portuguese. Certificate in Management Studies, part time, wide range of entry qualifications acceptable: over-25s with suitable business experience need not always have formal qualifications.

Bromley College of Technology
MSC-sponsored Real-Time Computer Programming and Applications, full time. MSC-sponsored Secretarial Course, part time through Job Training Scheme. Electronics Servicing for City and Guilds award, part time, for those employed in the industry and those with a keen interest in it. BTEC Post Experience courses, part time, for people aged 21-plus – main entry

criterion is 'ability to benefit'. Options are Computer Studies, Improve your Financial Decision Making, Making Sense of Marketing. Evening study options include Word-Processing (Introductory to Advanced), Computer Literacy, Audio-Typing, Medical Shorthand.

Cambridge College of Further Education
Job Training Scheme funded by MSC. RSA Book-keeping/ Accounts,evenings. GCSE, evenings. Foundation Certificate in Accounting, day and evenings, can lead to Association of Accounting Technicians' course. Institute of Marketing Certificate and Diploma, evenings, applicants with sales/marketing experience but without usual qualifications may be admitted. Tee-Line Shortand, Typewriting and Word-Processing, beginners to RSA III, day and evenings. Cake Decoration, for those aiming at high standards for celebration cakes, evenings. Patisserie, afternoons, to meet requirements of hotels, hospitals, etc. Cookery for Hotels and Restaurants, City and Guilds 706/1, part time day release. Breadmaking and Flour Confectionery for City and Guilds 120, part time, for new entrants to/older workers in bakery industry. Wine and Spirit Association Certificates, part time, useful preparation for work in wine trade, hotels, etc. Applications Programming Certificate for City and Guilds 417, part time, to suit computer operators wishing to progress. Community Care in Practice, for people employed, or preparing for work, in the community, part time. Pre-School Playgroups Association Foundation course, part time, school hours only. Nursery Assistants course, for those wishing to work with the under-fives, City and Guilds 730, Certificate for Teachers in Further and Adult Education, City and Guilds 734, Certificate in Teaching Students with Special Needs in Further Education, RSA Diploma in the Teaching of Communications, RSA Certificate for Vocational Preparation Tutors – modes unspecified.

Cambridge: Cambridgeshire College of Arts and Technology
BTEC HND Business Studies, entry concessions possible for over-21s (most students have at least O-levels), work experience taken into account. BTEC HND Software Engineering, over-21s without formal qualifications but with relevant work experience considered. BTEC HND Illustration – 'students with exceptional artistic ability or relevant industrial experience may be accepted with less than the minimum qualifications'. P/t and short course options include Camera Work and Graphic Reproduction; Computer Applications in Phototypesetting; Photocomposition – Film and Paper Assembly; Photocomposition – Keyboard Systems and Phototypesetting; Print Familiarisation, Lithographic Printing and Platemaking (Art and Design Department). Also Motor Vehicle Welding, Diesel Engine Servicing, Motor Vehicle Electronics, etc. (Engineering Department). Secretarial and Word Processing courses (Management and Business Studies Department). P/t vocational courses are offered in the following subject areas (details from

college): Science, Computing, Engineering, Mechanical and Production Engineering (short courses), Management and Business Studies, Construction, Printing, Foreign Language Training for Business.

Canterbury College of Art – see Kent Institute of Art and Design

Chatham: Mid Kent College of Further and Higher Education
(Also at Rochester and Maidstone.) BTEC National Diploma and HND, sandwich, Computer Studies. Mature students without the usual academic qualifications may be admitted in special circumstances. BTEC HND Business Studies, full time, same rules as for Computer Studies. Certificate of Qualification in Social Work, full time, for applicants aged 20-50. Those over 25 do not need formal academic qualifications, though they must satisfy the college that they can meet the academic requirements of the course. All candidates must have had at least a year's working experience since leaving school (not necessarily in social work). Applications from mature students/ethnic minorities particularly welcome. Association of Accounting Technicians' Course, part time – over-21s without usual entry requirements may apply. BTEC Business Studies or Business Studies (Finance), part time, over-21s without usual academic entry requirements may apply. Institute of Legal Executives, part time, over-30s with appropriate experience may be exempted from educational entry requirement. Institute of Purchasing and Supply Foundation Course, part time – over-25s with relevant experience may be exempted from educational entry requirement. BTEC Certificate in Management Studies, part time – over-25s who have held a suitable post for at least three years may be admitted without formal academic qualifications. NEBSS Certificate/Diploma in Supervisory Studies, part time – for employed/potential supervisors,with background to enable them to benefit from the course. Institution of Industrial Managers (formerly Works Managers), part time – over-27s with at least four years industrial experience may be admitted without academic entry requirements. Institute of Personnel Management, part time – over-23s with at least two years relevant experience may be accepted without the minimum academic qualifiations. Computer Programming, part time, introductory to advanced. MSC-sponsored Business Computing, part time. NC/CNC Machine Tool Setting and Operation, and NC/CNC Part-Programming, part time – for mature students, to update their knowledge. Shorthand, Typewriting and Word-Processing, part time, various levels, Medical Reception, part time, open to those without experience in the medical field. Open Learning (see 'Open and Distance Learning Courses').

Chichester: West Dean College
(Independent college.) Three full time restoration courses in association with the British Antique Dealers' Association – Antique Furniture, Antique Porcelain and Ceramics, Antique Clocks – and two full time professional

restoration courses – Musical Instrument Making, and Book-binding and the Care of Books. All five courses lead to Diplomas. The college authorities emphasise that Antique Ceramics Restoration and Antique Clocks are 'advanced' courses, though they appear in this retraining section as they enable successful students to acquire a vocational training. Also short (one-week or weekend) courses in creative subjects with earning potential – e.g. Cabinet-Making, Calligraphy, Stained Glass, Working with Precious Metals.

Antique Ceramics Restoration: viewpoint
'This course combines a very good basic training in the history of ceramics with practical experience at the same time. We often work from museum photographs of articles in their original condition. Any restoration should be accurate, and ethics come into it. The restoration must be unobtrusive, yet quite obvious when you look at it from, say, about a foot. When I leave,I'll find a job that isn't purely commercial, which combines craft with the antiques trade.'

[Student, Restoration course at West Dean College]

Working with Precious Metals: viewpoint
'I'm making a silver coffee pot, which is the most complicated thing I have tackled so far, but I do make other things – boxes, bowls, spoons, small things to make and sell or give as Christmas presents or 25th wedding anniversary presents. The fact that West Dean runs weekend and five-day courses means that they cater both for the person with leisure to fill and those who may want to turn a hobby to professional use, perhaps when they are between careers. If you choose, they can train you to a competent professional level.'

[Student on Working with Silver short course, West Dean College]

Chichester: West Sussex Institute of Higher Education
Nurse training in association with Chichester and Graylingwell School of Nursing, for candidates aged 18-42; courses leading to Registered General Nurse, Registered Mental Nurse, Enrolled Nurse General and Enrolled Nurse Mental. See Nurses' Central Clearing House in the address list at the back of this book for the address to which to apply.

Colchester Institute
MSC-sponsored Import/Export Clerks, full time. MSC-sponsored Systems Analysis, full time. MSC-Sponsored Advanced Office Technology, full time. MSC-sponsored BTEC Certificate in Electronics, full time. Mature students welcome and no upper age limit to any of the Institute's courses – admission at the discretion of individual course tutors. Courses that attract late starters are Teaching English as a Foreign Language, full time; Diploma in Vehicle Restoration, full time; Diploma in Book Conservation, full time; Diploma in

Leisure and Recreation Studies, full time. Open Learning (see 'Open and Distance Learning Courses').

Vehicle Restoration: viewpoint
'I left school with really no idea what I wantd to do, and ended up restoring and tuning pianos,which I enjoyed. In the last few years, it's obviously been a dying trade because of the advent of electronic instruments, so when I saw this car restoration course advertised, I jumped at the chance – the philosophy of restoration is very much the same. Though the metalwork, and particularly the welding, involves a lot more than I first thought, the woodwork tools and usages are all the same. What the course has done for me is to give me a lot of skills which will mean I can't be out of work when I leave here. Firms specialising in car restoration are springing up all over the country. I think people are simply getting fed up with the boxes car manufacturers are producing nowadays, all alike in three sizes.'
[Student, Vehicle Restoration Course, Colchester Institute]

Book Conservation: viewpoint
'We also offer a two-year Diploma in the Conservation of Books and Archive Materials, from which students move into a wide variety of jobs: in County Record Offices and the Public Records Office, in Trinity College, Dublin, and another one works with the National Trust, looking at the problems of book collections in big country houses. Two former students set up independently in Cambridge. Another is off to Glasgow University Library; another went to the National Library in Florence – a lovely place to work. Book and Archive Conservation is an area where it's been estimated in this country alone there will be over 100 jobs coming up in the next five years; in fact there's an absolute mountain of work piling up all the time – millions of documents in need of conservation.'
[Spokesperson, Book Conservation, Colchester Institute]

Croydon College
Wide range of Adult Training opportunities for people on Community Programmes, designed to suit each person's needs. Options include: Construction, Book-keeping and Financial Administration; Electro-Mechanical Engineering; Computing; Community Health and Social Work; Plumbing, Painting and Decorating; Counselling; Supervisory Skills. (See also 'Small Business and Self-Employment Courses'.) BTEC HND Business Studies, full time, possible entry concessions for over 21s. Extended Certificate of Qualification in Social Work (CQSW), full time, but hours 10 a.m. – 3 p.m. only to suit people with home commitments. Certificate of Qualification in Social Work, full time, conventional hours. For both CQSW courses, those over 25 need not have O-levels but must show evidence of ability to undertake academic work and, ideally, have some relevant experience. Estimating and Quantity Surveying, full time, for over-21s with

building industry experience. Bookbinding, part time, day or evening. Printmaking, part time,(selection by portfolio for practising artists). Certified Diploma in Accounting and Finance for graduates or equivalent, but over-21s may be considered on the grounds of relevant experience. BTEC HNC Business Studies/Public Administration, part time – over-21s without usual qualifications may be accepted at Course Director's discretion. BTEC Certificate in Management Studies, part time – over-25s may be accepted with three years relevant management experience.Certificate in Marketing, evenings – over-21s with three years practical marketing experience need not offer formal qualifications. Institute of Personnel Management Course, part time, day and evening or evenings only – Part 1 entry open to people with two A-levels *or* two years practical experience. Institute of Purchasing and Supply Foundation Course, evenings – people aged 26-plus working in purchasing need not offer GCEs. NEBSS Certificate in Supervisory Management, for candidates of minimum age 21-plus and with supervisory potential. Shorthand/Typing, afternoons or evenings – candidates must be competent in English Language. Service of Food (Silver Service Waiting), evenings, no formal entry requirements. Wine and Spirit Education Trust Certificate/Higher Certificate, no formal entry requirement. Computer Literacy and Computer Programming, evenings, no formal entry requirement. CNAA Certificate in Further and Adult Education, part time, for those wishing to teach in further and adult education. BTEC National Certificate in Heating, Ventilating and Air Conditioning, part time day and evening, for draughtsmen/women or site technicians wishing to extend career prospects. City and Guilds Craft Studies in Electronic Engineering, part time, day and evening. Mature, experienced students may be admitted at Part II level. Mechanical Engineering Craft Studies for City and Guilds 201/5 awards, open to mature students with engineering background. Machine Tool Setting and Operation for NC/CNC, leading to City and Guilds 230 award; mature students employed in production engineering considered. Motor Vehicle Craft Studies for City and Guilds 381 award, part time, day or evening, no formal entry requirements. NB: many of these courses are designed for young students, but the college willingly considers mature entrants when space is available.

Adult Training Strategy: viewpoint

'There is a wide range of courses on the Adult Training Strategy at Croydon College for people from a Community Programme/Unemployed background, including Pitman's Office Skills; AEB Book-keeping; RSA Business Courses; Cambridge University Information Technology and Computer Courses; CSLA Sports Awards courses; Youth and Community Guidance courses; Interpersonal and Counselling Skills courses; Elderly Care courses; Crèche Workers courses; City and Guilds courses in Carpentry and Joinery, Construction, and in Painting and Decorating. The Adult Training Strategy at Croydon College can also get numbers of Community Programme/

Unemployed people on to a wide spectrum of traditional further education curricula on an infill basis.'

[Spokesperson, Croydon College]

Epsom: North East Surrey College of Technology

MSC-sponsored Accounts/Book-keeping, full time; Access to Information Technology, part time; Computer Programming, full time; Secretarial Refresher, full time; Clerical Update, full time. BTEC HNC Building Services Engineering (Controls), full time. BTEC HNC Scientific Instrumentation, full time. BTEC HND Business Information Technology, full time. BTEC HND Science (Applied Biology), full time. BTEC HND Construction, full time. BTEC HND Computer Studies, full time. Horticulture for City and Guilds award, part time, in association with Merrist Wood Agricultural College, no formal entry requirements. Medical Reception, part time, no formal entry requirements. Typing, Shorthand, Word-Processing, part time, no formal entry requirements. NEBBS Certificate in Supervisory Management, part time, for potential supervisors/managers, BTEC Certificate in Management Studies, evenings, for those who have varied academic backgrounds, or who are over 25 with at least three years experience in a post of responsibility. Certified Diploma in Accounting and Finance, evenings. Those over 25 may be allowed to enrol if they have attained a position of responsibility in a career other than accountancy. Short part time courses with earning potential, leading to a College Certificate and City and Guilds award include Fashion, Soft Furnishing,Toymaking, Tailoring, Machine Knitting. Flexilearning (see 'Open and Distance Learning Courses').

Guildford College of Technology

MSC-sponsored Job Training scheme in many areas: details from college. Mature students with five O-levels may apply for the Diploma in Fine Bookbinding, full time. Those with three O-levels may apply for the Design Technician in Printing full time course.

Hatfield Polytechnic

MSC-sponsored Professional Updating for Women, three days a week in college, one day a week with an employer, one day per week on an Open University distance learning pack; hours 10 a.m.-3 p.m. to suit school days. Day nursery facilities available. (See also 'Degree and Advanced Courses'.)

Havering Technical College

Open Learning, includes Shorthand and Typing (see 'Open and Distance Learning Courses').

Hemel Hempstead: Dacorum College

Offers a series of courses, designed to suit individual needs. Courses start every term and require attendance two hours daily for duration of studies. Subjects include Keyboarding Skills, Typewriting (I and II), Word-Processing, Shorthand (Beginners, 50-plus, 80-plus), VDU Operation, Book-keeping, Wages Preparation.

High Wycombe: Buckinghamshire College of Higher Education
BTEC HND Engineering, full time, BTEC HND Information Technology, full time, BTEC HNC Electronic Engineering, part time. BTEC HNC Mechanical/Production Engineering, part time. BTEC HNC Computer Studies, part time. For these, the college 'particularly welcomes applications from mature students who, whilst not necessarily possessing formal qualifications, have appropriate industrial experience which is relevant to the course.' Certificate of Qualification in Social Work (CQSW), full time – minimum age of entry is 21 and there is no upper age limit. Previous social work experience is essential for those under 23 and over 40 and desirable for others. There are no formal educational requirements for candidates aged 27-plus. BTEC HND Business Studies, full time or sandwich; exceptionally those without formal qualifications aged 21-plus may be admitted. BTEC HNC Business Studies, part time, regulations as for full time. BTEC HND Business Information Technology, full time – applications from mature students welcomed. Institute of Personnel Management Course, evenings – candidates without normal qualifications considered if at least 23 with at least 24 months personnel or related experience. National Examinations Board Course in Supervisory Studies, part time, for potential supervisors/managers over 21; no formal entry qualifications.BTEC Certificate in Management Studies, part time, day and evening; those over 25 may be admitted without formal qualification if they have had at least three years experience and are holding/have held a position of responsibility.

Ipswich: Suffolk College of Higher and Further Education
Certificate of Qualification in Social Work, full time – candidates 23-45. Diploma in Residential Day Care, full time, for candidates aged 18-50. Academic qualifications are not required for the latter course.

Social Work: viewpoint
"I previously worked in engineering and held down my last job, as a chief estimator, for 18 years. Over the last seven or eight years, I realised I was very much a square peg in a round hole. I was attracted by social work because I had served as a borough councillor dealing with problems, so with my children aged 13-21 and responsibilities in economic terms diminishing, I realised it was 'now or never' if I was going to make a break. There was a lot of heart-searching and worry, but we've made it, and there's no looking back now.'

[Student on CQSW course, Suffolk College]

Diploma in Residential and Day Care: viewpoints
'I'd done quite a bit of work with unemployed people and also with a community relations council. When I was made redundant, I went back to college for a course in cost accounting, thinking I might go into business, but that didn't work out, and I finally decided that it would be worth me going into social work as a paid occupation. The course is valuable, particularly the placements. For instance, the placement I'm on now is with old people. Having met a lot of old people living at home, when I was working as a volunteer, I find it's a very different environment when they are resident in a home. You have 50 or 60 people to consider and you have to cater for their needs 24 hours a day.'

[Student, Residential and Day Care course, Suffolk College]

'There are eight to ten thousand homes in this country providing residential care for children, old people, handicapped and mentally ill people, in the voluntary, private and social services sector. They all need properly trained staff, though it's worth emphasising that staff do not necessarily have to 'live in' and may take sleeping-in duties on a rota basis. Residential social work is as practically demanding as hotel management, whilst also calling for personal and emotional qualities. A residential setting is a complex organisation, and management responsibilities include food, heating, upkeep of property, management of grounds, organisation of day and night shifts, and most important, catering for the needs of individuals. Residential social workers contribute substantially to the therapy and psychological help given to people in homes. In addition, day care provision for all client groups is now rapidly expanding and is providing excellent career opportunities for people who wish to work regular hours.'

[Spokesperson, Suffolk College]

Kent Institute of Art and Design
(The college is an amalgamation of Canterbury College of Art, Medway College of Design and Maidstone College of Art.) In the past, colleges have been prepared to consider under-qualified candidates with relevant work experience and a good portfolio of work in art/craft/design. Policies are not likely to change in this respect as the result of amalgamation and mature students should always enquire.'

King's Lynn: Norfolk College of Arts and Technology
MSC Job Training Scheme – choices offered are: Clerical/Office Skills; Retail Distribution and Warehousing; Health and Community Care; Hotel and Catering; Agriculture/Horticulture; Road Transport; Motor Vehicle Repairs; Construction; Engineering – Fabrication and Robotics; Hairdressing; Leisure and Tourism; Modular Electronics; Plant Operation; Food Technology (Processing) and Hygiene; Chemical and Plastics Technology; Business Enterprise. Also MSC Training Link course in Basic Skills and Vocational

Testing. All these MSC courses are full time, 9 a.m.-5 p.m.

Kingston Polytechnic
MSC-sponsored 'Women Into Management Course', full time – includes general management, finance, marketing, computing and in-company project. Two years' previous business experience at a responsible level required. Polytechnic Diploma in Theatre, Film and Television Design, full time. Formal academic qualifications not always necessary; previous experience in the theatre, film or TV (professional or amateur) needed. BTEC HND Business Studies or Mechanical Engineering, full time, over-21s with four or more years in suitable employment may be admitted without minimum qualifications. Polytechnic Diploma in Personnel Management – over-23s with suitable work experience may be admitted by test and interview. Diploma in Social Work/Certificate of Qualification in Social Work (CQSW), full time, for people aged 30-50 – formal academic qualifications not essential. (See also 'Degree and Advanced Courses'.)

Luton College of Higher Education
BTEC HND Business Studies, full time, entry concessions possible for those over 21 with suitable business experience. HND Business Studies with Bilingual Administration option; exceptionally those over 21 may be admitted wthout the usual entry qualifications at the discretion of the college. HND Public Administration, full time, entry concessions possible for those over 21 with suitable work experience or community experience. HND Computer Studies, full time – mature entrants with suitable work experience given special consideration. HND Business Information Technology, full time – same rule applies. HND Computer Aided Engineering/ HND Applied Electronics, Computer Engineering, Communications Engineering, all full time – mature students considered on merit. Wide range of part time courses, also Open Learning (see 'Open and Distance Learning Courses').

Maidstone: Mid Kent College – see under Chatham

Morden: Merton College
Beginners' Typing, part time, (a Return to Work course). Typing and Word-Processing, part time (a Return to Work course). Fashion Technicians, full time – practical sewing test for entry. Motor Cycle Engineering Mechanics, full time – aptitude test. Musical Instrument Repair, full time, aptitude test. Computer-Aided Engineering, full time. The college says: 'All our courses are open to mature students, and, for most, exemptions from entry requirements are available.'

Motorcycle Engineering: viewpoint
'I moved up to Lincolnshire because we could get a house there. I'm married

with a young child, but I never seemed to get a job in Lincolnshire. One place went bankrupt before I could get there and other jobs simply fell through. I've always wanted to work with motorcycles but I just didn't have any experience. Firms are willing to take on young people, but not adults without any experience because they're going to have to pay them too much to train. Then I got on to this course with an MSC allowance. They train you from the beginning, the whole thing – design, frames, cycle parts, engines, fuel injection, electrics. We do a couple of days practical in the workshops and three and a half days in the classroom, plus general studies, plus welding. Meanwhile my family commutes between my mother-in-law in Salisbury, my parents in Teddington and our home in Lincolnshire, but it should all be worth it in the long run.'

[Student, Motorcycle Engineering, Merton College]

Musical Instrument Repair: viewpoint

'I spent 15 years as a self-employed cabinet maker, doing French polishing and antique restoration, and it was my love of music that brought me to this course. My friends are musicians as well. I felt I wanted to repair guitars and make guitars, which is a natural progression from my experience as a cabinet maker (though in fact we learn to repair a very wide range of instruments here). We cover general woodwork and general metalwork, and work on brass instrument repair, woodwind instrument repair, non-fretted stringed instrument repair, the violin family, fretted stringed instrument repair and we also do work on pipe organ design and maintenance.'

[Student, Musical Instrument Repair, Merton College]

Newbury College

Restart and various MSC-sponsored Adult Education courses,all free to and specifically for unemployed people. 'Adult job-changers are welcome to enrol for any of the college's courses on a full time or part time basis. The opportunities for job change, whether in technological subjects or business studies, are too numerous to list in detail, says the college.

Norwich City College of Further and Higher Education

College Certificate in Community and Welfare Studies, full time or part time, minimum age 25, with an interest in working with people. HND Business Studies, full time, and HND Computer Studies, full time – applicants over 21 may be accepted if they can show ability to benefit from the course. Other HND possibilities include Computer-Aided Engineering, Electronics, Hotel Management, and Information Technology. The college hopes to offer HND Business Information Technology. Mature students are accepted on an infill basis on all college courses: options could include College Craft Catering Diploma, full time, (several City and Guilds awards included), City and Guilds Hotel Reception, full time, BTEC National Certificate in Land Use (Valuation and Property Management), full time –

mature students with relevant experience considered without qualifications. City and Guilds Technician in Electronic Servicing, full time – mature students with active interest considered for entrance test. Certificate/ Diploma in Furniture-Making, full time, entry by aptitude test. City and Guilds Recreation and Leisure Studies, full time. 'Re-Entry to Nursing', evenings, for qualified nurses. Secretarial courses including general, legal, medical, linguist, private and post-graduate, full time. Beginners' courses in typing, shorthand and word-processing, part time. Retraining and updating in office skills, part time day and evening. Also Open Learning (see 'Open and Distance Learning Courses').

Portsmouth College of Art, Design and Further Education
Mature students may be accepted under 21-hour rule for the following: BTEC National Diploma in Design (Communications); BTEC National Diploma in Design (Three-Dimensional); BTEC National Diploma in Business Studies (Distribution); Pre-degree Art Foundation. Open Learning (see 'Open and Distance Learning Courses').

Portsmouth Health Authority: Queen Alexandra Hospital
Mature Registered General Nurse training course, open to local candidates aged up to about 45. thirty-hour week, from 9 a.m. to 3.30 p.m. (other duties covering the 24-hour period).School holidays off. Candidates are expected to do some relevant work, paid or voluntary, before being considered – e.g., work in an old people's home or as an auxiliary in a nursing home.

General Nurse Training: viewpoint
'I think the main advantage we have is a worldly experience. When you get into your 30s you have had your children, you have elderly grandparents, your own parents are becoming more middle-aged. Mature nurses have a lot to offer in the sense that we can empathise with the patients and their problems. The disadvantage is that we tend to get more emotionally involved: as mothers and as wives, and as children of elderly parents, we can perhaps sympathise with patients a lot more easily. People have said, 'Oh I think you must be mad. You've got a husband, you've got a home, your children have grown up – what on earth are you doing studying nursing?' I think it's fulfilling a part of my life that I missed out on earlier on.'
[Mature student nurse, Queen Alexandra Hospital]

'Men are just as welcome as women to come forward, but originally the course was for women with children at school. We test them for tenacity and do tend to send people away saying, 'If you haven't done any studying since school, go off and do a bit'. We try to get them to demonstrate some sort of discipline of work, so perhaps they may become home helps or help in an old people's home. They never get in the year they apply because we have so many applicants. They bring experience of life, patience and the wish to go in and be good, basic, caring nurses. In time, they become more ambitious, but essentially I don't think they ever lose that basic caring attitude, whereas at 18, you're raring to get on.'

[Spokesperson, Queen Alexandra Hospital School of Nursing]

At the time of writing, this is one of only four schools of nursing offering an extended (school hours only) Registered General Nurse Training, though the current shortage of young entrants is prompting many nurse training schools to investigate the possibility of organising courses on a part-time basis, like the one described at Portsmouth. In addition, the Nurses' Central Clearing House Handbook includes many nurse training schools, which accept candidates for full-time nurse training up to the ages of 45 or 50. For details, write to the Nurses' Central Clearing House, PO Box 346, Bristol BS99 7FB.

Portsmouth: Highbury College of Technology

The college did not send information on mature student entry, but its prospectus includes various courses in areas noted for second career opportunities – e.g: Technical Authorship, evenings; Diploma in Driving Instruction, part time; Secretarial and Computer courses, full time and part time.

Reading: Bulmershe College of Higher Education

Certificate of Qualification in Social Work, full time, for candidates aged 22-50: those over 25 need not necessarily have formal qualifications but must have academic potential and all are expected to have had some experience in paid or voluntary social work. Certificate in Community and Youth Work, full time: only a small number of candidates under 23 are taken – they must have at least five GCE O-levels. Those aged 23-plus must be able to demonstrate a good standard of written ability as well as experience as a volunteer worker, part time or full time, equivalent to a full year's work. This college gives the impression of being friendly and keen to make it easy for adults to take advantage of a second chance to study. (See also 'Degree and Advanced Courses'.)

Rochester: Mid Kent College – see under Chatham

St Albans College

Business and Secretarial Skills Retraining/Refresher course. Modular: options include Typewriting, Audio Typewriting, Word-Processing, Computer Awareness, Computerised Accounting, Book-keeping, Shorthand, etc. Flexible attendance – all classes between 9.15 a.m. and 3 p.m.

St Albans: Hertfordshire College of Art and Design

BTEC HND Design (Modelmaking), full time, for students from varying backgrounds, previous relevant experience helpful. (Also Art Therapy and Dramatherapy – see 'Degree and Advanced Courses'.)

Modelmaking: viewpoint

'We are always prepared to consider people, whoever they are and whatever their qualifications. Probably most students come from some design course or other, but we have had film cameramen, people with degrees in geology, people retraining from being made redundant, a number of people from the armed forces, and so on. The course has an excellent relationship with the business and a good employment record. We look at examples of things students have made and also for the potential to deal with other people. Often the client does not have a clear picture in his or her mind as to the nature or purpose of the model to be made, and relies on the modelmaker to interpret and develop the idea. There are about 2000 professional modelmakers in Britain, working for architects and designers and working in film and television as well.'

[Spokesperson, Hertfordshire College of Art and Design]

St Albans: Hertfordshire College of Building

Short courses with earning potential, students of all ages eligible: Signwriting and Lettering, Practical Painting and Decorating, Practical Paperhanging, Cabinet-Making for Beginners, Upholstery in Furniture Construction, Home Concreting and Patio Construction.

Southampton Technical College

MSC Job Training provision awaited as this book went to press, but college emphasises an interest in adult students. New Technologies – a variety of opportunities exist for adults to update skills and knowledge in: Computer-Aided Design; Computer-Aided Engineering; Robotics; Information Technology. Also Introduction to Computing and Access to Information Technology provision. Secretarial training, from beginner to advanced, including 'Refresher'. Playgroup Foundation and Advanced courses, part time, for people aged 21-plus. Modern Languages centre (French, German, Spanish, Italian), all levels. Upgrading studies in supervisory management. Open Learning (see 'Open and Distance Learning Courses').

Southend College of Technology

Separate brochure of day and evening courses for adults. Includes: Office Skills Refresher, part time, 9 a.m.-3 p.m; New Technology Typing (Word-Processors, Electronic Typewriters, etc.), part time; Word-Processing, from beginner to advanced, part time, day or evening; Audio Typing for beginners and improvers, part time; Teeline shorthand for beginners, evenings. MSC-sponsored Administration/Secretarial skills courses. Music for Adults (includes evening 'Rock College' if you want to start your own group). Women Only evening courses in Car Maintenance and Electricity for Everyday Living. Wide range of Engineering courses includes Electronic Computing Workshop, Computer Machine Tool Programming, Electronics and Microprocessors for Motor Vehicles (evenings). Courses for teachers (RSA, City and Guilds). Better Care courses for those running residential homes. First Aid for home and in industry. For unemployed people, the college states: 'Every college course is open to you, and we are working with the DHSS to simplify arrangements for claiming benefit while you learn. Most unemployed adults are entitled to study for up to 21 hours a week without losing benefit, and we now have a system which should avoid any difficulty in doing just that.' Open College (see 'Open and Distance Learning Courses').

Stevenage College
MSC-sponsored Book-keeping, full time. MSC-sponsored Secretarial, full time. Extended Certificate of Qualification in Social Work (CQSW), course for people with home responsibilities (school hours only) and/or without conventional qualifications. Care Assistants' course for mature students, for City and Guilds 325. One day a week in college, one day a week in placement, three terms.

Extended Social Work Course: viewpoints
'I worked in a Labour Exchange. I just seemed to administer rules and I felt I wasn't helping the people on the other side of the counter ... I was a foster parent. I heard about the course from a social worker friend who had been on it ... I'd taken an Open University degree and there were no opportuniites where I lived, so as I had done community work before I married, I moved to Stevenage from Dorset so I could take this course.'

'The college takes into consideration that most of the people on the course have children and make allowances for that. They also offer a lot of support for those who haven't the academic background ... Being a more mature student gives you a wider scope and a wider field to talk about. Mothers and elderly people feel we're more in tune with what they are going through.'

'We start the course with a preliminary placement. I was in an area social work placement. Then we have a community work placement (I worked with Asian women in a local area), a residential placement (I worked in a psychiatric unit), and then I was part-time in college and part-time on placement in a medical social work department at a local hospital.'

[Students, Social Work Courses, Stevenage College]

'Students come on the course saying 'I've only been a Mum for 10 years', 'I've only been a foster-Mum', 'I've only been looking after my handicapped children'. We find they come with a lot of talent and a lot of life experience, which is more important than A-levels. In the first year of the course, they catch up on the students with A-levels and the course is a blend of theory and practice; studying social work subjects like child care, mental health, family therapy, social policy and the law, at the same time as putting it into practice in the field. Social work involves counselling, but you are working from a legal perspective. It's a very important role as a local government officer.'

[Spokesperson, Stevenage College]

Sutton College of Liberal Arts
Computers, part time. Typewriting, part time. (See also 'Small Business and Self-Employment Courses'.)

Watford: Cassio College
Introductory and Certificate courses in: Counselling, part time, Introduction to Bereavement Counselling, part time; Dental Surgery Assistants, part time; Typing, part time; Learn Professional Journalism, part time; Updating Office Skills, part time; Word-Processing and Electronic Typing, evenings; PICKUP and short courses in cookery, bakery and specialisms within these areas, for people wishing to update knowledge and skills. Cookery for the Catering Industry, for City and Guilds 706/1, mode unspecified. NEBSS Supervisory Studies, mode unspecified. Range of specialised short courses (one-day or part time evening) in subjects that range from specialist Sugar and Chocolate Work to Telephone Techniques. (See also 'Small Business and Self-Employment Courses' and 'Open and Distance Learning Courses'.)

Watford College
BTEC HND Business Studies (Advertising and Marketing, Business and Financial Administration, Personnel Management, Executive Secretaryship options), full time. Those over 21 with relevant work experience but without conventional qualifcations may be admitted. Diploma in Advertising, full time, mature candidates with relevant business experience may be accepted on merit. Diploma in Publishing, full time, normally graduate or similar entry; exceptional candidates admitted with other qualifications. Printing, Photography and Packaging courses, various modes and entry requirements. Secretarial and Business courses, various modes and entry requirements, including a part time day secretarial course. NEBSS Certificate in Supervisory Studies, part time, no academic entry requirements, for potential supervisors aged 21 and over. BTEC Certificate in Management Studies, part time, no academic entry requirements for candidates aged 23 and over. Certificates in Personnel Practice, Marketing, Sales Management, Production Planning, all part time, entry requirements variable. Wide range of Automobile Engineering courses, full time and part time, including 'Multi-Skills Centre' with facilities for studying body repair, mechanics, electrics, restoration, model engineering, welding, etc. During 1988 plumbing, heating, carpentry, painting and decorating, bricklaying, plastering, tiling and glazing should be added to Multi-Skills. Open Learning (see 'Open and Distance Learning Courses').

Welwyn Garden City: De Havilland College

MSC-sponsored course, 'Access to Information Technology': Automatic Systems – CNC Machine Tools, full time; CNC Machining and Computer Aided Design, full time; Computer-Aided Engineering, full time. MSC-sponsored Job Training Scheme, full time (9 a.m. to 4.30 p.m.) for candidates aged 19-30, out of full time education for at least two years, with two A-levels and five O-levels and a good commercial background. BTEC HNC Engineering Software, part time – appropriate A-level background required, but applications from those with relevant work experience can be considered. Retraining for mature students: Keyboarding for Supervisors and Managers, full time: Intensive Secretarial, mornings only: Refresher in Secretarial Skills, school hours only. Journalism and Media Studies (A-levels with vocational slant and City and Guilds Media Techniques award), full time, – mature students with five O-levels welcome. Science for Industry (A- and O-levels with laboratory practice), full time, part time or under 21-hour rule – mature students welcome, including those without formal qualifications. Social Care (A- and O-levels and work experience in social care), full time, part time or 21-hour rule. BTEC National Diploma in Health Studies, full time (suitable preparation for nursing, midwifery, occupational therapy, physiotherapy entry). Special consideration given by the local School of Nursing and Operating Department Assistants' training school to students who complete this course successfully; open to all candidates with three or four O-levels and mature students welcome – those without qualifications interviewed and advised. Counselling, part time.

Wimbledon School of Art

CNAA Diploma in Higher Education for Theatre Wardrobe, full time, includes costume design as well as costume making. Selection by interview. Candidates must submit examples of their work, which must include evidence of ability in sewing. NB: the college points out that this is an Advanced course.

Central England

Abingdon College
BTEC Certificate in Management Studies part time – over 25s with suitable experience but no formal qualifications may be eligible. BTEC Certificate in Business Administration, part time – same regulations apply. London Chamber of Commerce and Industry's Private Secretary's Certificate and RSA single-subject examinations, full time. Mature candidates with industrial/commercial experience and a good education may apply. MSC-sponsored Audio-Typewriting course, full time – age limits 19-40, with O-level English Language (grades A-C) or equivalent. Open Learning (see 'Open and Distance Learning Courses').

Birmingham – Polytechnic
Certificate of Qualification in Social Work (CQSW), full time – over 25s need not have GCEs if they have experience of social work practice, but will be assessed for academic potential. Diploma in Careers Guidance, full time – over25s with relevant employment experience may be accepted without usual academic qualifications. Certificate in Foundation Studies in Art and Design – exceptionally talented applicants may be taken as special admissions (without O-levels). Institute of Personnel Management Course, part time – course entry requirements relaxed for those aged 23 with at least two years' relevant experience. Certificate in Individual and Family Counselling, part time, candidates working in voluntary counselling considered as well as nurses, health visitors, social workers, youth workers. Certificate in Playwork, part time, for experienced playworkers. (See 'Degree and Advanced Courses' for full time and part time courses with special provision for mature students.)

Birmingham: Bournville College of Art
P/t courses for all ages, some with earning potential – e.g: Bookbinding; Ceramics; Fashion (for beginners or advanced dressmakers); Photography; Silversmithing and Jewellery; Technical Illustration.

Birmingham: Newman and Westhill Colleges
At Westhill College: Certificate in Community and Youth Work, full time for

those who are at least 20. Over-23s may offer alternatives to academic entry requirements.

Bridgnorth and South Shropshire College of Further Education
Updating for unemployed people in Automation and Robotics, part time plus home-based study. Computer-Aided Design – no previous computer experience required, basic drawing skills an advantage, evenings. Computer Numerical Control lathes course for people who have knowledge only of conventional machining methods, evenings. Computer-Aided Engineering, part time, modular (some costs may be reimbursed by MSC). BTEC national award courses, full time, for young people, but open to mature applicants with relevant industrial/commercial experience – e.g: Business and Finance; Engineering; Electronics; Caring Services; Computer Studies; Secretarial and Office Technology. Specialised courses include Tourism and Catering, leading to City and Guilds and RSA awards.

Chesterfield College of Technology and Arts
MSC-sponsored Modern Office Skills, full time. MSC-sponosred BTEC HNC Computer Technology, full time. Open Learning (see 'Open and Distance Learning Courses').

Corby: Trensham College – see under Kettering

Coventry: Henley College
Basic Skills Training (for people having difficulty in getting work, owing to lack of attainment at school). Technical Writing. Engineering Skills in CNC/CAD. New Engineering Skills in High Technology. Computing. Office Skills and Technology. Microcomputer Servicing and Maintenance. Food Preparation. Leisure and Recreation Management. Mature students also welcome on BTEC HND in Hotel, Catering and Institutional Management. Modes not specified – ask college.

Coventry Polytechnic
Polytechnic Diploma in Social Work/Certificate of Qualification in Social Work, full time – possible entry concessions for those aged 25-plus withsome practical experience in social work (paid or voluntary). BTEC HND Physical Science, full time – enquiries welcomed from mature students, including those with limited entry qualifications or appropriate industrial experience.

Coventry Technical College
BTEC Continuing Education in Software Engineering. HNC in Instrumentation and Control. HND in Mechanical and Information Engineering. All suggested by the college for people changing direction. Modes not specified, ask college.

Derbyshire College of Higher Education
BTEC HND Business Studies, full time – over 21s may be admitted without usual entry qualifications if they have commercial experience and relevant academic background. BTEC HND Design (Crafts: Studio Ceramics), full time – mature students with a high level of portfolio work may be admitted without usual entry qualifications. BTEC National Certificate and Higher National Certificate, sandwich, in Narrow Fabric Manufacture (UK Centre for tuition in this field). Mature applicants must satisfy the college of their ability to benefit from the course. Certificate in Community and Youth Work, full time – applications welcome from over 23s without the usual academic requirements who can demonstrate appropriate experience. BTEC Higher National Diploma in Computer Studies, full time – 'The over-riding consideration in admitting you to the course will be evidence that you are likely to be able to complete the course satisfactorily'. P/t courses include Institute of Personnel Management, Institution of Industrial Managers,Certificate in Supervisory Management (NEBSS), Design for Printing. P/t and evening classes with earning potential include Lettering, Enamelling, Silversmithing, Jewellery-Making.

Dudley College of Technology
MSC-sponsored Adult Preparation Training under 2l-hour rule and New Job Training Scheme; options include Reception Skills, Computer Applications, Literacy/Numeracy, Effective Communication and Confidence Building, Electronics, Typewriting, the Electronic Office, Construction Skills (includes Welding, Building, Carpentry, Bricklaying, Plumbing), Community Care, Word-Processors, Computers in Business, Job-getting Skills, Introduction to Self-Employment, Selling Skills, Audio-Typewriting, Keyboarding and Communications. Cookery, part time, for City and Guilds award. Soft Furnishing, part time, for City and Guilds award. Union of Educational Institutions Certificate in Dress (beginners or returners), part time. Fashion for City and Guilds award, part time. Basic Hairdressing for mature students,for City and Guilds award, under 2l-hour rule. Glass Making and Decoration, full time, part time evenings or under 2l-hour rule. RSA Diploma in the Teaching of Community Languages, part time or evenings, for students who are teaching community languages – e.g: Urdu, Punjabi, Gujerati – or are eligible for such work. BTEC Certificate in Business Administration, full time, and possibly under 2l-hour rule – entry at tutor's discretion. Also similar opportunities to study Production Control, Supervisory Management and Industrial Management. BTEC National/Higher National Business Studies – flexible entry requirement for mature students with suitable experience. Association of Accounting Technicians Course, part time, entry requirements flexible for over-21s. Book-keeping and Clerical Work, 10a.m.-3p.m. daily. Mature students may also apply for: Medical Reception, full time, (two O-level entry); Legal Secretaries, 10a.m.-3p.m. daily (O-level English Language required); and Intensive

Secretarial, 10a.m.-3p.m. daily (O-level English Language required). Wide range of Office Skills, part time – e.g: Word-Processing, Audiotyping, RSA, Pitman and Teeline Shorthand. Motor Vehicle Craft Studies (includes Welding, Fabrication and Vehicle Engineering), evenings – for mature, movitated students, for City and Guilds award. Electronics Servicing, evenings – for mature, motivated students, for City and Guilds award. MSC-sponsored Business Computing, full time. Computing for Women, 10a.m.-3p.m. (four O-levels needed, including Maths and preferably English). Wide range of part time and evening Computer and Information Technology, NC/CNC Part-Programming, and similar updating courses. Flexistudy (see 'Open and Distance Learning Courses').

Hinckley College of Further Education

Alternative Programme for unemployed people, under 21-hour rule. Students may join or leave at any time and take as many subjects as they like, as long as they do not exceed 21 hours college time per week. Options include: Typing(Beginners, Advanced and Word-Processing); Cookery for the Catering Industry (for City and Guilds award); Computer Studies; Soft Furnishing and Upholstery; Motor Vehicle Maintenance; Photography/Video; Antique Restoration; Woodwork; Community Care Practice (for City and Guilds award); Shorthand; Creative Writing; Reprographics. Open Learning (see 'Open and Distance Learning Courses').

Kettering: Trensham College

(Also at Corby.) 50-50 retraining in construction and engineering under 21-hour rule. Various courses under MSC adult training strategy. Office Systems Procedures, clerical updating, afternoons. Electronic Servicing for City and Guilds award, evenings, to suit mature students. Supervisory Studies for NEBSS Certificate – for potential supervisors over 20. Playgroup Foundation, part time, school hours only. Non-vocational courses with earning potential – e.g: Furniture Restoration, Tailoring, Clothing Craft – may lead to City and Guilds award. New Technology updating courses, part time, also Open Learning (see 'Open and Distance Learning Courses'). Mature students welcomed on 'infill' basis. Choices are 'too numerous to mention. We respond to requests'.

Kidderminster College of Further Education

Replan for unwaged adults, based on 21-hour rule. Students may take any number of options as long as combined hours do not exceed 21 hours a week. Options include: Supervisory Management; Selling; Retailing; Hairdressing and Cosmetology (Unisex); Business Accounting and the Use of Computers; Car Maintenance; Carpentry and Joinery; Introduction to Electronics. Hairdressing, for the City and Guilds award, for mature students during school hours only. Mature students also welcome on full time Hairdressing and Cosmetology. People with work experience welcome on Intensive Secretarial, full time.

Leamington Spa: Mid Warwickshire College
Replan for unemployed adults – start any time, no qualifications needed. Options include: Computing/Computer Literacy; Shorthand and Typing; Office Skills; Word-Processing; Welding; Painting and Decorating; Building Skills; Community Care; Lesiure and Recreation; Intensive Secretarial Studies, lOa.m.-3p.m., under 21-hour rule, for people with home responsibilities. Community Care, full time, for Certificate in Welfare Studies, or Practical Caring Skills, part time, for City and Guilds award. Food and Management Studies, part time, for City and Guilds award. Flexistudy; Open College planned (see 'Open and Distance Learning Courses').

Lichfield College
This college plans considerable expansion of adult and continuing education. Currently has many part time day and evening courses with earning potential – e.g: Dressmaking; Pottery; Upholstery; Cabinet-Making; Cookery. Creative Studies in Embroidery and Pottery for City and Guilds award. Photography for City and Guilds award. Mode not specified – ask college. Open Learning (see 'Open and Distance Learning Courses').

Newark Technical College
Individually planned mature students' Secretarial course/mature students' Clerical course – may be full time, part time or under 21-hour rule. Can lead to awards of LCCI, RSA, BTEC, EMFEC, Pitman, and/or GCSE. Wide range of Computer and Information Technology courses, evenings. Recreational Studies, full time, for potential supervisors in leisure industry – age limits 20-37 with good sporting and academic attainments. Security Services, full time, for potential supervisors – age limits 25-50, proven integrity, general fitness, adequate education (GCE/CSE). Playgroup Leaders' Basic course, evenings. Creative Studies (Fashion and Design, Embroidery, Ceramics, Cookery), full time or part time, can lead to City and Guilds award. Music and Musical Instrument Technology – 'The Department welcomes students of all ages to a wide range of full-time and part-time courses'. Music Preparatory course, full time, admission by audition and interview. Musical Instrument Electronics course, full time, leads to BTEC National Diploma. Candidates need O-level/Grade 1 CSE Maths, Physics and English and ability in Music. Piano Tuning, Maintenance and Repairs, full time – mature students accepted aged up to 35. No academic or musical qualifications demanded, but GCEs helpful. Violin-Making and Repairing, full time – mature students accepted up to age 35, knowledge of practical woodwork and technical drawing desired. Selection by interview. Woodwind Making and Repairing full time – open to mature students aged up to 35, selection by interview and practical test.

Newcastle-under-Lyme College

Participates in Staffordshire Replan scheme. Job Training Scheme submission with MSC – contact college for details. Centre for the Open University and for Staffordshire Basic Education Unit.

Northampton: Nene College

BTEC HND Business and Finance, full time – over-21s may be admitted with less than usual entry qualifications. BTEC HND Graphic Design, full time – students without usual entry qualifications should have at least three years relevant experience; exceptionally, those with considerable aptitude and potential considered. Advanced Diploma in Fashion, full time – mature students with relevant industrial experience or unusual aptitude and potential may be considered. Certificate of Qualification in Social Work (CQSW), full time – emphasis on recruitment of mature students with relevant experience. Over- 25s may be exempted from academic entry requirements.

Nottingham: South Nottinghamshire College of Further Education

Women Only courses in Information Technology, Community Care Practice and Management. Details from college. Open Learning proposed (see 'Open and Distance Learning Courses').

Oxford Polytechnic

HND Business Studies, full time – over-21s with relevant work experience and suitable academic background may be admitted without usual entry qualifications. Certificate of Qualification in Social Work (CQSW), full time, preferred age range 23-45 with some relevant experience; entry concessions for over-25s.

Redditch College

Design for Print, part time, for unemployed adults. BTEC National Diplomas in Business Studies or Distribution, full time – entry concessions for over-19s at Principal's discretion. Pre-Nursing and Caring Services, full time, for young students, but over-19s admitted at Principal's discretion. Pre-Social Work, full time – mature students welcome. BTEC HND Computer Studies, full time – over-19s admitted on the basis of experience and/or aptitude. BTEC HND in Business Studies (Travel and Tourism), full time – over-19s admitted at Principal's discretion. Office Skills (Beginner/Refresher) under 21-hour rule, for RSA/TVEI qualifications. Clerical Skills, under 21-hour rule, for unemployed adults aged up to 25, for RSA awards. Adult Preparation: training for unemployed, part time – a range of skills may be sampled. Pre-School Playgroup Introductory Course and Leadership Course, part time. Sales and Selling, evenings, for those wishing to enter the full-time selling course. Wide range of part time courses in fields as diverse as Computers and Export. Leisure courses with earning potential – e.g: Book

Illustration; Creative Writing; Dressmaking; Woodwork. Flexistudy (see 'Open and Distance Learning Course'). It is proposed that this college will merge with North Worcestershire College in September 1988 to become North East Worcestershire College: this could affect the range of courses available.

Retford: Eaton Hall International

Combines distance learning and residential block study methods. Licentiate Diploma in Teaching English as a Foreign Language: 3O-week Distance Learning Programme, four-week residential block, for Trinity College London Diploma. Diploma in Teaching English for Specific Purposes: six-month Distance Learning Programme, four-week residential block, for Eaton Hall Diploma (being validated by RSA).

TEFL/TESL Courses: viewpoints

'I've come from university. I graduated in July, spent eight or ninemonths unemployed, couldn't find anything for a Geography graduate, and then saw this advertised in the paper and was able to arrange a loan from the bank. One of the fascinating things about TEFL is that you can really go anywhere to work when you are qualified. You just take your pick – the world's your oyster'.

'I thought 'I can't go on this course. I'm not a graduate. I'm not a teacher.' But I wrote a letter, and very kindly I was accepted, and it shows that everyone has a chance if they try hard enough. My own early life was spent as an officer in the Merchant Navy. From that I graduated into handling ships as a ships' agent,and that's my job now, in Singapore, the second busiest port in the world. I hope to set up a languages school in Japan with my wife and brother-in-law when I retire.'

'I'm an industrial chemist and hopefully I shall be getting involved in the field of specialised English teaching. I applied for a job abroad as an English teacher before I even enrolled on the course. I was luckily accepted. Then I decided I should get some qualifications behind me so that I would be a better teacher.I have now finished and leave for Japan next Tuesday.'

[Students TEFL/TESL courses, Eaton Hall International]

'The demand for teachers stems from the world's thirst for English. It is now indisputably the world language. The last figure I saw was that six hundred million people were using the English language every day as part of their lives. On top of that you've got English pop records, English TV and radio programmes, American and British films all over the world – so access to English is something everybody's familiar with and people in most countries want. We have a never-ending stream of requests for teachers who have completed our course to go overseas.'

[Spokesperson, Eaton Hall International]

Solihull College of Technology

MSC-sponsored Basic Cookery, full time. MSC-sponsored Waiting, full time. Cookery for City and Guilds 706/l awards under Job Training Scheme. Hairdressing, Floristry, Horticulture, Information Technology, all under 21-hour rule, for City and Guilds awards. Graphic Design for Print/Video Media, Commercial Photography, Commercial Photography/Graphics, Fashion/Knit – all under 21-hour rule. Computer Programming, for City and Guilds award, evenings (beginners). Basic Fabrication and Welding, Refrigeration Engineering, Motor Vehicle Maintenance, CNC Machining, Introduction to Basic Electronics and Computing – all under 21-hour rule, for City and Guilds awards. General and specialised Secretarial training for beginners and those needing updating, under 21-hour rule. Wide range of Languages, part time and evenings, including French, German, Spanish, Arabic, Chinese and Japanese. Language Laboratory of tapes (see 'Open and Distance Learning Courses').

Conventional Japanese: viewpoints

'I spent some time in Japan and I've an interest in the country. The object, though, is to get a basic knowledge of Japanese to use in in business, to try and get a better job.' Communicating between a firm here and Japan – interpreter, possibly, depending on how good my Japanese becomes.'

'I would like to learn the language so that I could go out there and live. I'd like to set up a job, stay there and work for a year and then come back and get my degree in Japanese.'

'It's certainly easier than French – we're only speaking it phonetically and not learning the written language, so it's easier than you might think.'

[Students, Solihull College of Technology]

'We noticed there was a demand for Arabic, so we started courses in that, and following the success of that, we decided to offer Japanese, particularly in view of the Japanese interest in British Leyland and other quite large companies in this area. We find that often students have some connection with the country – they've got Japanese wives, or they've been abroad to Japan. Some businessmen are involved in meeting Japanese people so we know they'll need their Japanese phrases. One former student told me 'I've got the best company I could have in terms of colleagues at work because most of them are Japanese.'

[Spokesperson, Solihull College of Technology]

Stafford College of Further Education

BTEC HNC Typographic Design, sandwich. Adults with relevant work experience and good portfolio may be accepted without formal academic qualifications.

Stoke-on-Trent: Cauldon College

Retraining for Catering course, under 21-hour rule – can lead to City and Guilds 706/l (Cookery for the Catering Industry, Part l) and 707/l (Food and Beverage Service, Part l). Students may continue for a second year and take City and Guilds 706/2 and 707/2. Most Construction Crafts are also offered to City and Guilds level. (See also 'Open and Distance Learning Courses').

Stoke-on-Trent: North Staffordshire Polytechnic

BTEC HND Design (Ceramics), full time. Mature students without usual academic qualifications but with industrial experience may be accepted. BTEC HND/HNC Business and Finance, full time or part time. Over-21s may be accepted without usual academic qualifications. BTEC NC Ceramic Technology, full time – unqualified students accepted at Polytechnic's discretion. BTEC HNC/HND Ceramic Technology, full time or part time – unqualified students with considerable appropriate experience accepted at Polytechnic's discretion. Institute of Personnel Management, part time – candidates 23-plus with at least two years' appropriate experience and who satisfy the IPM for student membership may be accepted without usual qualifications. Institute of Purchasing and Supply, part time – potential managers, supplies controllers, senior storekeepers, etc. who satisfy the IPS may be accepted without usual qualifications. Institute of Industrial Managers, part time – over-27s with at least four years experience who hold/have held a post of responsibility may be accepted without usual qualifications. Supervisory Studies for NEBSS Certificate – for potential managers over 21.

Stourbridge College of Technology and Art

BTEC HND Graphic Design, full time; those with at least two years in the graphic communications industry considered without usual qualifications. Preparatory Caring and Health Service course, full time – for young students, but mature students considered. Association of Accounting Technicians, full time – for young students, but others considered.

Sutton Coldfield College of Further Education

Mature students accepted on an infill basis to general courses, as well as on MSC-sponsored courses. No details supplied – contact college.

Tamworth College of Further Education

BTEC HNC Business and Finance part time – over-21s without formal qualifications but with suitable experience may be admitted. (The college says: 'Many of the most successful candidates have been older people returning to college for refresher or retraining courses.') BTEC ND Business and Finance, full time, and NC Business and Finance, part time – flexible entry requirements. RSA Diploma for Personal Assistants, full time. Mature students without formal qualifications but with relevant experience may be admitted. Beginners' Shorthand and Typing for mature students – school hours only. Wide range of Secretarial evening classes. Institution of Industrial Managers Certificate, evenings – over-27s with at least four years industrial experience and employment in a post of responsibility may be accepted without formal qualifications.

Thame: Rycotewood College
BTEC Continuing Education Certificate in Design (Crafts). This course concentrates on the design and making of fine bespoke furniture. Applications are invited from mature students (above the age of 25) and with a minimum of three years' work experience. BTEC HNC Service Engineering Management, full time – suited to technicians with experience in agricultural engineering; mature students may be accepted without usual entry qualifications.

Warley and West Bromwich: Sandwell College
Amalgamation of the former Warley College of Technology and West Bromwich College of Commerce and Technology.) (1) Warley Campus. MSC-sponsored Secretarial, Clerical and Business Studies under 21-hour rule. Construction, Electrical and Electronic Engineering, Fabrication Engineering, Vehicle Work – selected classes under 21-hour rule. Non-vocational evening classes with earning potential include Wood-Turning, Car Maintenance, Dressmaking, Cookery, Tailoring, Soft Furnishing, Community Care – full time or 21-hour rule, mature students welcome. Child minders, evenings. Mechanical Engineering Craft Studies, under 21-hour-rule. (2) West Bromwich Campus. BTEC HNC Business Studies – sympathetic consideration for those aged 21-plus with suitable work experience but without usual entry requirements. General Office Skills (Beginners or Updating) under 21-hour rule. Institute of Chartered Secretaries and Administrators, part time or evenings – candidates aged 23-plus without usual qualifications may be considered. BTEC ND/NC Hotel, Catering and Institutional Operations, full time – mature students with appropriate experience may be accepted without usual entry qualifications. International Health and Beauty Council courses, full time, entry requirements may be relaxed for more mature candidates. Furniture Craft, full time, for adults who wish to change careers. Speech and Drama Teachers' Diploma, evenings, mainly for mature students. Performing Arts, under 21-hour rule. Introduction to Journalism, under 21-hour rule. Counselling, part time or evenings – mature students especially welcome. Institute of Marketing Certificate, evenings – over-25s with at least three years' marketing experience may be accepted without usual entry requirements. Institute of Industrial Managers' Certificate, part time – over-27s with at least four years' appropriate experience may be accepted without usual entry requirements. Institute of Purchasing and Supply Foundation, part time – over-26s with relevant experience need no formal qualifications. Institute of Management

Services Certificate, part time – over- 25s without formal qualifications accepted if they satisfy selectors they will benefit. Supervisory Studies for NEBSS Certificate, part time – for over-21s who are potential supervisors. Computing and Information Technology, full time or part time, from Beginners to Advanced. Evening classes with earning potential – e.g: Photography Assistant, Creative Radio, Radio Drama, Pottery, Millinery, Soft Furnishing, Dressmaking.

Wellingborough College
Automobile Engineering (three evenings weekly) for City and Guilds award for More Mature Students. Computer courses, from Beginners to Advanced, part time. Introduction to Social Work, part time. BTEC Diploma in Caring, under 21-hour rule. Shorthand and/or Typewriting part time. Skills Workshop (for office staff who feel out of touch with the modern office world), school hours only. Sight and Sound keyboard training, part time. Receptionist/Telephonist Skills, part time. Further Education Teacher Training, evenings – for over-23s, qualified in the subject they want to teach. Many leisure courses with earning potential – e.g: Picture Frame Making, Dressmaking, Photography, Bee-keeping, Writing. Electronic courses, from Beginners to Advanced, part time and evening. Electronic and Microelectronic Systems, TV and Video, Electronic Measurement and Control. NEBSS General, for industry and commerce. NEBSS Recreational Management.

Wolverhampton: Bilston Community College
Soft Furnishing and Upholstery, for City and Guilds award, evenings – practical sewing ability needed. Catering and Food Service, for City and Guilds awards, part time, day and evening – for mature unemployed people. Licensed Trade Catering, part time, for established licensees, also suitable for those joining the trade. Design and Decoration of Flour Confectionery, for City and Guilds award, evenings. Diploma in Play Leadership, part time. Foundation Course for Playgroup Supervisors, part time. Computer Programming and Information Processing; Information Technology; Background to Technology – all for City and Guilds awards, full time or under 21-hour rule. Adult Skills, Manufacturing, under 21-hour rule; choose from Welding, Electrical Installation and Maintenance, Domestic Electrics, Microelectronics, Turning, Milling, Grinding, Car Body Repair, Trailer Making, Vehicle Electrics, Car Maintenance, Engine Reconditioning, Engine Auxiliary Reconditioning, Computer Controlled Machining (CNC, CAM), Computer Aided Design (CAD), Computer Programming, Brass Decorative Sheet Metal Work,Small Portabuildings Manufacture, Activity Toys Design and Manufacture,Domestic Appliance Repair, Decorative Metalwork. Fashion for City and Guilds award, part time. Hairdressing for City and Guilds awards, under 21-hour rule. Nursing and Caring Skills (for home nursing), part time or evenings. Hospital Play Specialist's course, part

time. Office Skills, under 21-hour rule. Secretarial skills, wide range, part time. Preliminary Certificate in Welfare Studies, part time and under 21-hour rule – can lead to more advanced courses. Social and Community Service, under 21-hour rule. RSA Diploma in the Teaching of Community Languages, part time – for those with an A-level in the target languge, or who have reached the level of a full secondary education in it. Wide range of languge courses, part time. ESF-sponsored training for women: Women Re-Entrants, Vocational and Language Training for Women, Women and New Technology, Women in Science and Engineering, Women in Supervision and Management, Women and Self-Employment, Women and Craft, Design Technology – all full time, but only 20 hours a week. Many evening courses with earning potential – e.g: Vehicle Painting and Customising, Renovating Furniture. Open Learning and Flexistudy (see 'Open and Distance Learning Courses').

Hospital Play Therapy: viewpoint
'Candidates should usually be 20-plus and have substantial experience with children – for example, previous training in nursery nursing, nursing, teacher training, play leadership, or perhaps the Diploma in Residential Care. It is not essential to be employed by a hospital, though courses provide both day-release training for therapists in post and initial training for would-be play therapists. Their work in encouraging play helps children adjust to a strange and sometimes frightening environment and familiarise themselves with hospital apparatus and procedures, as well as advising the hospital on the selection of play materials, liaising with nursing and medical staff and encouraging parents, volunteers and parents to participate in play'.
[Spokesperson, National Association of Hospital Play Staff]

Wolverhampton: Wulfrun College of Further Education
ESF-sponsored Kitchen Design (women only) and Media Technicians (women only), both full time. Computer-Aided Design. Desk Top Publishing – mode not specified. Mature students welcome on infill basis to all courses. Homestudy (see 'Open and Distance Learning Courses').

The following colleges in the Central region supplied information in 1987 about their retraining courses but no response was received to 1988 enquiries. Readers may nevertheless wish to make individual contact:

Birmingham College of Food and Domestic Arts
Bromsgrove: North Worcestershire College
Derby College of Further Education
Henley-on-Thames: King James's College of Henley
Hinkley: North Warwickshire College of Technology and Art
Leicester Polytechnic
Lincolnshire College of Art and Design
Loughborough College of Art and Design
Loughborough Technical College

Nottingham: Basford Hall College
Nottingham: Trent Polytechnic
Stoke-on-Trent Technical College
Witney: West Oxfordshire Technical College

Northern England

Altrincham: South Trafford College of Further Education
BTEC Certificate in Business Administration – modular, combining college and home study for people over 21, or those with at least three years' experience in a responsible position in industry or commerce. BTEC National Certificate in Business and Finance, under 21-hour rule. Secretarial skills, part time and evenings, under 21-hour rule. Typewriting for Beginners and Refresher students, Shorthand, Word Processing, Audiotyping – mode not specifed, Photography, evenings, for City and Guilds award. Embroidery, part time, for City and Guilds award. Jewellery, part time, for City and Guilds award. Languages: French, German, Spanish, Japanese, Italian, Modern Greek, Urdu, Russian – evenings. Leisure courses with earning potential include Dressmaking, Furniture Restoring. Courses under 21-hour rule in Catering for City and Guilds craft awards, also City and Guilds Hairdressing, City and Guilds Beauty Therapy, BTEC Health Studies, Foundation Art.

Ashington: Northumberland College of Arts and Technology
MSC-sponsored Scope programme, various options, part time. MSC-sponsored courses include: Closed Circuit Television Construction, full time; Clerk of Works course – Mechanical and Electrical Engineering, full time; Office Skills (one day a week); Word-Processing (half day a week); Wider Opportunities for Women (three days plus one day placement a week); BTEC National award (day- release – ask college for details of subjects). (See also 'Open and Distance Learning Courses' and 'Small Business and Self-Employment Courses'.)

Barrow-in-Furness College of Further Education
MSC-sponsored Updating in Modern Office Technology (distance learning). Practical Woodwork/Practical Brickwork/Practical Painting and Decorating – evenings, open to all ages. Electronics and Mechanical Engineering, various levels and modes – some open to all ages; includes updating – e.g: Robotics and Computer Numerical Control courses. Secretarial, Computing and Management courses, various levels and modes – some open to all ages. Certificate and Diploma in Industrial Management – mode not specified.

Supervisory Studies for NEBSS Certificate, part time – for potential supervisors. City and Guilds Further Education Teachers' Certificate, part time – for those with technical or professional qualifications wishing to teach in further education. Courses to suit individual mature students can be devised for part time day or evening study. Many leisure courses with earning potential – e.g: Dressmaking, Millinery, Machine Knitting, Cookery, Pottery. Open Learning (see 'Open and Distance Learning Courses').

Blackburn College

MSC-sponsored Private Secretarial Course for mature students with O-levels or equivalent, full time. London Chamber of Commerce and Industry's Private and Executive Secretary's Diploma, full time – mature students accepted at College's discretion. Vocational Preparation for unemployed people, options include Engineering, Motor Vehicle crafts, Electrical Installation, Construction Trades, Computing, Motor Vehicle Painting, Clerical Skills and Office Practice, all under 21-hour rule. City and Guilds Further Education Teacher's Certificate, part time – for potential and practising adult education teachers/trainers with qualifications relevant to the subject they want to teach. Management Studies, part time and evenings – entry concessions for people aged 25-plus with appropriate experience. City and Guilds Certificate in Media Techniques (Press and Radio Skills) and Certificate with Urdu and/or Gujerati and/or Arabic Languages full time or part time (candidates must have GCE O-level/GCSE or equivalent in at least four subjects at grades A, B or C, and for Urdu/Gujerati/Arabic options, evidence of A-level equivalent studies in the appropriate language is required). Institute of Personnel Management, part time and evenings – entry concessions for people with relevant experience. Supervisory Studies for NEBSS Certificate, part time – no formal entry requirements. Institute of Marketing Certificate, evenings – entry concessions for mature students with relevant experience. Institute of Purchasing and Supply, part time and evenings – entry concession for people aged 25 with relevant experience. Open Learning (see 'Open and Distance Learning Courses').

Bolton Institute of Higher Education

MSC-sponsored BTEC HNC Computer Studies,full time. MSC-sponsored Diploma in Systems Analysis, full time. MSC-sponsored Diploma in Computer Programming, full time.Other fresh start possibilities include: College Diploma in the Care of the Mentally Handicapped Adult, full time; Certificate in the Further Education and Training of Mentally Handicapped People, full time; BTEC HND Business Studies, full time (over-21s with relevant experience and education may be admitted without the usual academic qualifications). The college says: 'On the basis of your previous experience, you may also be granted exemption from certain modules; this would be subject to approval by BTEC.' BTEC HND Graphic Design, full time (candidates with related industrial experience may be considered without the usual academic qualifications).

Bradford and Ilkley Community College

BTEC HND Business and Finance/Secretarial Linguist's/Public Administration, full time – entry concessions possible for mature students. Certificate in Youth and Community Work, full time – entry concessions possible for over-25s. BTEC National Diplomas, full time – entry concessions possible for mature students – Building, Business, Computer Studies, Design, Leisure Studies. Family and Community Care, full time, for City and Guilds award – mature students particularly welcome, no formal entry requirement. Nursery Nursing, full time for NNEB Certificate – over-21s may apply without formal qualifications. Intensive Office Studies, full time – particularly appropriate for mature men and women seeking clerical posts. Pre-Nursing, full time – special provision may be made to accept mature students without formal qualifications. Textile Merchants' Special Certificate, full time – entry concessions for mature students. Preliminary Course in Art and Design, part time – applications invited from mature unemployed people. BTEC Certificate in Textiles, part time – special admission arrangements for mature students. Students accepted on infill basis on all Art and Design courses. Community Sports Leader's Award, part time – no pre-entry qualifications, approved by Central Council of Physical Recreation. Short courses in Outdoor Pursuits for would-be leaders with relevant experience, part time. In-Service course in Social Care, part time – for people with six months experience in a caring job, or in voluntary work. City and Guilds Further Education Teacher's Certificate, part time – for intending/practising teachers in FE. Wide range of BTEC Engineering courses (various specialities) for candidates who can show they can expect to be successful. Basic Technology Courses, part time, for women, school terms only – no academic qualifications required. City and Guilds Engineering updating courses: e.g., CAD/CAM. Wide range of BTEC Business Studies courses for candidates who can show they can expect to be successful by virtue of other studies/work experience. Institution of Industrial Managers Certificate, part time – entry concessions possible for over 27s with four years' industrial experience. Supervisory Management, part time – for over 21s with management potential; leads to NEBSS Certificate. BTEC Certificate in Management Studies, part time, unit-based – suitable for potential managers, entry concessions for candidates 25-plus with three years' experience. Languages, part time – French, German, Italian, Polish, Russian,Spanish, all levels. Wide range of Secretarial Skills/Office Technology courses, part time, all levels.

Bridlington: East Yorkshire College of Further Education

ESF-sponsored Tourism, Leisure and Recreation, Catering and Hotel Management, Control Technology and Caring in Institutions courses (apply for details). Mature students' Electronic Engineering, full time. Mature students' Private Secretary's Update, full time. Art Education, under 21-hour rule. Open Learning (see 'Open and Distance Learning Courses').

Burnley College
MSC-sponsored Business Studies Secretarial (details from college). Projected Introduction to New Skills and Women into Technical Education courses (details from college). Open College (see 'Open and Distance Learning Courses').

Consett: Derwentside Technical College
MSC-sponsored Electronics, full time. MSC-sponsored Information Technology, part time. Community Care Practice, part time – for mature people employed/hoping to be employed in the caring field. Office Skills for the Adult Unemployed, part time (Shorthand, Typewriting, Audio, Word-Processing, Office Practice, Business Communications). Art and Design Skills for the Unemployed, part time (Three-Dimensional Studies, Painting and Drawing, Screen Printing, etc.). Workshops in Electronics, Computers, Maths, Literacy, Numeracy, Drama, Languages. Wider Opportunities for Women; CNC Machine Operation; Part-Programming; Access to Information Technology; Catering. Modes not specified – ask college for details.

Dewsbury College
Scope programme (includes skills sampling – Construction, Engineering, Clerical, Retailing, Computer Skills). Motor Vehicle Fabrication, under 21-hour rule. Industrial Sewing and Design, under 21-hour rule. Construction trades (various), under 21-hour rule. Catering and Caring Skills, under 21-hour rule. Electrical and Electronic Skills, under 21-hour rule. Open Learning (see 'Open and Distance Learning Courses').

Durham: New College Durham
The college states: 'all college courses are open to all – ask for the prospectus.' MSC-sponsored Scope courses with 'tasters' of Computing, Word-Processing, Basic Office Administration, Typing, Book-Keeping, Social and Community Care, Construction Crafts, Motor Vehicles. MSC-sponsored Robotics, full time. MSC-sponsored Microprocessor and Industrial Control Systems, full time. MSC- sponsored Secretarial Skills, full time or part time. BTEC HND in Accountancy and Finance; Leisure Administration (Music and Entertainment Industries and Sport and Recreation streams); Tourism Management and Travel Management; RSA Personal Assistants' course and Bilingual Secretarial course. Mode is not specified for any of these – ask college. Certificate in Marketing, evenings – those with three years' Marketing experience may enter without exam qualifications. RSA Teacher's Diploma in Typewriting, Shorthand, Office Procedures – over-25s with English O-level and appropriate skills eligible without usual qualifications. Various part time and evening Shorthand, Typewriting,

Word-Processing, Office Skills courses. Certificate in Industrial Management, part time, entry requirements relaxed for over-27s with four years' industrial experience. Supervisory Studies for NEBSS Certificate, part time – no entry qualification but students must be over 21 and able to benefit from the course. Institute of Management Services Certificate, part time – over-21s admitted by discussion with course tutor. Adult Education Teachers' course – candidates must have subject qualifications and an interest in teaching adults. City and Guilds Further Education Teachers' Certificate – candidates must have subject qualifications and intend to teach or train personnel in commerce, industry or public service. BTEC Computer Studies, evenings, and Information Technology for managers, evenings – for people with three years' experience in responsible position in industry/commerce and able to cope with course work. The Cookery Certificate (can lead on to the Cook's Professional Certificate), evenings – no formal entry requirements. City and Guilds Fashion award, evenings – candidates need a good grasp of dressmaking skills. Updating in Computing, Electronics, Robotics and New Technology, part time to suit individual career plans. Open Learning (see 'Open and Distance Learning Courses').

Gateshead Technical College

Conservation of Fine Art, full time – open to people with previous conservation experience or degree or certain A-level qualifications. Comuter-Aided Engineering, Computer-Aided Draughting, Computer Numerical Control, Computer-Aided Production Management, Robotics, Digital Electronics, Word-Processing, Computerised Business Systems – at various levels and in various study modes. MSC-sponsored Selling courses, part time (evening version available) – suitable for beginners. Industrial Electronics, evenings for mature students. Machine Tool Setting and Operation, leads to City and Guilds award – mature students without usual qualifications but with appropriate experience may apply. Leisure classes with earning potential: subjects include Dressmaking, Decorative Ironwork, Cordon Bleu Cooking, Machine Knitting. Open Learning (see 'Open and Distance Learning Courses').

Grimsby: Humberside College – see under Hull

Halifax: Percival Whitley College of Further Education

MSC-sponsored Typing and Office Technology, full time. MSC-sponsored Shorthand for Typists and Office Technology, full time. ESF-sponsored Clerical and Computing course, full time (people aged 18-24 only). ESF-sponsored Women in Electronics, full time. ESF-sponsored New Technology in Engineering, full time (people aged 18-24 only). ESF-sponsored Introduction to Building, full time (people aged over 25 only). ESF-sponsored Self-Employed Gardening, full time (people aged over 25 only). ESF-sponsored Open Workshop, full time (for students with special needs):

training in Manufacturing, Catering,Retailing, Building Maintenance, Market Gardening, Sewing, Repair and Maintenance. Wide range of 21-hour rule courses. Open Learning and Flexistudy (see 'Open and Distance Learning Courses'). The college writes: 'With the introduction of the New Adult Training Strategy this year, it is very difficult to be precise about what will be on offer, but it is the general policy of the college to make courses as accessible as possible to adult students.'

Huddersfield Polytechnic

ESF-sponsored Women into Technology, school hours only: includes Design and Materials, Computing, Electronics, Chemical Science. BTEC HND Business and Finance, full time (opportunities for students without academic qualifications if their experience is very relevant). BTEC HND Science (Chemistry), full time. Mature students encouraged, but must offer usual entry qualifications. Foundation course in Accountancy, full time – mature students without usual entry qualifications may be admitted. Diploma in Careers Guidance, full time – over-25s with valuable employment experience may be considered with less than usual entry requirements. DipHE (Engineering), full time – mature students may be admitted with less than usual entry requirements. Diploma in Social Work/Certificate of Qualification in Social Work (CQSW) – minimum age of entry is 25; formal entry requirements not specified. An extended part time CQSW is also available for people with home commitments. City and Guilds Further Education Teacher's Certificate, part time – for potential FE teachers and trainers with qualifications relevant to their subject(s). Institute of Linguists' course, part time, for those who have studied French beyond A-level or similar level. Institution of Industrial Managers Certificate, part time – entry concession for over-27s with four years' experience. BTEC Certificate in Management Studies part time – entry concessions for over-25s with three years' experience. Supervisory Studies for NEBSS Certificate – for candidates over 21 with supervisory potential, no formal entry requirement. BTEC HNC Business Studies – entry concession possible for over-21s.

Hull: Humberside College of Higher Education

(The college also has a site at Grimsby). MSC-sponsored HND Computer Software Engineering full time – for people with HND/HNC in relevant engineering discipline or equivalent plus suitable industrial experience. BTEC Diploma in Exhibition and Museum Design, full time – mature students who do not meet academic entry standards considered on the basis of portfolio of work. BTEC HND Business Studies (Private Secretarial, Accounting, Business Administration, Industrial Administration, Leisure Studies and European Marketing options), full time or sandwich – mature students who do not meet academic entry standards considered; French essential for European Marketing option. BTEC HND in the Science and Technology of Food – candidates with less than usual entry requirements considered. DipHE, full time (can lead to degree) over-21s considered without formal qualifications. Certificate of Qualification in Social Work, full time – over-25s need not have formal entry qualifications but should have some appropriate experience. Certificate in the Further Education and Training of Mentally Handicapped People, full time – over-21s need not have formal qualifications, but must have had some appropriate experience. Open Learning (see 'Open and Distance Learning Courses').

Leeds: Jacob Kramer College

Vocational Fine Art/Crafts, part time – for mature students unable (for reasons of age, qualifications, family commitments) to pursue full-time education within the HE sector. Unemployed students accepted under 21-hour rule.

Leeds: Park Lane College of Further Education

Secretarial Training/Retraining, part time and under 21-hour rule, including Shorthand, Typewriting, Audio-Typewriting, Word-Processing, Secretarial Duties. Mature students also accepted on Medical Reception and Private Secretarial courses, full time. Access to Information Technology, evenings. RSA Computer Literacy and Information Technology, modular, part time and evenings. Word-Processing for beginners, part time and evenings. MSC-sponsored Wider Opportunities course includes Wages/Salaries, Book-keeping, Keyboarding, Typing, Word-Processing, Telephone Reception skills, Office Skills, Job-Seeking Skills. The college is a regional centre for Travel and Tourism and has full time and part time courses for late entrants to this type of work.

Leeds Polytechnic

Skills Training and Career Development (over-25s who have been unemployed for six months, part time. Can lead to one-year full time courses – e.g: Diploma in Administration Studies; Diploma/MSC in Health Education; Diploma in Institutional Management; Hotel and Tourism Studies; Diploma in Management Studies; Diploma in Personnel Management. Certificate of Qualification in Social Work for Graduates, Certificate in Teaching of Typewriting and Word-Processing (part time), Postgraduate Diploma in Office Systems, Bilingual Diploma in Information Administration. Business Automation for unemployed 18-25 – year-olds, under 21-hour rule. BTEC HND Finance and Accounting/Business Studies, full time – exceptionally, mature students without formal qualifications but with relevant work experience may be accepted. Polytechnic Diploma/Certificate in Sports Coaching Studies, full time – for those with recognised ability in the field of coaching/performance and/or who have been recommended by the respective governing body of the sport. Certificate in Education for intending teachers of Craft, Design and Technology, full time (for craftsmen/women with experience in industry, English and Maths O-level and the Full

Technological Certificate of the City and Guilds of London Institute in an appropriate woodworking/metalworking trade, or BTEC HND/HNC equivalent; candidates must be 23 by 1 October in the year when their course begins). BTEC HND Hotel, Catering and Institutional Management, full time – exceptionally, mature applicants with a sound general education and/or good relevant experience may be considered. Polytechnic Diploma in Modern Languages and Business Studies, full time – mature students with alternatives to the usual qualifications, and French or German equivalent to A-level standard, are considered. Certificate of Qualification in Social Work, full time – candidates without formal qualifications will be required to take an educational attainment test.

Liverpool Institute of Higher Education
Diploma in Occupational Therapy, full time. Students over 26 considered on merit (usual entry requirement five O-levels and twoA-levels plusFirst Aid Certificate).

Liverpool: South Merseyside College
MSC-sponsored Clerk of Works course full time, for people aged 22-plus with City and Guilds Advanced Craft Certificate, or BTEC/SCOTVEC ONC or equivalent qualification. Applicants without formal qualifications but with extensive experience, preferably supervisory, considered.

Manchester Polytechnic
Mature students very welcome – send for free 'Mature Students' Handbook'. (Also see 'Degree and Advanced Courses'.) Foundation Course leading to Polytechnic Certificate in Visual Studies, full time – entry concessions for mature students and those of exceptional merit. Polytechnic Certificate in Recreational Arts for the Community, full time – no entry requirements for mature students other than commitment and ability to work in at least one art form. Diploma in Careers Guidance, full time – various entry qualifications. Certificate of Qualification in Social Work (CQSW), full time – entry concessions for over 25s, paid or voluntary social work experience needed. Polytechnic Certificate in Youth and Community Work, full time – entry concessions for over 25s with relevant practical experience. BTEC Diploma in Clothing Machine Technology, full time – entry test for mature students. BTEC HND Technology of Food, full time – entry concessions for mature students. Polytechnic Certificate in Meat Technology and Inspection, full time – entry concessions for mature students with approved industrial experience. BTEC HND Hotel, Catering and Institutional Management, sandwich – entry concessions for mature students with appropriate industrial experience. DipHE, full time – can lead to degree; entry concessions for mature students, from whom applications are especially welcome. BTEC HND Science (Chemistry), full time – sympathetic consideration to candidates with alternatives to usual entry

qualifications. BTEC HND Computer Studies, full time or sandwich – entry requirement concessions for mature students with relevant work experience; aptitude test possible. BTEC National Certificate in Polymer Technology – entrance examination for candidates without conventional qualifications. Extensive range of part time courses welcoming mature students which can be used as a bridge into full time courses.

Science Laboratory Technology
'I took a laboratory technician's apprenticeship with Rolls-Royce at Crewe and found myself stationed in the plastics and rubber laboratory, so naturally I was doing polymer science at college, part-time. First I did the TEC (now BTEC) sciences courses,then I came to Manchester to do the Higher BTEC and went into polymer science and technology. At the end of that course I was made redundant from Rolls-Royce – but my combination of work experience and college study made it possible to join degree students, and get a degree in two years instead of four years'.

'People don't expect middle-aged Mums like me to want day release but, having started out as a medical laboratory technician and gained ONC before I left to marry and have a family, I was determined to pick up where I left off. I found I got quite a lot of opposition. When I first applied for the job, I think they wanted somebody who'd just be an extra pair of hands, but I wanted to make a career, so after a lot of persuasion, I managed to get day release for the Institute of Medical Laboratory Sciences course.'

[Students, Faculty of Science and Engineering, Manchester Polytechnic]

'Mature students bring their own experience in. It may sometimes happen that in a class, the group will be studying a particular topic and when the lecturer asks if there are any questions or comments, a mature student will say 'Oh, we don't do it at work that way now, we do it this way' – in which case the lecturer will be able to make use of that particular student's experience for the benefit of the class as a whole.'
[Spokesperson, Faculty of Science and Engineering, Manchester Polytechnic]

Manchester University
Extra-Mural Department: Career Studies Unit with MSC-sponsored programme of short courses – e.g. Foundation (Job-hunting Skills), Personal Evaluation and Presentation, Small Business Suitability, Computer Workshop, ,Understanding Management, Effective Management, Executive Recruitment.

Manchester: University of Manchester Institute of Science and Technology (UMIST)
Conversion course in Computation/Computation and Optics, full time – leads to MSc, attracts some late starters.

Manchester: Withington Centre for Community Education
Modern Office Skills Retraining, Garment Manufacturing (could attract MSC sponsorship), both full time. Open Workshops in Modern Office Skills, Maths, English, Book-keeping, Basic Skills, English as a Second Language, Business English. Leisure courses with earning potential include Floristry for City and Guilds Certificate, Dressmaking, Tailoring, Machine Knitting, China Painting, Cookery and Cake Decoration, Information Technology. Flexistudy (see 'Open and Distance Learning Courses').

Middlesbrough: Longlands College of Further Education
College has MSC – and ESF-funded courses but did not give details. Also states that mature students are welcome on an infill basis to its regular courses. Open Learning (see 'Open and Distance Learning Courses').

Middlesbrough: Teesside Polytechnic
MSC-sponsored Computer-Aided Engineering, full time. MSC-sponsored Management, full time.

Newcastle-upon-Tyne Polytechnic
MSC-sponsored DipHE Business Information Technology, full time. MSC-sponsored BTEC HNC Engineering – Computer-Aided Engineering, full time. MSC-sponsored BTEC HNC Engineering – Optoelectronics, full time. MSC-sponsored Institute of Production Control Diploma, full time. Entry concessions are possible for mature students on most courses. (See also 'Degree and Advanced Courses'.)

Peterlee College
MSC-sponsored Scope programme, various options, part time. MSC-sponsored New Technology/Wider Opportunities for Women, part time. Practical Secretarial skills, under 21-hour rule. Engineering: short updating courses under 12 or 21-hour rule, including Robotics, CAD/CAM, Welding, Electronics, Motor Vehicle Engineering, etc. Computing Workshop, day and evening. Can lead to City and Guilds Information Technology award. Flexistudy and Open Learning (see 'Open and Distance Learning Courses').

Preston: Lancashire Polytechnic
Opportunities for mature students on most courses, mainly at higher level (see 'Degree and Advanced Courses'). Foundation/Introductory courses include Accountancy, Management, Mathematics and Statistics, and there are pre- degree courses (see 'Pre-Entry Sample and Access Courses') and Open College courses (see 'Open and Distance Learning Courses'). Polytechnic Diploma in Social Work/Certificate of Qualification in Social Work (CQSW), – few formal entry requirements for over-25s; evidence of recent study advantageous. MSC-sponsored full time Conversion course to Microbiology. Associate Student access to all courses (see 'Degree and

Advanced Courses') provides a useful means of retraining. ACOL Analytical Chemistry course for updating.

Rotherham: Rockingham College of Further Education
Department of Industry-funded courses for redundant employees: options include Microtechnology, Community Care, Sign Writing, Horticulture, Jobbing Building, Painting and Decorating, Catering – full time, all for City and Guilds awards. ESF-sponsored Basic Catering and Book-Keeping (unemployed people over 25) under 21-hour rule. ESF-sponsored Community Service (unemployed people over 50) under 21-hour rule. ESF-sponsored New Office Technology Skills (age limits 18-25) under 21-hour rule. Wide range of leisure courses with earning potential – e.g: Cake Decoration, Cookery, Fashion, Toymaking, Upholstery, Creative Writing, etc.

Retraining After Redundancy
'Before I started on this Microelectronics course, I was a crane driver. I'd thought of doing Heavy Goods Vehicle driving, but I'd done a little bit inside CB Radio and I wanted to take a Radio and TV course, but there wasn't one available, so I chose this instead. It's proved to be a little bit heavy going but very interesting, and there's another stage of the course where we might be able to think about setting up on our own. I'd thought of doing the small jobs, like repairing home computers.'

'After being made redundant after 30 years, I took a Hairdressing course, but I haven't been able to find any work in that line. I think they're looking for more experience. I saw the Community Service course advertised, and I thought 'Well, you can't know too much,' so I decided to come along. We've had a lot of visits – to the courts, the prison, the youth detention centre – and we're learning first aid and home nursing and going out on work experience. I've gained a lot of knowledge. I'd like a part-time job, but I'm quite happpy to go and do something voluntary and get my satisfaction that way. If I got into the hospital scheme, perhaps I could start by helping the hairdresser.'

[Students retraining at Rockingham College]

'My feeling was, and I've been proved right, that there are a lot of people in the over-50 age group who felt they were on the scrap heap. They'd been made redundant because of the rundown in the steel works and other areas of work and they felt that they were probably of no more use to the community. We decided that we would like to try a community service course for unemployed people and, with the possible openings for community service, we thought it might be an appropriate course for the over-50s. They study rights and responsibilities, social problems, community problems, learn basic caring skills and first aid and caring for the sick, and they will shortly go out on work experience, a day a week in old people's homes, children's homes, the probation service, with young offenders – in community work generally.'

[Spokesperson, Rockingham College]

Rotherham College of Arts and Technology

Workshop for the Unemployed, part time, with opportunities to learn a wide range of skills, from Woodwork to Industrial Sewing, and from Light Crafts to Welding. Special Workshop, one day a week, with English Language support for students whose first spoken language is Mirpur Punjabi. Women's Workshop, one day a week from 12.30-3.30p.m., sampling Joinery, Painting and Decorating, Motor Vehicle Maintenance, Welding, Domestic Appliance Repairs, Electronics and Wood and Metal Turning with a woman teacher. PHIT – (Physically Handicapped into Information Technology), under 21-hour rule – to prepare for training in Computer Studies and Information Technology. Industrial Electronics, under 21-hour rule – leads to City and Guilds award. Electrical Engineering, under 21-hour rule – leads to BTEC National award. Electronic Servicing, part time, day and evening – leads to City and Guilds award. Security and Emergency Alarm Systems, part time, day and evening – leads to City and Guilds award, very suitable for people wishing to retrain for a new career. Cleaning Science, part time – leads to City and Guilds award, can lead to work in hotel housekeeping, as warden of sheltered accomodation, in hospital domestic supervision, etc. Computer-Aided Engineering, various levels, evenings – to update engineering tradespeople and technicians. Microelectronics, various levels, evenings, to update electrical/electronic tradespeople and technicians. Ceramic Technician's Certificate, part time – mature students accepted at discretion of Head of Department. Construction courses, part time: Brickwork, Carpentry and Joinery, Plumbing – all leading to City and Guilds awards, mature students accepted at discretion of Principal. Basic Course in Youth and Community Work, evenings – for people 21-plus with at least six months' experience of voluntary youth work. Further Education Teacher's Certificate, for people aged 22-plus, who are intending to teach in FE or are engaged in training – leads to City and Guilds award. Teaching and Training People with Mental Disorders, evenings, with seven one-day visits, leads to City and Guilds award. Community Care Practice, part time, for people, 21-plus who wish to obtain employment in the Caring field – leads to City and Guilds award. Playgroup Leaders and Assistants, part time, for people wishing to work in that field. Social Care Preparation, full time, includes A-levels and City and Guilds award.

Salford College of Technology

Certificate in Residential and Day Care, full time – entry concession for over-23s with relevant work experience. Pre- Employment Common Unit of the Certificate in Social Service, full time – entry concessions for over-25s with relevant experience. Association of Accounting Technicians, full time – exceptionally, entry concession for candidates over 21. BTEC HNC Business and Finance, part time – exceptionally, entry concession for over-21s. BTEC HNC/HND Business and Finance or Public Administration, full time or part time – exceptionally, entry concession for over-19s with relevant experience. College course in Conveyancing, full time, O- and A-level entry, for students of 21 and over. BTEC Post Experience Certrificate of Business Administration, part time, for Professional Footballers aged 21 and over entering business. Certificate in Accountancy, part time – entry concession for mature students. Acounting Techncian's Certificate, part time – for students 21 and over with good command of English. Institution of Industrial Managers Certificate, part time – entry concession for over-27s. Institute of Purchasing and Supply Foundation, part time – entry concession for over-25s. Certificate in Production and Inventory Control, part time – entry concession for over-25s. Institute of Health Service Administrators, part time – for people with professional health service qualifications (medicine, nursing, paramedical, ambulance); or entry concessions if over 30 and working in health service administration. Certificate in Business Management, part time – entry concession for over-25s at discretion of Principal. Institute of Personnel Management, part time – various entry requirements, including two years' personnel experience in a post of responsibility. Diploma in Training Management, part time – various entry requirements, including relevant training experience. Institute of Marketing Certificate, part time – various entry requirements, including three years' experience. Preparation for Professional Social and Community work, part time or evenings – A-level standard, employed or seeking employment in Social or Commmunity work. City and Guilds Further Education Teacher's Certificate – for candidates over 23, adequately qualified in the subject(s) they want to teach. Keyboarding and/or Word-Processing: short courses, part time. Languages: French, German, Spanish, all levels, part time. Computing, all levels part time. Cleaning Science, part time, leads to City and Guilds award; for work in hospital domestic services, with hotels, local authorities, contract cleaning companies. Microprocessors and Micro-electronics: various short courses, open to anyone needing retraining. MSC-sponsored 'Step up' retraining opportunities, full time for unemployed people: options are Computer Numerical Control, Computer-Aided Design, Quality Assurance, Robotics, Electronics, Microcomputer Applications; when combined with appropriate industrial experience, scheme leads to BTEC HNC Engineering. BTEC Post Experience Units in Computing and its applications – open to over-21s with significant work experience. Chiropody, full time – mature students entry concession, dependent on age/background.

Salford University
Information Technology in Modern Management, full time.

Sheffield: Rother Valley College of Further Education
MSC-sponsored Modern Office Administration, full time. ESF-funded Information Technology, full time. Non-metallic Moulding and Casting, full time. Motor Vehicle Craft Studies, full time. Courses under 2l-hour rule include: Bricklaying and Woodwork, Catering and Food Studies, Art, Craft and Photography, Agriculture, Horticulture (including greenhouse work), Recreation and Leisure Studies(leads to City and Guilds award), Modern Office Skills, Motor Vehicle Craft Studies Part II, Fibrous Plaster and Fibreglass work, BTEC Commercial Computing Certificate, BTEC Electronics/Computing Certificate, BTEC Continuing Education units, (e.g. Using Word-Processors, Working with People). Mature students accepted on infill basis on wide range of full-time courses. Many part time day and evening leisure courses with earning potential- e.g: Welding, Photography, Woodwork, Catering, Horticulture, Stained Glass Work. MSC/CP Scheme (local only): 'Care of the Dependent Adult'.

Sheffield: Shirecliffe College
'All our courses are open to mature entrants.' Diploma in Community Care,full time – specifically designed for mature students. Diploma in Signwork, full time, leading to City and Guilds Certificates – entry at discretion of college after aptitude test and interview. Diploma in Furniture, full time – entry at discretion of the college. Courses under 2l-hour rule in Brickwork, Carpentry and Joinery, Machine Woodworking, Painting and Decorating, Plastering, Mechanical Services, Welding, Maintenance of Building Services Equipment and Gas Installation Technology. Supervisory Studies for NEBSS Certificate, part time – open to potential supervisors. Computer Studies through Access to Information Technology scheme, plus exam courses leading to City and Guilds and BTEC awards.

Southport College of Art and Technology
Adult Training Programme for unemployed people, part time under 2l-hour rule; includes: Introduction to Information Technology, Catering, Reception Skills, Typing for Beginners, Word-Processing, Audiotyping, Shorthand, Book-keeping, Electronic Office, Photography, Design Skills, Hairdressing, Looking After People, Housekeeping, Crafts, Horticulture/Gardening, Electronics/Electrical Systems, Building, Painting and Decorating, Carpentry and Joinery, Plumbing and Heating, Household Repairs, Small Appliance Maintenance, Basic Engineering Skills, Fabrication and Welding, Motor Vehicle Maintenance. Access to Information Technology, evenings: wide range of computer courses. Older students and those with industrial experience welcome on most full-time courses – e.g: BTEC National Diploma in General Art and Design, full time; Nursery Nursing Examination Board, full time; City and Guilds Certificate of Travel Agency Competence, evenings; adult job-seekers welcome. Leisure courses with earning potential include: Vehicle Restoration, Dressmaking, Creative

Writing, Horticultural Maintenance, Theatrical Costume. Open Learning (see 'Open and Distance Learning Courses').

Sunderland Polytechnic
MSC-sponsored Diploma in Training Management, full time. BTEC HND Design, full time – entry concessions possible for mature students with relevant industrial or commercial experience. BTEC HND Business Studies or Business and Leisure Studies, full time – exceptionally, entry concessions possible for mature students. Certificate in Community and Youth Work, full time – entry requirements waived for suitable mature students with relevant experience. Polytechnic Diploma in Social Work/Certificate of Qualification in Social Work (CQSW), full time – minimum age of entry 30; no formal entry requirement. Engineering for Women, full time, leads to Polytechnic Certificate – entry concessions for mature students with relevant experience. Polytechnic Diploma in Personnel Management (IPM Stage I equivalent), part time – successful candidates may progress to stages II and III. NEBSS Certificate in Supervisory Management,part time – for candidates aged at least 21. HNC Naval Architecture, HNC Applied Biology, HNC/HND Computer Studies – all part time; entry concessions possible for mature students. Certificate in Community and Youth Work, part time – applications from candidates over 21. (Also see 'Degree and Advanced Courses'.)

Warrington: North Cheshire College
(Amalgamation of former Padgate College of Higher Education, Warrington College of Art and Design, Warrington Technical College and local Adult Education Centres.) 'All our full-time courses are open to mature students,' they say. Options include: Medical Secretarial, BTEC National Diploma in Computer Studies, BTEC Certificate/Diploma in Leisure Studies, BTEC Certificate in Science, BTEC National Diploma in Engineering, Nursery Nursing for NNEB, Family and Community Care, BTEC National Diploma in Health Studies. (See also 'Degree and Advanced Courses'.)

York: College of Ripon and York St John
Diploma in Occupational Therapy, full time – mature students over 24 may be eligible for entry concessions (but competition is keen).

The following colleges in the region supplied information in 1987 about their retraining courses but no response was received to 1988 enquiries. Readers may nevertheless wish to make individual contacts:

Blackpool and Fylde College of Higher and Further Education
Darlington College of Technology
Doncaster Metropolitan College
Grimsby College of Technology
Hartlepool College of Technology
Huddersfield Technical College

Leeds: Airedale and Wharfedale College
Leeds: Kitson College of Technology
Liverpool Polytechnic
Newcastle College of Arts and Technology
Sheffield: Granville College
South Shields: South Tyneside College of Further Education
Sunderland: Monkwearmouth College of Further Education
Wakefield District College
York: Pocklington Institute of Further Education

Wales and Western England

Aberystwyth: Ceredigion Further Education College
(Amalgamation of Aberystwyth College of Further Education, Cardigan College of Further Education and Felinfach College of Further Education.) BTEC First Diploma in Business and Finance, full time, National Diploma in Business and Finance (Business, Secretarial, or Media Studies – Bilingual options),full time – mature students on all these courses accepted at Principal's discretion. Royal Society of Arts Diploma for Personal Assistants, full time – mature students with relevant business/secretarial experience accepted at Principal's discretion. Postgraduate and A-level Bilingual Secretarial course full time – unqualified mature students accepted at Head of Department's discretion. Intensive Secretarial course, full time – suitable for mature students who wish to train/retrain for a secretarial career. Private Secretarial course, part time – suitable for those with some knowledge of office skills who wish to resume a career. Signwork, for City and Guilds award, full time – no entry qualifications other than natural aptitude and interest.

Barnstaple: North Devon College
The college says: 'We welcome mature students to all of our full-time courses. Already mature students have been offered places on Art and Design,Catering, Hairdressing, Nursery Nursing.' Foundation Art Course, full time – mature students welcome to apply for the one or two-year General Art and Design course. Other opportunities include City and Guilds, BTEC and NNEB courses.

Bath: Norton Radstock College of Further Education
Courses for unemployed adults and those on community programmes, part time. Options include Hairdressing, Commercial/Clerical skills, Agriculture, Engineering, Computer Use, Horticulture, Crafts. Basic Engineering Competence, full time, leads to City and Guilds 2O1, suitable for those who wish to update skills. Welding Craft Practice, evenings, leads to City and Guilds l65, suitable for people with no previous welding knowledge. Horticulture, part time, leads to City and Guilds awards in various subjects-e.g: Amenity Horticulture, Decorative Horticulture; suitable for unemployed adults. Car Maintenance for the Owner-Driver, part time, includes

servicing and preparation for MOT – could have earning potential. MSC-sponsored ITEC unit – free courses for unemployed in subjects like Industrial Control by Computers, Introduction to Information Technology, Print Your Own Magazine (desktop publishing). Leisure courses with earning potential include Creative Writing, Painting and Drawing. Flexistudy courses (see 'Open and Distance Learning Courses').

Bridgewater College
MSC-sponsored Secretarial Skills, full time. MSC-sponsored Secretarial Refresher, full time. MSC-sponsored Receptionist Skills, full time. Caring and Services, full time – for those wishing to work in the Social Services. RSA Counselling Skills course, mode unspecified. Open Learning (see 'Open and Distance Learning Courses').

Bristol: Brunel Technical College
MSC-sponsored General Catering, full time, leads to City and Guilds 706/2,707/1 and Wine and Spirit Trust Certificate. HCIMA catering courses, part time, suitable for adult job-changers or 'women returners'; mode unspecified. Beauty Therapy, full time, open to anyone over 18, leads to five City and Guilds awards. Hotel Reception, full time – anyone over 18 welcome.MSC-sponsored Adult Engineers Training Scheme (AETS) Radio Licence retraining, full time for people with previous aircraft maintenance experience; CAA-approved Aero Electronics, full time, leads to Category 'R' (Radio) Licence; mature student entry by interview, practical aircraft maintenance engineering experience often accepted in lieu of formal qualifications, or advice given on suitable preliminary courses. CAA-approved Airframes and Engines, full time, leads to Category 'A and C' Licence, for prospective aircraft maintenance engineers in civil aviation. BTEC Electronics and Communications Engineering courses for National/Higher National awards – mature students may be accepted on the basis of an interview (no age restrictions). MSC-sponsored Microelectronic Engineering, full time, for BTEC Certificate in Electronic Engineering. Fundamental Electronics, part time – for those who use electronic equipment and want to know how it works, no entry qualification. Links with St Paul's Outreach Centre (Inner City Project) – two former students of this centre are now on full time Electronics Servicing courses. Course in Essential electricity, part time, for City and Guilds award – open to anyone in 16-50 age range, no formal entry qualifications.

Aeronautical Engineering for Mature Students
'One of our students, a woman in her late 20's said she always wanted to work on and with aircraft, but was persuaded at school into a more 'ladylike' career. She became a State Registered Nurse and a Ward Sister. Nevertheless, she felt this was not her true vocation and decided life was passing her by. She came to the college, obtained her CAA Airframes and Engines

Licence (not without a little struggle because she was not a 'natural') and then emigrated to Australia. Another male student finally achieved his CAA-approved Aircraft Maintenance Licence when he was 41. He was originally rejected for the course because he lacked the minimum entry requirements, but we advised him to take a part-time course for some BTEC Level l units. These gained him entry to the CAA course. As his LEA would not give him a grant, he supported himself by working in the evenings and at weekends. He did so well that he was awarded the Society of Licensed Aircraft Engineers and Technologists prize, and subsequently obtained work wih Birmingham Executive Airways.'

[Spokesperson, Brunel Technical College]

Bristol: Filton Technical College

MSC-sponsored Export/Marketing, full time. BTEC National Certificate, part time or evenings (options in Business Studies, Banking, Accountancy Technician's work). Entry concessions possible for mature students. BTEC Pre-Higher National Certificate Conversion course, part time or evenings. Entry concessions possible for over-21s with GCE O-level English Language. Access to Information Technology 20-hour intensive courses, weekends/evenings. Supervisory Studies for NEBSS Certificate part time/ evenings, no formal entry requirements for potential supervisors. Trade Union Studies, part time, for workplace representatives. Association of Accounting Technicians, part time or evenings, entry concessions for over-21s with two years' accounting experience. Finance Houses Association, evenings. Entry concessions for mature students. Wide range of Secretarial and Professional Institute courses – possible entry concessions for mature students. Flexistudy (see 'Open and Distance Learning Courses').

Cardiff: South Glamorgan Institute of Higher Education

'We accept mature students on all our courses.' The college has indicated the following courses as attracting mature students: BTEC HND Design, full time. BTEC HND Business Studies and ND Business Studies, full time. BTEC HND Catering and ND Catering, BTEC HND Science (Medical Laboratory Sciences), full time. BTEC ND Dental Technology, full time. BTEC HND Science Applied Biology, full time. BTEC ND Science, full time. BTEC HND Technology of Food, full time. BTEC ND Food Technology, full time. BTEC HND Hotel, Catering and Institutional Management, full time. BTEC ND Hotel Catering and Institutional Operations. Dip. General Catering, full time. Dip. Baking (Technician), full time. Dip. Baking (Craft), full time. BTEC ND Construction, full time. BTEC HNC/HND Engineering (Electronics and Communications), full time. BTEC HND Engineering (Electronic Products: Manufacture and Test), full time. BTEC ND Engineering (Electronics and Communication), full time. BTEC NC Engineering (Electronics), part time. BTEC HND Engineering (Plant and Engineering

Services), full time. BTEC Dip. Technology (Engineering), full time. CGLI Electronics Servicing, full time. Diploma in Social Work/Certificate of Qualification in Social Work (CQSW), full time – entry concession for over-25s. Certificate in the Education and Training of Mentally Handicapped People, full time – entry concession for over-23s, but one year's paid or voluntary work experience essential. Working Together with People who have a Mental Handicap, sandwich. Candidates must be over 25, with five O-levels and at least two years' work experience with mentally handicapped people. MSC-sponsored part time course for Wardens of Sheltered Housing Complexes. Chiropody, full time for State Registration. Ladies Hairdressing/Beauty, full time, leads to IHBC and City and Guilds awards, entry by interview and test. Beauty Therapy and Hairdressing, full time, leads to seven awards including Remedial Cosmetology and Theatrical Make-up – candidates need three O-levels and success in test and interview. Certificate in Printed Communication, full time – candidates normally need equivalent of CSE Grade 3 in three subjects: courses can lead into BTEC course or employment in Reprographics. (See also 'Degree and Advanced Courses'.)

Cheltenham: The College of St Paul and St Mary
Teaching English as a Foreign Language, full time, leading to RSA Preparatory Certificate, or Licentiate of Trinity College, London; Teaching English as a Foreign or Second Language; RSA Further Education Certificate (graduate, or graduate-equivalent, or teacher entrants). (See also 'Degree and Advanced Courses'.)

Chippenham Technical College
MSC-sponsored Technical Authorship, full time. Modular Office Skills, to suit student, part time. Publicity Production, full time and under 21-hour rule. Caring Skills, full time and part time. Managing the Office, part time, can lead to BTEC award. Making Numbers Work For You, part time, can lead to BTEC award. Improve your Financial Decision-Making, part time, can lead to BTEC award. Mature Students' Typewriting, part time. Word-Processing, part time. Advanced Hairdressing, full time or part time. Supervisory Management, part time. ESF-sponsored Welding and Sheet Metalwork, full time. Mature students accepted on infill basis on many of the college's courses – unusual options include Horse Management and Training, full time, and Equestrian Studies for BTEC award, full time. Wide range of part time courses with earning potential in and around Chippenham includes: Computing, Cookery, Copper Enamelling, Dressmaking, Machine Knitting, Photography, Picture Framing, Pottery, Sewing Machine Techniques, Silversmithing, Upholstery, Writing for Profit, Book-Keeping, Business Studies, Electronics, Shorthand, Typewriting. Also Flexistudy (see 'Open and Distance Learning Courses').

Exeter College
Courses under the 21-hour rule: Leisure and Recreation, Catering, Management Training. Concessions for mature students without usual entrance qualifications on many courses. 'The main condition is *evidence* that the person in question is likely to succeed.'

Haverfordwest: Pembrokeshire College of Further Education
MSC-sponsored Catering, full time. All courses open to mature students on infill basis. (See also 'Small Business and Self-Employment Courses'.)

Llanelli: Carmarthenshire College of Technology and Art
MSC-sponsored Business Information Technology, full time. ESF-sponsored Business Technology, full time. Open Learning (see 'Open and Distance Learning Courses').

Pontypridd: the Polytechnic of Wales
MSC-sponsored HNC Computer-Aided Engineering, full time. MSC-sponsored HNC Engineering Design, full time. MSC-sponsored HNC for Science Graduates, full time. Also Open Learning (see 'Open and Distance Learning Courses'). Mature students without conventional entry requirements may be considered for many BTEC (and degree) courses at the discretion of the Polytechnic, and are advised to seek advice from the appropriate Course Leader before applying.

HNC Electronics Conversion Course for Science Graduates
'After O-levels I joined the Navy, and was an electrical mechanic on helicopters for three years. Then I left to work in a hospital's Pathology Department, where I became interested in Microbiology. Subsequently I took a university degree in Microbiology, but when I graduated I was unable to get a job. My Jobcentre in Newport told me about this Electronics course for unemployed graduates at the Polytechnic of Wales, and though I found the Maths and Physics difficult, I think I'm coping all right now. In my industrial placement, I hope to work in a hospital, with the long-term plan of combining my Microbiology degree and this Electronics course, to work in Medical Electronics.'

[Student, BTEC HNC Conversion course, Polytechnic of Wales]

'We have been running this course for science graduates to take the HNC Electronics for several years and it is very popular – often we have 50 or 60 candidates for 18 places. We interview them all, looking not just for academic ability but practical skills – whether they'd done anything in the way of a constructional project during their degree course. On past records, about 75% have obtained jobs in electronics on completing the course, in all sorts of areas, from electronic design, technician engineer, computing, medical electronics, to geophysical work connected with oil exploration.'

[Spokesperson, Polytechnic of Wales]

Poole: Dorset Institute of Higher Education

BTEC HND Business and Finance, full time. BTEC HND Business and Finance, (Tourism) full time. BTEC HND Business Information Technology, full time. BTEC HND Hotel, Catering and Institutional Management, full time. BTEC HND Computer-Aided Engineering, full time. BTEC HND Practical Archaeology, full time. BTEC HNC in Electronics, full time. Most full-time courses are open to those mature students without formal qualifications who can present evidence that convinces admissions staff that they have the capacity and ability to succeed in and benefit from the course.

Salisbury College of Technology

MSC-sponsored Clerks of Works Course, full time, for candidates aged 22-plus with an approved craft training. Modern Technology: opportunities to learn or re-learn skills in Computer-Aided Engineering, short courses in Computer-Aided Draughting and Design (CAD). Introduction to Numerical Control (CNC). Further Numerical Control (CNC). Quality Assurance (QC). City and Guilds Further Education Teacher's Certificate, for practising or potential teachers/trainers in colleges, commerce, industry, public service – part time or evenings. Call Order Cookery, under 21-hour rule. Mature students welcome on infill basis to all part-time courses (send for part time prospectus). BTEC Continuing Education Units in Business Administration and Management. Many leisure courses with earning potential, part time or evenings – examples: Picture Frame Restoration, Modern Furniture Repair and General Woodwork, Dressmaking, China Repair, Tailoring, Typing Skills, Machine Knitting, Small Outboard Engine Maintenance, Creative Writing, Bookbinding, Better Driving.

Street: Strode College

MSC-sponsored Secretarial, full time. Mature students accepted on infill basis: possible subjects include Typewriting, Shorthand, Word-Processing, Hairdressing, Beauty Consultants, etc. Pre-School Playgroups Foundation course, part time. Wide range of leisure courses with earning potential – e.g: Cookery, Dressmaking, Machine Knitting, Quilting, Poultry-Keeping, Upholstery, Woodwork. Open Learning (see 'Open and Distance Learning Courses').

Swansea: Gorseinon College

MSC-sponsored Community Care, full time, for City and Guilds award. MSC- sponsored CAD/CAM/CNC courses, full time. MSC-sponsored Languages for Industry, full time. MSC-sponsored Information Technology for Business, full time. Hydraulics and Pneumatics, mode unspecified.

Taunton: Somerset College of Arts and Technology
MSC-sponsored HNC Industrial Design, full time. MSC-sponsored Modern Office Practice, full time. MSC-sponsored Secretarial Refresher/Upgrading, full time. MSC-sponsored Accounting Technicians course, full time, leads to BTEC Certificate. Consideration given to mature students for all courses; they find BTEC HND Graphic Design, full time, and BTEC HND Textile and Surface Pattern Design, full time, attractive choices. Selection by interview and portfolio work. Open Learning (see 'Open and Distance Learning Courses').

Graphic Art Design for Mature Students
'I was a draughtsman in the Portsmouth area, and I left my job and got a postman's job in Somerset so that I could find the time during the day to develop my art. I'd been working alone, mainly in cartooning, but about four years ago, I decided to try and get into art college, to just find out what I wanted to do, and develop various styles. It was the best thing I could have done and at the right time. If I'd left school and gone into art as all my friends did – well, most of them wasted it totally, and none of them are in art now. I know exactly what I want to do and I'm totally committed to it. I've also found the business studies side of my course very interesting: there are a few things that never crossed my mind. My plan is to buy my way into a group of established artists in a London agency, and I've discussed it with the business studies chap here and he gave me advice on it.'

[Student on HND Art course, Somerset College of Art and Technology]

'When we are choosing mature students for Art and Design courses, the main factor we look for is commitment. To decide to give up your job and take a minimum of three years' training is a pretty big decision for anybody. Certainly the first (Foundation) year is not likely to be very easy from the financial point of view, though the HND course will be supported by a mandatory award. Mature students, too, need to be able to see the career prospects ahead. Having made their decision, they have to be very sure about what they want. Provided they can produce evidence of really good work, it wouldn't matter that they were, say 36 with no O-levels, even for a grant, when it came to the Higher National Diploma.'

[Spokesperson, Somerset College of Art and Technology]

Tiverton: East Devon College of Further Education
The college offers MSC-sponsored courses and courses under the 21-hour rule, but does not give precise details. It specifies Technology, Engineering, Leisure and Recreation, Business Studies and Secretarial courses as attracting late starters.

Weymouth College
Diploma in the Conservation of Stonework, full time, open to candidates

with qualifications or experience necessary to benefit from the course; included History of Sculpture, Carving, Stone Working and Building Technology, Conservation and Restoration. Open learning (see 'Open and Distance Learning Courses').

The following colleges in this region supplied information in 1987 about their retraining courses, but no response was received to 1988 enquiries. Readers may nevertheless wish to make individual contact.

Cardiff: Rumney College
Cheltenham: Gloucestershire College of Arts and Technology
Deeside: North East Wales Institute
Llandridnod Wells: Radnor College of Further Education
Weston-super-Mare College of Further Education
Ystrad Mynch College of Further Education

Scotland and Northern Ireland

Belfast College of Technology
Courses for unemployed adults, part time, includes Computing Skills, Word-Processing, Programming in BASIC, Photography, Gardening, Motor Vehicle Maintenance, Home Electrics, Brickwork, Plumbing, Decoration, Woodwork, Garment Making, Domestic Machine Knitting, Contemporary Affairs, Communication Skills.

Clydebank College
MSC-sponsored programmes (subjects not specified). SCOTVEC National Certificate modular courses: you can choose your own modules and make up a 21-hour course of study.

Dumfries and Galloway College of Technology
MSC-sponsored Catering Crafts, full time. MSC-sponsored Catering, full time. Mature students over 21 may be granted entry concessions on SCOTVEC HND/HNC full time courses – popular options are Business Studies, Computer Studies, Information Studies and Secretarial Studies. Courses that may be of additional interest are: the SCOTVEC NC programme for Medical Secretaries, full time, over-21s may be granted entry concessions; and the Institute of Clerks of Works Mature Candidates' Course – evenings, for people over 40 with at least five years' relevant experience. There are 21-hour opportunities in Engineering and Science. Skills Training Programme for unemployed people, shift workers, housewives, retired people in a wide range of options, such as Brickwork, Carpentry and Joinery, Painting and Decorating, Interior Design, Screen Printing, Upholstery, etc.

Dundee: Duncan of Jordanstone College of Art
Up to 10% of admissions to First Year General Course in Art and Design may be without formal qualification, on the basis of outstanding portfolio of work and by satisfying selectors of the candidate's ability to complete the course. Diploma in Home Economics, full time, welcomes mature students, as does SCOTVEC HND Catering, Hotel and Institutional Management, full time.

Edinburgh College of Art

Up to 10% of exceptionally gifted students may be admitted to courses without formal entry qualifications, on the basis of portfolio suitability, essay and/or interview. The college states that: 'The Central (Art) Institutions are empowered to admit a very small number of students annually who do not hold the requisite academic qualifications but whose portfolios of work are of an exceptionally high standard. In support of applications for Courses in Art, candidates are required to submit a portfolio of their own unaided work. The College's assessment of the standard and promise indicated by the portfolio of work is of great importance in arriving at the final selection of candidates.'

Edinburgh: Napier College

HND Legal Studies, full time – those aged 21-plus may be granted entry concessions. Diploma in Careers Guidance, full time – those aged 25-plus with at least five years' relevant work experience may be granted entry concessions. SCOTVEC HND Business Studies, full time – those aged 21-plus may be granted entry concessions. Unusual opportunities include: College Diploma in Book and Periodical Publishing, full time – candidates must have two A-levels or two H-grades; College Diploma and Membership of the British Institute of Interior Design, full time – candidates must have two A-levels or three H-grades; SCOTVEC HND Printing (Administration and Production), full time, candidates must have two H-grades.

Edinburgh: Queen Margaret College

Mature students with non-standard qualifications accepted on SCOTVEC HND Hotel, Catering and Institutional Management Course, full-time. Mature students welcomed on Diploma in Drama, full time,and SCOTVEC HND Information Studies, full time, with entry concessions in some cases. Diploma of the Society of Chiropodists, full time,accepts mature students (high success rate noted by the college). (For other paramedical opportunities, see 'Degree and Advanced Courses'.)

Glasgow College

SCOTVEC HNC Legal Studies, full time – possible entry concessions for students aged 21-plus. SCOTVEC HND Business Studies, full time. possible entry concessions for students aged 21-plus. Diploma in Personnel Management, full time – possible entry concessions for students aged 27-plus with at least four years' relevant experience. SCOTVEC HND Secretarial Studies, full time – possible entry concessions for students aged 21-plus. Wide range of part-time courses for Professional Institute qualifications.

Inverness College of Further and Higher Education

Study Programmes are organised on a modular basis; in theory, thereore, anyone can take any module. Assessment is by continuous monitoring (no exams). You select modules to make up your own study programme, and unemployed people can take up to six half-day modules under the 21-hour rule without losing benefit. Study areas specifically recommended for unemployed/mature people are in Hotel and Catering Administration, Food Trades, Home Crafts, Mechanical and Petroleum Enginerring. Open Learning (see 'Open and Distance Learning Courses').

Newry: Newcastle College of Further Education
Pre-School Playgroups, part time, for City and Guilds award. Open Learning under consideration.

Newtownabbey Technical College
Adults are welcome to enrol for any course in the college, full time or part time, and there is no upper age limit. Adult Unemployed Initiative, part time – options in: Vehicle Maintenance, Welding, Metalworking Skills. BTEC First and National Diplomas, full time, and Certificates, part time in Business and Finance, Engineering and Construction. Over-19's without minimum qualifications admitted at Principal's discretion. Wide range of part time courses leading to RSA (Certificate of Continuing Education) and City and Guilds awards – e,g: Computer Programming, Welding Engineering, Motor Vehicle Crafts, Plumbing, Heating and Ventilating, Radio and Television Electronics, etc. – for school-leavers but open to adults on infill basis. Office skills/secretarial subjects, part time and evenings, in Shorthand, Typewriting, Audio Typing, Word-Processing, etc. Leisure courses with earning potential, part time, include Creative Embroidery, Dressmaking, Recreational Metalwork, Recreational Brickwork, Recreational Woodwork, Recreational Car Maintenance, Video Techniques. Many of the above can be taken through Open Learning courses (see 'Open and Distance Learning Courses').

Glasgow: The University of Strathclyde
At the Scottish Business School, MSC-sponsored courses for people who are unemployed or under notice of redundancy, and meet the entry criteria for each course. Management Development Course, full time, six weeks, for people with managerial experience in industry or commerce. Management Update Programme, first week full time, following 10 weeks part time, for people who have been unemployed less than six months and are seeking entry either or re-entry to management. Women Into Management, part time (half a day a week for 12 weeks), for women who are seeking either entry or re-entry to managerial positions in industry, commerce and the public sector.

The following colleges in this region supplied information in 1987 about their retraining courses but no response was received to 1988 enquiries. Readers may nevertheless wish to make individual contact:

Aberdeen College of Commerce
Aberdeen: Robert Gordon's Institute of Technology
Armagh College of Further Education
Ayr College
Belfast College of Business Studies
Cumbernauld College
Down College of Further Education
Edinburgh: Telford College of Further EducationGlasgow: The Queen's College
Glasgow: Springburn College
Hamilton: Bell College of Technology
Limavady Technical College
Lurgan College of Further Education

SMALL BUSINESS AND SELF-EMPLOYMENT COURSES

Ideas and courses that teach marketable skills and profitable ways of using them

Introduction

Working for yourself is very tempting to anyone who gets tired of the 'work–mortgage–work' lifestyle that one person I interviewed described so aptly. But it can, sadly, disintegrate into a 'work–no mortgage–work' lifestyle that is worse than punching a time clock, unless you are very careful about the kind of business or self–employment operation you are going to set up, and make quite sure there will be a profit left over to live on when you have paid all the setting–up and running costs.

That same temptation beckons even more seductively when rejection – as so many people feel it to be – through redundancy makes a nonsense of a career plan, qualifications, overtime, initiative and all. 'If I employed myself, so the argument goes, 'I wouldn't have to rely on whether the marketing department was efficient or not. I wouldn't have to price my products so highly that they couldn't compete. I could offer extra services (delivery/gift-wrapping/late-night opening).'

And then the 'How could I fail?' syndrome takes over, with its beguiling view of grateful customers recommending newcomers, so that advertising could be cut; national publicity bringing hordes of new clients to the door; banks competing to lend you money.

Of course, for some people, that is just the way it happens. We've all read stories of computer whizz-kids making a small fortune selling computer games to the big firms; people facing ruin who just happen to be able to knock off a best-selling novel in time to beat the bailiffs; worker communes providing local services that make a profit out of factory offcuts; people making money out of second-hand school uniforms or off-peak cheap transport.

Equally, though, we all tut-tut in sympathy from time to time over the 'local boy makes bad' stories in our newspapers, reading how people have lost all their pools winnings/redundancy money/cash from remortgaged homes in disastrous enterprises that, on the face of it, sounded safe enough propositions.

What, perhaps, should be given more publicity when people are thinking about self-employment and small businesses are the enterprises that rub along because their owners are prepared to put in inordinate amounts of work. It may be true, as the MSC advertisements tell us, that 'Inside every employed person is a self-employed one'. But is that person going to be able to cope with unsocial hours and the need to work without sick pay or holiday pay; to cope with the mingled tensions of having to see the bank manager for extra credit, quote for a crucial order and fend off the VAT return for another week? These are the aspects of self-employment that really take their toll of enthusiasm, rather than the question of under cutting from competition or unpaid tax bills mounting up for five years.

Small businesses rarely fail with a bang. It is more a question of of exhaustion setting in, coupled with the unwilling recognition of the fact that there are not 60 hours in the day, or 12 days in the week, and that no amount of ambition, courage and determination will keep you awake over your knitting machine/lathe/order for 250 canapés for the Mayor's reception when you are actually so tired you can't stand up, let alone do work to fine tolerances.

If this all sounds rather downbeat, then it's better to be prepared for it now, rather than when you have taken on the responsibility for your own (and perhaps other people's) employment. Not having a boss has its compensations, but you must be prepared for the fact that there isn't anyone around to say 'How awful!' when you have a problem or a tragedy and need to take a few days off. Good friends, who will step in when you are carted off to hospital with appendicitis, are a must – sympathy or no sympathy, your clients will still be depending on you, and may be forced to go elsewhere for supplies or service if you let them down. (Incidentally, though the NHS will whip out your appendix with instant and splendid efficiency, you will find you can't even keep a business afloat from a hospital bed surrounded by 20 others – so private medical insurance has extra value for the small businessman/woman, bringing not only speed of treatment but privacy, a phone and, if you're able, the chance to instruct your helpers or even see your most valued customer if you're laid up.)

Insurance, in fact, is a word to keep closely in mind when you are thinking of going self-employed, and I don't only mean the kind of official policy you take out to protect you against employers' liability, accident or illness. You need to consider the kind of business you are in, and imagine what kind of trouble might lose you an important customer. How can you provide yourself with a safety net?

For instance, suppose your business activity includes delivery of a large number of heavy packages of brochures by road as soon as they are printed, and your van breaks down. Have you a network of good friends who will lend you transport, or a contact in the local car hire firm who will rent you a van instantly, or do you really understand how the Red Star parcels system works? (Red Star once saved *my* neck when I left a vital tape-recording neeed for the next day's radio programme up in Derby; the interviewee found it and despatched it instantly to my local station!)

It's this kind of tip that you're likely to be given on a small business course, along with advice on costing, on record-keeping, on advertising and promotion, and on legal, insurance and tax problems. If you want to be able to concentrate on making a success of your business, you need to go on a course to teach you the basics of management, so that you can keep the mechanics of the business ticking over without effort, leaving your 'fine tuning' to be given to the product or the service you are offering. You can't afford time to worry about whether you've put aside the right percentage of sales for VAT, or ordered enough invoice forms to see the quarter through.

On college small business coures, you can, for example, learn about computers, using *their* computers and *their* discs, rather than trying to teach yourself on your own new and very expensive equipment at home after a day's work. If your business happens to rely on regular supplies of materials from outside suppliers, a business course leader can help you devise an ordering and stock control system that will ensure items are automatically re-ordered before you run out. That's when you'll be advised about setting up a back-up provision, for getting materials when there is a rail, road or postal strike.

BEP, GEP, NEP, and PEP are government initiatives to help new businesses get started. BEP stands for Business Enterprise Programme, typically offered by Northumberland College of Arts and Technology on the basis of a day a week's attendance over seven weeks. PEP stands for Private Enterprise Programme, and Bracknell College has provided details of their one-day seminars. Each deals with a different aspect of business, so if you want just to learn about the Financial Control of an enterprise, you can book for that day, or if you want to learn about Computers in the Small Business, you can book for that day. Though these are MSC-sponsored programmes, Bracknell College points out that candidates who don't meet the eligibility rules for a free course are still able to join the courses by paying a course fee.

GEP is the Graduate Enterprise Programme, a management training course for recently qualified graduates. Entry is competitive and the scheme includes four weeks at a Business School (free, and with a training allowance for the student) plus further counselling and advice when the business is launched. NEP is the New Enterprise Programme, a much extended version of the above, aimed at people who are seen as having realistic business plans with the prospect of employing at least ten people in two years. Again courses are run at business schools and last 16 weeks, with four weeks in residence. For both GEP and NEP entry is very competitive: you should do as much research as you can in advance to make sure your project is viable and likely to show an income with scope for expansion even after all costs and a profit margin have been allowed for.

Costing is a crucial part of any small business, and it includes adding in what you think is a reasonable rate per hour for your services – something some would-be self-employed people underestimate. Try comparing what you earned when on the minimum hourly rate in your previous job or comparing what is being offered in the lowest-paid jobs in the situations vacant columns with the amount you think you'll get, so that you can work out how much business you will have to turn over before you get a living wage.

For some people, it will be quite enough if they cover their costs and get a modest rate per hour for their work, because they're doing something they enjoy while also building up skills, whether they're in dressmaking or installing fitted kitchens. It is nevertheless worth remembering that, these days, many people have been glad to develop a sideline into a lifeline when redundancy has struck. So be businesslike about your affairs, even if you personally see your self-employment project as pin money. For those who need to make a survival wage from the start, the government's Enterprise Allowance Scheme is a great help. As the regulations stand as we go to press, you can claim £40 a week for up to 52 weeks to help you get your business started. There are rules to abide by: you must apply before you start the business and you must have access to £1000 of capital (could be a bank loan), as well as being unemployed – any Jobcentre has a leaflet with details. This is the sort of thing you would be told about on any good self-employment or small business course, where you will also, as a rule, be put in touch with either the nearest Small Firms Information Service, or given the name of a counsellor at the college to whom you can turn for advice when you are establishing your enterprise.

Before directing you to courses and examples of people who're going self-employed, let me recommend two handbooks by Godfrey Golzen, who has made something of a speciality of advising future entrepreneurs. *Going Freelance* (Granada) is particularly strong on ideas for second incomes, while *Working for Yourself* (Kogan Page) has more emphasis on setting up a business.

This section of *Make a Fresh Start* is mainly concerned with college courses which deal with the nuts and bolts of setting up any kind of business – raising money, keeping books, selling, dealing with tax and insurance and so on. You may like to consider one of these factual business courses in association with a course to gain a new skill. But there are also courses in specific kinds of businesses – running a guest house, a newsagent's, setting up a publishing enterprise. Personal reports cover:

An Income from the Lane: Aylesbury College
Antique Clock Restoration: West Dean College
Heavy Goods Vehicle Driving: RTT Training Services, Mendlesham

and more personal stories about people who may choose to use their skills in self-employment can be found in the 'Retraining and New Skills Courses' section. If you can't think of a business idea, take a look through subjects that colleges suggest have 'earning potential' and you may find there's a skill you can learn that could be marketed in your locality.

Always check with your Jobcentre on the latest government initiatives to help people set up in business for themselves. As new schemes are announced and local colleges get involved in them, course titles may change but the Jobcentre should know not only what's on offer now but what may be planned for next term.

London and Middlesex

Colleges appearing in this section are listed below by district, except where the location of the college is obvious from its name. This should help you to discover the most accessible college offering the course that you want.

Avery Hill, Mile End, Dartford (Kent) and Woolwich	Thames Polytechnic
Barking and West Ham	North East London Polytechnic
Barnet, Enfield and Haringey	Middlesex Polytechnic
Camden and Islington	North London Polytechnic
Deptford	South East London College
Elephant and Castle	London College of Printing
Leicester Square	College for the Distributive Trades
Tooting	South West London College
Waterloo	Morley College

College for the Distributive Trades
'Your Own Shop', part time.

London College of Printing
Diploma in Publishing Production, full time, for people who want to set up in book or magazine publishing.

Middlesex Polytechnic
MSC-sponsored Business Enterprise Programme, part time.

Morley College
Running a Workers' Co-operative, evenings. How to Survive Information and Work Overload, evenings. Many leisure courses with earning potential (see 'Retraining and New Skills Courses').

North East London Polytechnic
Short courses in Small Business management – content and mode to suit individual needs.

North London Polytechnic
MSC-sponsored short courses in Business Management.

Paddington College
MSC-sponsored Business Enterprise programme, part time – for those in self-employment or small business or those wishing to do so.

South East London College
Guest House and Small Establishment Management, part time, for City and Guilds award. Cooks' Professional course, part time or evenings for City and Guilds award – suitable for those planning to set up their own catering service.

South West London College
Community Entrepreneurs' Training Programme, part time – for people involved in organisational or management role in community-based employment project; specially useful for people from ethnic minority self-help projects.

Thames Polytechnic
ESF-sponsored Women Into Business, full time – women under 25 only.

Uxbridge College
MSC-sponsored Women Towards Management, part time, beween 9 a.m. and 4 p.m. May be used as foundation of knowledge for managing your own business or for progress within an organisation. MSC Enterprise Programme. Enterprise Awareness Days (one-day). Business Enterprise Programme (six-seven days) and Private Enterprise Programme (day-long modules) for those setting up or developing their own businesses.

The following colleges in London supplied information in 1987 about their small business courses, but no response was received to 1988 enquiries. Readers may nevertheless wish to make individual contact:

Hackney College
Tottenham College of Technology

Southern and Eastern England

Aylesbury College
At their Hampden Hall, Stoke Mandeville Centre the college's short course unit offers a variety of intensive courses lasting from one to five days. Subjects include: Starting Your Own Smallholding; Taking a Small Farm; Going Self-Employed in Rural Enterprises; Flower Arranging for Restaurants, Shops and Offices; Producing Food Organically; Garden Design and Planning; Principles of Vegetable Growing. There is a 'back to nature' approach to Pig-keeping, Goat-keeping and many others subjects.

An Income from the Land
'My husband and I plan to have a small amount of land and keep chickens, bees and a couple of sheep, and also grow vegetables, but mostly we'll sell free-range eggs. Our idea is to sell our house and get something a bit run down to do up, which means we would have a bit of money left over to do what we want. But my husband still wants to commute to London, so we can't go too far.

From this course, I've sorted out the animals we want. I was quite keen on having a house cow, but I've changed my mind about that. I didn't like the idea of the calf every year that you have to do something with. I would perhaps have gone in for the wrong things without this course'.

'I'm a barrister, but I've wanted to be a farmer ever since I was five, and I was very surprised to find you could learn about farming 'in dribs and drabs' of a few days here and there. I had always imagined you'd have to do a full-time course, which would take you away from what you were already doing. At the moment I'm in the marvellous position of being able to carry on with my current employment while I learn about something else. Hopefully, by the time I've spent a bit of time doing a few courses I'll be in a position to move out of my current job and into something else without any fear that it's going to fail.'

[Starting Farming students, Aylesbury College]

'The courses are held several times a year and they are for all kinds of people: from those who want to make the most of owning a house with a big garden to those who want to buy smallholdings and those who have a fancy to keep goats or geese. The length of a typical beginners' course is four to five days. You can't hope to cover everything in that time, but students should be able to see if their idea is feasible. We try to give them the basic husbandry principles and some financial details as well, to point them in the right direction. We have had every kind of student, from airline pilots to post office workers. There is increasing evidence of professional and business people who have been made redundant coming along and, if they sell a house in a very desirable commuter area, then with their redundancy payment as well they can afford to go and buy a property in a much cheaper area. We try to make sure that they go ahead with their eyes open.'

[Spokesperson, Short Courses Unit, Aylesbury College]

Bracknell College

(NB: The following courses are *free* to those who have been in business for less than 12 months; see also 'Costs and Grants' section). Private Enterprise Programme: Financial Control, part time; Basic Accounting, part time; Book-keeping, part time; Computers in Business, part time; Accounting and Finance, part time; Marketing, part time; Legal Requirements of the Small Business, part time; Computers in the Small Business, part time; Taxation, part time.

Bromley College of Technology

MSC-sponsored Beginning in Business course, part time. BTEC PostEx-perience courses (various options), teaching useful business/management skills, part time and under 21-hour rule. The college has s Small Business Club.

Chichester: West Dean College

(Independent College.) West Dean/British Antique Dealers' Association courses in: Restoration of Antique Clocks, full time; Restoration of Antique Ceramics and Porcelain, full time; Restoration of Antique Furniture, full time. NB: these are advanced courses. Also numerous short full time courses in subjects with earning potential, like Upholstery, Cabinet Making, Blacksmithing, Pottery, Cane Seating, Silversmithing, etc. (See 'Retraining and New Skills Courses'.)

Antique Clock Restoration

'I've always been interested in clocks, but there just isn't anybody doing this kind of course in Scotland, where I live, so it seemed a good idea to come down here and study and then go back when I was reasonably accomplished and could set up in business. There are probably only one or two other people who would represent any competition to me and there are lots of nice clocks about to restore. If you are a good restorer, people will pay for it, because they know your work will last for a very long time.'

[Student, West Dean College, Chichester]

'Students don't need to have previous training in clock-making, but they do need to be dextrous and demonstrate an aptitude for the intricate work. Clocks for restoration are supplied by antique dealers, museums and private owners. The West Dean/BADA Diploma in Clock Restoration is awarded to students on successful completion of the course. Final assessments are based on continuous assessment of practical work, a written paper and a visual recognition test. Diplomas are awarded on satisfactory completion of the course.'

[Spokesperson, West Dean College, Chichester]

Cambridge: Cambridgeshire College of Arts and Technology
This college has a Business Development Unit, running a wide range of short courses including: Be Your Own Boss; How to come up with an Idea for a Business; Keeping the Books; Assertiveness Training for Managers; Law of Employment; Contract Law; Developing Personal Effectiveness.

Croydon College
MSC-sponsored Setting Up a Business, part time, for participants in Community Programmes. Also part time RSA Business Enterprise Skills course,for people from a Community Programme/unemployed background under the Adult Training Strategy.

Epsom: North East Surrey College of Technology
Accounting for Small Businesses, evenings. Microcomputers in Business, part time or evenings. Thinking of Starting a Guest House? – occasional course. Management and Care Training Course for Proprietors and Managers of Voluntary and Private Residential Homes, part time.

Havering Technical College
MSC-sponsored Business Workshops for people intending to become self-employed. Book-keeping for the Small Businessman, part time. Start Your Own Business, part time. Word-Processing, part time. Information Processing, part time.

Hemel Hempstead: Dacorum College
Start Your Own Business, short course. BTEC National Certificate in Business and Finance. Modes not specified, ask college.

Mendlesham: RTT Training Services Ltd
(Independent college.) Range of courses connected with Road Transport and Road Transport Management – in particular: courses for RSA Certificate of Professional Competence to run National/International Road Transport Operations: and intensive courses for HGV I, II, III and PSV licences. Various short courses that might be combined with driving for self-employment, e.g: Prospecting for Sales, Distribution Management.

Heavy Goods Vehicle Driving
'The duration of HGV training is subject to an assessment of a candidate's ability, but it can last from about five to 15 days. I would expect an average ability candidate to be able to pass the Class I HGV driving test in about 10-12 days. The course consists of 30% theory – the theory of driving, observation and planning, the Highway Code, safety regulations, mechanical conditions and the tachography – and the other 70% is on the road. Taking the test is all part of the training package.'

[Spokesperson, RTT Training Services, Mendlesham]

Morden: Merton College
Licensed Conveyancers, details on request. Starting Your Own Business, part time. Book-Keeping for the Self-Employed, part time. Law for the Self-Employed/Taxation for the Self-Employed/Computer Uses in the Small Business – apply to the college for details. Wide range of evening computer courses for small business owners.

Norwich City College
Proprietors of Private and Voluntary Homes for the Elderly, evenings. Proprietors of Private Residential Homes for the Elderly and Handicapped, residential one-week full time.

Slough: Langley College
Book-keeping for the Small Businessman, part time. Start Your Own Business, part time. Word-Processing, part time. Information Processing, part time.

Watford: Cassio College
The short course unit runs a series of one-day and part time evening courses including Book-keeping, Accountancy, Retail Customer Care, Consumer Law, Retail Security and Loss Prevention, Telephone Techniques. Small Business courses are also offered through Open Learning (see 'Open and Distance Learning Courses'), including subjects like Pub Management, Running a Guest House, etc. The Department of Adult Studies runs 'Starting and Running a Small Business', mode unspecified.

Welwyn Garden City: De Havilland College
Starting and Running Your Own Business, evenings. Accounting for Small Businesses, evenings. Computer-based Accounting, evenings. Introduction to Salesmanship, evenings. Communication for Managers, evenings.

The following college in this region supplied informtion in 1987 about small business courses, but no response was received to 1988 enquiries. Readers may nevertheless wish to make individual contact:

Portsmouth: Highbury College of Technology

Central England

Bridgnorth and South Shropshire College of Further Education
City and Guilds 491, Guest House Management.

Coventry: Henley College
Guest House Management, part time. Supervisory Skills. Presentation Skills. Occupational Selection Testing. Report Writing. Computer-Assisted Language Learning, mode unspecified.

Derbyshire: College of Higher Education
'Small Business courses are arranged periodically in response to local needs', says the college.

Dudley College of Technology
MSC-sponsored Small Business courses,referred to as MAC, BEP, PEP and MEP, says college. Self-Employment,full time. Mini-Business, evenings. Management Extension programmes for redundant executives; include three weeks' intensive training in Small Business Management plus 23 weeks with a small business solving a particular problem.

Kettering: Tresham College
Wide range of Open Learning Small Business packages (see 'Open and Distance Learning Courses'). Also short courses one and two days) in varied range of topics,including Acounting for the Non-Accountant, Marketing for the Small Business, Trading Opportunities Overseas.

Kidderminster College
Enterprise Skills for Self-Employment, under 21-hour rule – includes: Raising Finance, Market Investigation,Selling, Advertising, Financial Control, etc. Also support services for new enterprises, and Small Business Club.

Leamington Spa: Mid Warwickshire College of Further Education
MSC-sponsored Self-Employment, evenings. All the followingavailable in the evening: Tax/Payroll Matters for the Small Business, Introduction to

Computers in Small Business, Be Your Own Boss, Book-Keeping for the Small Business. Food and Management Studies for mature students, under 21-hour rule, suitable for those who want to set up their own food business, go into catering or run a private guest house.

Newark Technical College
Managing Your Own Business, evenings. Managing the Finances for Your Own Business, evenings. Management workshops for Small Businesses, mode unspecified. Computers for Small Businesses, mode unspecified.

Redditch College
Small Business Service: part time courses to suit individual small firms. Retail Management, evenings, for independent retailers. DIY Credit Control course, to assist companies to reduce the amount of outstanding credit.

Solihull College of Technology
Starting and Running Your Own Business, evenings. Book-Keeping for the Small Business, evenings. Marketing on a Small Budget, Marketing Workshops, Computing for Small Businesses, Business Law for Small Businesses – these are follow-up courses; details from the Small Business Unit.

Stoke-on-Trent: North Staffs Polytechnic
Small Business Development programmes, mode varies.

Tamworth College
Range of small business courses – including: Self-Employment, Small Businesses, Book-keeping for Small Businesses, Computerised Accounting for Small Businesses, Computerised Payroll for Small Businesses, Marketing and Advertising for Small Businesses, Salesmanship and Customer Relations.

Warley: Campus, Sandwell College
Be Your Own Boss, part time. MSC-sponsored Business Development course, full time. BTEC Post Experience Units, part time, in different aspects of business management – e.g: Working with People, Word-Processing, Implementing Small Business Computer Systems, etc. Small Business Club.

West Bromwich: Campus, Sandwell College
MSC-sponsored Start Your Own Business, evenings. Small Business, afternoons or evenings. Selling for the Self-Employed, evenings. Book-Keeping for the Self-Employed, evenings. Employing Someone, evenings. Starting a Shop, evenings. Business Development course, evenings. Introduction to Managing a Newsagency, evenings. Merchandise Course for the News Trade, evenings. Small Business Club.

Wellingborough College
MSC-sponsored Business Enterprise Programme, evenings and weekends. MSC-sponsored Private Enterprise Programme – includes: Computers, Marketing, Accounting, Employing People. BTEC Small Business Units, part time – include: Options in Financial Control, Costing and Pricing, Raising Finance. A Shoe Repair course is suitable for those considering setting up in business (not sponsored).

Wolverhampton: Bilston Community College
Self-Employment, part time, in collaboration with Wolverhampton Business Consortium, under 21-hour rule: covers Book-Keeping, Marketing, Finance, communications, Law, Pricing and Costing. Co-operative Business Enterprise, part time, covering all aspects of a successful co-operative business start up. Engineering Skills Expansion for the Prospective Self-Employed, part time. 'Many other short courses are run by the college's Business Development Unit (tel. 0902 43065) relevant to the training and updating needs of new and expanding businesses. Courses include Accounting, Marketing, Computing, Supervisory Skills, etc'.

Wolverhampton Polytechnic
MSC-sponsored Private Enterprise Programme includes Market Exploration and Exploitation Techniques, Budeting, Costing, Project Appraisal, Record-Keeping and Information Technology. Under the PICKUP programme, the college offers courses in Management Information Systems, Desk Top Publishing, Marketing for Small Business, and Computer-Aided Design. Modes variable.

Wolverhampton: Wulfrun College of Further Education
Self-Employment and Small Business courses. Twelve week courses for unemployed wanting to start self-employment – basic skills.

The following colleges in this region supplied information in 1987 about their small business courses, but no response was received to 1988 enquiries. Readers may nevertheless wish to make individual contact:

Bromsgrove: North Worcestershire College
Derby College of Further Education
Loughborough College of Art and Design
Nottingham: Trent Polytechnic
Witney: West Oxfordshire Technical College

Northern England

Altrincham: South Trafford College of Further Education
Start Your Own Small Business, evenings. Business Law for the Small Business, evenings. Marketing for the Small Business, evenings. Microcomputing in Business, evenings. Book-Keeping and Taxation for the Small Business, evenings. Finance for the Small Business, evenings.

Ashington: Northumberland Technical College
MSC-sponsored Business Enterprise Programme, one day a week. MSC-sponsored Private Enterprise Programme one-day problem-solving courses.

Bradford and Ilkley Community College
Small Business Development Unit. General introductory course to Setting Up in Business, part time and evenings. Practical Accounting, part time and evenings. Setting Up and Keeping Books, evenings. Purchasing and Stock Control in the Small Business, part time. The Use of Microcomputers in the Small Business, part time. Marketing and Selling in the Small Business, part time. Business Correspondence for the Small Business, part time.

Bridlington: East Yorkshire College of Further Education
ESF-sponsored Small Business Course, full time. Catering and Hotel Management, full time.Start Your Own Business. In-House audit and training in Business Systems and Use of Information Technology, mode unspecified.

Burnley College
(See 'Open and Distance Learning Courses'.)

Consett: Derwentside Tertiary College
Series of short courses in Small Business Planning, Financial Management, Small Business Book-Keeping, part time or evenings.

Dewsbury College
Small Business Unit, offers Self-Employment Programme, evenings, plus 'after-care' service. Small Business Workshop – taster programme, part

time. Small Business Development Programme (for businesses with three or more employees), part time. Book-Keeping for the Small Business, evenings. Business Computing, part time. Marketing for the Small Firm, evenings. Finance for the Non-Accountant, part time. BTEC Continuing Education awards, various units, part time. (See also 'Open and Distance Learning Courses'.)

Durham: New College Durham
Small Business Unit offers a range of courses, including: 'Taster Course', one or two-hour sessions; Self-Employment course, part time. Self-Employment course, evenings. Small Business Profitability, evenings; Practical Book-Keeping and Accounts, evenings; Microcomputer Applications for Small Businesses, evenings; etc.

Gateshead Technical College
Self-Employment courses, part time and evenings, some MSC-sponsored.

Halifax: Percival Whitley College of Further Education
(At Calderdale Business and Innovation Centre.) Enterprise Allowance Seminars (for anyone applying for the MSC Enterprise Allowance), full time. Small Business Information Workshops, full time. Part-Time Programme in Self-Employment, part time. Small Business Programme, full time.(See also 'Open and Distance Learning Courses'.)

Leeds: Park Lane College
Being Your Own Boss, evenings. Being Your Own Book-Keeper, evenings.

Manchester University
Extra Mural Studies Department, Career Studies Unit. Small Business Suitability, one-week full time assessment course for self-employment

Middlesborough: Longlands College of Further Education
BTEC Continuing Education Units, leading to Certificate in Business Administration. Operational Salesmanship.

Newcastle-upon-Tyne Polytechnic
Small Business Unit. 'Various programmes available both day and evening, for people who have just started or are contemplating their own businesses. Also programmes for people who are unemployed but have transferable skills,placing them (after short training courses) within small companies with potential for growth.'

Peterlee College
Start a Small Business, part time as part of SCOPE programme (see 'Pre-Entry Courses').

Rotherham: Rockingham College of Further Education
Running Your Own Business, evenings. Accounts for the Small Business, evenings. The Licensee's Complete Wine Course, part time, for people who wish to enter the Licensed Trade (offered when there is sufficient demand).

Sheffield: Rother Valley College
Business Enterprise Programme and Private Enterprise Programme Seminars, under 21-hour rule. BTEC Continuing Education courses, under 21-hour rule – select from Computer Studies, Improve your Financial Decision-Making, Managing the Office, Using Word Processors, Working with People, Computer Programming, Methodology, Computer Systems. Run Your Own Guest House and Bed and Breakfast Business. Run Your Own Dressmaking Business. Arts and Crafts (including Stained Glass Work) for Self-employment. Modes not specified.

St Helens School of Management Studies
Extensive range of short courses and block-release courses, *normally residential*. Among those likely to be of interest to potential or existing small business operators are Retail Management, Retail Food Management, An Introduction to Effective Storekeeping, Effective Salesmanship, Purchasing Management. (Also see 'Retraining and New Skills Courses'.)

Salford College of Technology
Small Business Operations, full time, for people considering starting and operating small businesses. BTEC Post Experience Certificate of Business Administration, part time, day and evening, for professional footballers entering business.

Southport College of Art and Technology
Managing a Residential Care Home, part time. Guest House Owners' Course, mode unspecified. The College Short Course Unit now offers 'tailor-made' courses for local commerce and industry – e.g: Supervisory Skills, Interpersonal Skills, First Aid, Counselling Skills, etc.

Sunderland Polytechnic
Range of short courses in the Business School – options include Starting your Own Business, Running a more Profitable Business, Finance for Non-Financial Managers, etc. Other short courses suitable for the small business owner may be offered by the Micro-Technology Centre. Ask college for details.

The following colleges in this region provided information in 1987 about their small business courses, but no response was recieved to 1988 enquiries. Readers may nevertheless wish to make individual contact:

Barnsley: East Barnsley Community Education Unit
Blackpool and Fylde College of Further and Higher Education
Darlington College of Technology
Doncaster Metropolitan Institute of Higher Education
Grimsby Technical College
Leeds: Airedale and Wharfedale College
Leeds: Kitson College of Technology
Middlesbrough: Teesside Polytechnic
Newcastle College of Arts and Technology
Sheffield: Shirecliffe College
South Shields: South Tyneside College
Wakefield District College

Wales and Western England

Barnstaple: North Devon College
Short courses in Small Business. The college has its own Small Business Club.

Bath: Norton Radstock College
Self-Employment Skills, part time under Avon Training Agency's Community Programme Linked Training Scheme. Enterprise Unit at college, with full-time Adviser on Self-Employment, plus seven-day Business Enterprise Programme, covering all aspects of setting up in business, from Understanding Business Reords, Income Tax, National Insurance and VAT to Costing and Pricing. Also Mananagement Extension programme, whereby redundant executives are first trained in the techniques of Small Business management, then seconded to a small business for up to three months.

Bristol: Brunel Technical College
Wide range of part-time and short courses which could be a foundation for self-employment. (See also 'Retraining and New Skills Courses'.) Options include Painting and Decorating, Telephone Installation for Electrical Contractors, Commercial Cake Decoration and Finishing, Vegetarian Cooking, Licensed House Catering.

Bristol: Filton Technical College
BTEC Continuing Education Units in Small Business (include Computer Studies, Financial Decision Making, Marketing, Exporting) by Flexistudy (see 'Open and Distance Learning Courses').

Chippenham Technical College
Setting Up in Business, evenings. Cash Flow and VAT, part time. Salesmanship and Retailing Techniques, part time. Introduction to Microcomputers in Small Business, part time. Company Law and Finance, part time. Employment Law, part time.

Haverfordwest: Pembrokeshire College of Further Education
West Dyfed Small Business Centre supported by MSC, colleges, banks, employers and Pembrokeshire Business Initiative. Primarily operates on a home study basis. (See 'Open and Distance Learning Courses'.)

Llanelli: Carmarthenshire College of Technology
Business Information Technology Applications Packages for Self-Employment and Small Business, mode unspecified.

Salisbury College of Technology
Starting a Small Business. Business Enterprise Programme (BEP).Private Enterprise Programme (PEP). Small Business Finance and Development. Finance and Accounting for Non-Financial Managers. Guest House Management, for City and Guilds award, all evenings.

Street: Strode College
Start Your Own Business, evenings.

Taunton: Somerset College of Arts and Technology
Your Own Business courses, evenings.

Weymouth College
Starting Your Own Business, part time. The Business of Book-Keeping, part time. Wages, PAYE and Employment, part time. Running Your Own Business, part time.

The following colleges in this region supplied information in 1987 about their small business courses, but no response was received to 1988 enquiries. Readers may nevertheless wish to make individual contacts:

Deeside: North East Wales Institute
Gloucester: Gloucestershire College of Arts and Technology
Llandridnod Wells: Radnor College
Weston-super-Mare College of Further Education

Scotland and Northern Ireland

Belfast College of Technology
Small Business Administration, part time. Starting a Business, evenings.

Dumfries and Galloway College of Technology
MSC–sponsored one–day course in Implications of Self–Employment. Two Saturdays and evenings on MSC–Sponsored Self–Employment Course.

Edinburgh: Queen Margaret College
Business Development Centre. MSC–funded part time Small Business Course. Graduate Enterprise Programme, Business Enterprise Programme. MSC Enterprise Allowance Scheme awareness seminars. Specialised Lectures and Seminars. SCOTVEC Small Business Development. (See 'Open and Distance Learning Courses'.) Former trainees from this centre have established businesses as diverse as retirement homes and knitwear manufacture, shipping packing and fish–farming.

Glasgow University
The Centre for Entrepreneurial Development has a complete portfolio of full time and part time programmes for people wishing to start, expand or rescue small and new businesses.

Glasgow: University of Strathclyde
MSC–sponsored Business Enterprise Programme (covers Business Law, Marketing, Accountancy and Business Planning). MSC–sponsored Private Enterprise Programme (series of one–day seminars – wide choice includes Finding New Products, Selling Workshop, Book–Keeping, Taxation, Computers in Business, Employing People, Sources of Finance).

Inverness College
Starting and Running a Small Business, part time. Business Enterprise Programmes, Private Enterprise Programmes and College–based Programmes. Employment and Payroll, part time. Financial Record Keeping, part time. Costing, part time. Cash Handling, part time. Also Start–Up Support and Training in Health and Beauty, part time. Start–Up in Catering, part time.

Lisburn College of Further Education
Self–Employment and Small Business, evenings.

The following colleges in this region supplied information in 1987 about their small business courses, but no response was received to 1988 enquiries. Readers may nevertheless wish to make individual contact:

Aberdeen College of Commerce
Ayr College
Edinburgh: Telford College of Further Education

OPEN AND DISTANCE LEARNING COURSES

Ways of adding to your skills and qualifications 'At your own pace, in your own place'.

Introduction

For that useful phrase, 'at your own pace, in your own place', I have to thank Beverley Sand, whom I met at Wulfrun College of Further Education, Wolverhampton, where she was working as Home Study Adviser. She used it to explain the great changes that have developed from what used to be called 'correspondence courses', which have always been a lifeline for people who couldn't go to classes, and are approved by many professional bodies.

Traditional correspondence colleges are still in the business of providing home study courses, and remain very successful. There's a Council for the Accreditation of Correspondence Colleges, which you can read about later in this section, and many further education colleges buy in materials for their distance-learning schemes from correspondence colleges.

But the two big changes that have taken place to make Beverley Sand's description come true relate to the range of people who can study independently and to the range of subjects that can be catered for by distance-learning methods.

NEW COURSES – NEW CHOICES

At one time there was a very narrow range of examinations you could study for by post. Though some correspondence colleges offered their own preliminary certificates and diplomas, they were not necessarily recognised for college entry or student membership of professional institutes. Unless you had reached the stage of learning when you were ready to tackle the old GCE, or a similar level of national examination, there wasn't a great deal you could study that would lead to a recognised qualification. People needing courses below GCE level were rather left out in the cold.

Then again, while it was quite possible to study written subjects by correspondence course, you could do practical subjects like science only if you could make your own private arrangements with a further education college to use their facilities for the practical work.

Apart from the fact that people were often too shy to ask, this wasn't a lot of help for the people living out in the country, far from a college, or people on shifts, who were sleeping when the college was open. Not many people managed to take practical subjects like chemistry and biology by postal course. It wasn't very easy, either, to study languages purely on a correspondence basis, because you didn't know what they sounded like.

EXPERIMENTS AND SOLUTIONS

Gradually, though, the sources of distance learning began to devise solutions to these problems. The range of introductory courses increased. There were courses in study skills, and in basic maths and basic English for people who needed to catch up. As cassette recorders became cheaper, correspondence colleges issued some lessons (particularly for languages) on tape. Then the first practical kits for doing basic science experiments were produced. From being a slim envelope of printed papers, the correspondence course/home study/distance learning facility turned into quite a sizeable package. Some people refer to 'learning packages' today. Colleges will say, 'We issue a package of specially designed correspondence materials for open-learning students.'

OPENING UP THE SYSTEM

It was at about this time that the term 'open learning' started to appear in college prospectuses. While correspondence colleges were getting their act together and considerably widening the scope of what they offered, some further education colleges began to develop new ways of attracting students.

Enterprising lecturers, interested in catering for adults who had left school many years before, tried the idea of 'open' courses that anyone could join – no qualifications needed, no questions asked, no requirement to sign up for exams. Mind you, anyone who wanted to continue from the 'Introductory' levelcould build up units of study and reach a stage where they could take examinations – not conventional GCE-style exams, either, but specially devised examinations that took account of the way courses had developed. Assessment for the work done on the course played a large part in deciding the level of success,as well as any exam set (a method now copied in the new GCSE!).

The word 'open' as a way of describing a course became appropriated by all sorts of people. Further education colleges used it to indicate a course that had no entry requirements and didn't necessarily involve students in taking exams. Distance-learning colleges used it to indicate a course that could be studied at home – though it could be a course that did have entry requirements, and did involve students in taking exams.

Perhaps it's not surprising that students get very confused when they see the word 'open' in front of a course. It almost certainly means learning at your own *pace*. It could well mean learning at your own *place*. But it could mean learning *with* exams, or *without* – whichever you prefer. And nowadays, it could include accesss to a tutor, by appointment or on the phone.

CHOOSING AN OPEN LEARNING ROUTE

There are national, regional and local schemes to choose from. The course lists give examples of many local initiatives, but you also need to know about the national and regional systems, as they might prove more suitable for your needs.

There are the Open University, the Open Tech, and now the Open College, which is the most recent initiative. These are all *national* schemes.

Then there are the Open Colleges set up by groups of colleges: a single group can include colleges as widely separated as Manchester and South London. These are all *regional* schemes.

Often 'credits' for work you do in one regional Open College can be used at others, or to satisfy entry requirements for colleges outside the schemes.

Another use of the term 'open' is in 'open learning' courses offered by *individual* colleges. They are all *local* schemes. They may also use different course names. For example, anything that starts off with 'Flex-' is likely to be part of an open learning scheme.

All these courses, though, have one thing in common. They are designed to give more chances to more people. So,

- if you are unqualified and unready to take other courses
- if you're too shy to join in a class
- if your home responsibilities clash with class times
- if you work shifts and miss classes
- if you're disabled and can't get to college
- if you live in the country, far from a college

The 'open' systems, which do away with barriers like age limits, entry qualifications and classes in a set place or at a set time, could be a way of getting a fresh start despite your problems.

OPEN COLLEGE

Pioneered at Nelson & Colne College in Lancashire, this scheme was set up to let people into further education whether or not they had qualifications.

There are now a number of Open College Federations. These are groups of colleges that have got together to provide a range of courses open to every age group and in as many subjects as possible. Courses are usually at different study levels from absolute beginner to university entry level. Quite often, Open College students who reach a certain study level can go directly into university or polytechnic without needing A-levels and some universities and polytechnics work closely with a particular Open College Federation.

To do an Open College course, you don't need a reference from your old school or from your employer. You can choose an examination or a non-examination course. And you can sample subjects, change courses – or break off and re-start if necessary.

You may be able to take an Open College course using Open Learning methods (see below).

WHAT IS OPEN LEARNING LIKE?

In open learning you get printed lessons to study at home (sometimes practical kits, too, if your subject involves practical work). Increasingly, these are supplemented by audio and video cassettes where they are appropriate, and by newer developments, including Computer-Based Training (CBT and Interactive Video. You work through your assignment over a period that you agree with your open-learning tutor, who can advise you. You may be able to phone him/her to discuss problems, or there may be fixed times at college when tutors will counsel students in private. Some colleges arrange group tutorials for those open-learning students who want to attend them, but you don't have to go.

Working at your own pace is an important feature of open learning. Your work out when you will submit assignments. Only if you are working towards a specific date – for instance, an exam that takes place only once a year – do you have to keep up a certain pace. Even then, if something happens to hold up your work, you can agree to stop off for a while and return when the problem's solved, working for the next exam date. The only factor that really affects starting and stopping is the availability of tutors: for example, with a college-based course you can't begin in the summer holiday, as a rule.

Not every subject is available by open learning, but the range is increasing rapidly. By the time this book reaches the bookshops, more subjects may be offered by the colleges listed, including vocational and professional exam courses. Many colleges say they are 'planning open learning'. So it's always worth asking about this route if you can't, or don't want to, take a course that involves attending college regularly.

Open-learning student reports can be found for the following institutions:
Airline Studies: Academy of Travel Management (p. 00)

Flexastudy Accountancy: Redditch College
Homestudy O-levels: Wulfrun College, Wolverhampton
Flexastudy General: Filton College, Bristol
Distance Learning MBA: Strathclyde Business School

Many people have heard about the 'Big Three' national open learning initiatives and want to know more about them. They are the Open University, the Open Tech and the Open College. Though these are national initiatives, serving everyone in the UK, they are also separate, providing different kinds of course for different kinds of learner. Furthermore the Open Tech, unlike the other two, is not an organisation at all, but a now-completed government initiative involving over 100 different organisations. What they have in common is:

Anyone is eligible to start at a Foundation or Introductory level. You don't need qualifications. (But if you do have any exam qualifications you may be able to start further on in a course, getting exemptions from subjects you have already studied and passed.)

You do the work at home and you set the pace. You can stop and start, depending on your circumstances. No-one will badger you to spend more time studying than you can spare, but if you want extra help, there's a specially trained tutor to consult.

Course-work materials are provided, though you need a radio and/or cassette recorder, and/or TV and/or video recorder to use them (or access to this equipment – see 'College Links' below). They can include kits for science and other experiments, audio cassette tapes to listen to and TV programmes or videotapes to watch. As home computer ownership grows, some courses have materials on computer tape or disc that you can use.

COLLEGE LINKS

I have mentioned access to tutors when you need face-to-face or telephone help with problems. A variation on the 'college link' theme is that some further education colleges have Learning Workshops, where you can book time to use their computer or their video recorder to study an item from your learning package.

Let's look at the specifics of the three national open-learning initiatives:

The Open University has undergraduate ('first degree') courses and postgraduate courses. Units of these can be taken as associate student courses, if you only want to study one item in depth, or as a preparation or 'taster' for a full course. It also has an Open Business School, for managers and would-be managers, and in its Continuing Education Unit it provides courses for people who want to build on to their existing education. There are many special-interest courses for particular needs (see the University's entry). *Important:* No A-levels or other exam passes are needed to enter undergraduate courses or associate student courses. Only for advanced courses are you likely to need work or study qualifications but formal qualifications are not specified as a condition of entry.

Open University degrees are exactly the same as any other degrees when it comes to getting jobs that demand 'graduate status', or entering postgraduate courses of study or training, *except* that employers and college interviewers tend to give you extra consideration because you have shown you have self-discipline and staying power by getting a degree at home.

Learning packages sent to your home are backed up by audio and video cassettes and by television and radio programmes, and on many courses there's a summer school each year, where students meet and attend seminars, lectures and discussions.

For information, write to: The Open University, Walton Hall, PO Box 71, Milton Keynes, MK7 6AG and read the further entry in the Southern and Eastern England listing below.

The Open Tech, though now ended as an initiative, remains important because the organisations which took part are still providing the packages and services set up by the Open Tech Programme. Open Tech put the emphasis on running Updating and Skill Conversion schemes on a 'modular'or unit basis. You can take a unit at a time, to suit your needs. For example, an accounts clerk can learn to use a computer *before* the firm's accounts department is computerised. A production manager can study basic digital electronics through a course combining written lessons, a circuit board to which components can be added, and diagrams to follow. Open Tech courses are distinctly job-related and will help you expand the range of your expertise in a career area.

Courses are available across a wide range of activities, from catering to lift technology. Many employers buy Open Tech learning packages to use in updating their own staff but it's quite possible for individuals to buy them too (take a look at the range offered by Watford College, on p. 00, for instance).

You can take one module – to catch up on one missing skill – or combine half a dozen to retrain yourself. You might start studying an Open Tech module when unemployed, then get a job and want to divert to an Open Tech course related to that. In some career areas, you can get national certificates by taking certain groups of modules. But the Open Tech doesn't examine you for degrees in the way that the Open University does.

Open Tech courses are job-related. The emphasis is on using new technology and updating knowledge. Both the Open University and the Open Tech offer technological subjects, but the Open University tends to concentrate on *understanding* technology, and the Open Tech on *using* technology. You can pick out an item you need to learn about, like 'Laboratory Safety' or 'Flexography'. Unlike the OU the OT has no fixed start or completion dates.

For further information, use the Open Learning Directory *available in public libraries and at Jobcentres, which lists Open Tech training packages available, as well as a wide range of other quality open learning packages and services. Or, in in event of any difficulty, consult the Manpower Services Commission, Moorfoot, Sheffield S1 4PQ.*

The newest national initiative is the Open College. It extends the range of courses available for home study into areas like craft skills, caring skills and personal skills. For example, one of the first courses to be offered was 'It's a Deal: An Introduction to Effective Selling'. Another was 'Autocare', for people who want to learn to maintain a car in a safe and efficient condition and to carry out simple repairs. Technology courses ranged from a beginners' guide to electronics to computer-aided information systems in design.

There are many courses connected with business and management, including starting a new business. An interesting feature of the Open

College is that it really does begin at the beginning; there is a course to teach you how to study, and another on basic arithmetic called 'Make It Count'.

With all the courses you can assess your own progress, but some of them prepare students for the exams of national organisations like City and Guilds, BTEC and SCOTVEC. And you also have access to advice at Open Access Centres, based in colleges throughout the country. If you don't live near one, the Open College can link you to the National Distance Learning Centre, providing advice by post and phone. You can also buy courses directly, with a credit card, by calling the Open College hotline (0235-555444). There is a weekly television programme called the 'Open Exchange', which lets students phone in and get advice, comment on the courses and share experiences.

Some of the courses are 'bought in' from other open-learning providers. The actual package you get depends on the course. For instance, in a course for women seeking a change of directioncalled 'Women – the Way Ahead', you get a workbook, an audio tape, a paperback book and a videotape of case studies from the accompanying TV series. You're told that you need 30 hours of study to complete the course.

In contrast, the course on 'Pneumatics', aimed at maintenance personnel and technicians who want to update their skills (and beginners who want to learn about pneumatic equipment), consists of 15 study booklets and a practical home kit, including valves, cylinders and pipes. You're told you need to allow around five hours of learning time for each of the 15 units, plus six hours practical work towards the end of the course, and that the course should provide you with the knowledge to take the City and Guilds examination 230-3-25 in Pneumatic Systems.

For information, send for the (free) Open Book *guide to Open College courses, from The Open College, Freepost, PO Box 35, Abingdon OX14 34BR, or phone the Open College hotline (number given above). The book contains many useful addresses as well as information about the range of courses offered.*

CORRESPONDENCE COLLEGES

These, which blazed the trail for the wide range of home study and 'packaged' open learning courses now available at local authority colleges, continue to flourish.

Some of the colleges are highly specialised, offering courses in subjects like salesmanship, kennels management, accountancy and journalism. Others offer a vast range of subjects, from commercial courses to university degree preparation.

You can expect that any college accredited by the Council will conscientiously seek to offer value for money, and a realistic appraisal of a student's work. Accreditation is subject to periodic review. With the same subject, teaching methods can vary, so if you have a subject in mind that is taught by several colleges, it is worth getting literature from each one: then you can compare what's offered and how well it suits your personality and circumstances.

For information write to the Council for the Accreditation of Correspondence Colleges, 27 Marylebone Road, London NW1 5JS. Their Secretary will be pleased to send you the full list of over 30 approved colleges, with details of each college's range of subjects, if you write enclose an s.a.e.

Employers' associations may offer distance-learning courses which are not necessarily on the accredited list. If you are at all doubtful about a correspondence course, and it isn't on the Council's list, check with the employer for whom you want to work.

I suggested this to a reader who was enquiring about postal courses that would extend her prospects in the travel trade – particularly for work with an airline. She wrote for details of courses offered by the Academy of Travel Management – this is a subsidiary of British Airways. Here's what she wrote back after contacting them:

Airline Studies
'I got the Academy of Travel Management course in January of this year, and it was the best £64.50 I've spent. It was very interesting and I enjoyed learning it. I have now completed it (March) and am waiting for an exam date. I would like to thank you very much for introducing the airline school to me and I am confident that this certificate will be advantageous with me when I fill in job application forms at the end of the year.'
[Student, British Airways/Academy of Travel Management course]

Many of the 'Flexistudy' courses listed by further education colleges use distance-learning packages produced by a particular correspondence college, the National Extension College of Cambridge. Other local authority colleges have devised their own ways of combining correspondence course materials with face-to-face or telephone tutorials. Redditch College, for example, began its 'Flexastudy' courses over 25 years ago; if you read the description in the Central England courses section, you will see this method combines the use of traditional correspondence courses with tutorial help 'by appointment'. A similar system operates in Bristol at Filton Technical College. Here, then, are the regional lists: I've put the addresses of the national colleges into their respective lists, even though they do operate throughout the UK.

London and Middlesex

Colleges appearing in this section are listed below by district, except where the location of the college is obvious from its name. This should help you to discover the most accessible college offering the course that you want.

Bloomsbury	University of London
Ealing	Academy of Travel Management
Tooting	South West London College
West Norwood	South London College

Academy of Travel Management
(Independent College.) 'Study Plan' courses: Introducing Travel; The Basic Airline Course; Fares and Ticketing (1); Fares and Ticketing (2); Marketing and Automation.

Paddington College
Can supply a leaflet produced by the Central and West London Open College with addresses of 16 participating colleges. Contact Michael Sargent, the College Vice-Principal, who chairs the group of colleges forming the Open College. (NB: He also recommends the North London Open College, and says their directory is available from Sue Pedder, telephone 01-607 9393, which may be helpful for you if you live or work in North London.)

Richmond Adult and Community College
Open learning facilities in languages – French, Italian, Modern Greek; other languages may be available on request.

South London College
Part of the Open College of South London – works in association with the Polytechnic of the South Bank to provide courses for adults without conventional entry requirements; details from the college.

South West London College

Directed Private Study Unit combines distance-learning materials with short periods of face-to-face tuition and telephone advice sessions. Options include: Institute of Chartered Secretaries and Administrators Course; BTEC Higher National Certificate in Business Studies, British Ports Association Certificate. South West London College is a member of the Open College of South London, providing a range of courses for adults without conventional entry requirements; details from college.

University of London
First degrees and diplomas are available for those who study away from the campus in their own homes. It is not compulsory to take a correspondence course or attend classes at your local college if you prefer to plan your own degree studies (though many students do choose to take a correspondence course, and for one degree, the BSc in Economics, the University's Commerce Degree Bureau does provide postal tuition). There is,however a University Advisory Service which can guide students in the most appropriate qualification to work for, provide lists of correspondence courses, supply details of University syllabuses, outline library facilities and, in many subjects, supply reading lists and/or notes prepared by the University staff, advising on preparation for the examination. Short courses and lectures are regularly provided for registered External Students, and a list can be obtained from the Secretary for External Students. Candidates may study for the BD (Honours or Pass); BA (Honours or Pass) in Modern and Classical Languages, some Modern and Classical Oriental Languages, English, Geography,History (Classical and European), History of Art and Philosophy; LLB; BMus; BSc Econ; Diploma in Contemporary French Studies (postgraduate), Diploma in Clinical Pathology (postgraduate); Diploma in Education (for postgraduate students or those holding qualified teacher status); and Diploma in Public Administration (postgraduate or post-professional).

External Law Degree
'At school I was told I had the capability, but I just wasn't willing to apply myself, so I left with no qualifications at all,even though they had put me in for 10 O-levels and lined me up for three A-levels. I started work in a shop, then after learning typing and passing commercial exams, moved into a job as office junior with a law firm. I now work in the Legal section of a County Council, having obtained six O-levels and passed the examinations of the Institute of Legal Executives (which I studied for by evening classes). My ambition is to become a solicitor, so I am working for an External Law degree from London University. I shall follow this with the Law Society examinations. I've chosen to study by correspondence rather than go on with the evening classes because, even though my children can fend for themselves, I don't think it's fair to work full-time, then spend two hours for three evenings a week away from the house as well. By doing a correspondence

course I can be at home with the children. I feel also that the fact that correspondence courses demand so much written work must improve your chances in the exams. After all, the important thing is to be able to get the information down on paper, and, with work assessed through written essays all through the course, you become aware of your inadequacies in preparation and presentation.'

[Student, external LLB degree, University of London]

Southern and Eastern England

Basingstoke Technical College
Flexistudy courses for GCSE/A-levels now available.

Borehamwood: De Havilland College – see under Welwyn Garden City

Bromley College of Technology
Open Learning. Range of distance learning materials ranging from BTEC National Certificate in Telecommunications to Diploma in Engineering Management.

Canterbury College of Technology
Open College courses and a range of other open-learning courses – ask college for details.

Chatham: Mid Kent College of Further and Higher Education
(Also at Maidstone and Rochester.) Flexistudy: Fleximaths (Preparatory), GCSE English Language or English Literature, French,German, History, Economic History, Human Biology, Sociology, Accounts, Mathematics. O/A Psychology – Child Development. GCE A-level Economic History, English Literature, French, History, Law, Sociology. Not all subjects available at all three centres. A full range of vocational open-learning and Open College courses is also available. Contact the Open Learning Unit on 0634 830688

Colchester Institute
Flexistudy courses using National Extension College tutorial materials, plus college facilities where practical work is involved, plus tutorial help by phone or face to face.Options are: Return to Study, Fleximaths, 30-Hour Basic(Computing), Local History, Languages for Commerce and Industry, GCSE English Language and Literature, French, German, Spanish, Modern Mathematics, Biology, Chemistry, Physics, Psychology (Direct Studies), Sociology, History, GCE A-level English Literature, French, German, History, Mathematics, Biology, Sociology.

Crawley College of Technology
Open Learning: Management Development Programme; Management Update Programme.

Epsom: North East Surrey College of Technology
Flexilearning facilities in the Department of Community and General Education, with home-study packages plus tutorial support. Details from college. Open Learning courses in Managerial Studies offered by the Department of Management.

Hatfield: De Havilland College – see under Welwyn Garden City

Havering Technical College
Open Learning facilities with home study packages plus tutorial support by phone or face to face. A range of GCSE and GCE A-levels available: also Shorthand and Typing. 'We are an Open College, Access Gateway Centre and provide pre-course counselling and tutorial support during the course. We also have Independent Learning Suites on every site.'

Hemel Hempstead: Dacorum College
Open Learning Drop-In facility, offering the chance to brush up your Maths and English.

Luton College of Higher Education
Open Learning centre, providing the following courses in distance-learning form with tutorial support: Institute of Road Transport Engineers examination subjects; Institute of the Motor Industry examination subjects; Writing and Presenting Reports; Presenting Information Visually; Managing Your Own Learning; *Laboratory Safety; *Electronics; *Everyday Forms of Energy; *Food and Drink – a Biochemical Recipe; *Everyday Chemistry; *The Garden – Studies in Plant Growth; *Health Choices; *Introduction to Computing. (* indicates components of a conversion course for women moving from arts to sciences.)

Maidstone: Mid Kent College – see under Chatham

Milton Keynes: The Open University
See description given in introductory chapter. Provides home study facilities with specially written tutorial materials, practical kits for experiments, broadcasts on radio and television, audio and video cassettes plus support from tutorial groups and summer school. Undergraduate Programme for BA (Open) degree/degree with Honours, credit-based, with more than 130 courses, including the Open University Foundation courses with which students begin their studies. OU Foundation course credits are accepted by many universities, polytechnics and colleges in lieu of A-levels

for entry to their courses. Higher Degree Programme for taught masters' degrees and postgraduate degrees by research. Continuing Education Programme, incorporating the Open Business School, (in which two-thirds of students are employer-sponsored), professional courses for teachers and health and social welfare workers, postgraduate-level courses in Manufacturing and The Industrial Applications of Computers. Community Education packs – subjects such as energy conservation, school governing, planning retirement – and Personal Interest packs – in literature, music and art. (See 'Degree and Advanced Courses'.)

Norwich City College of Further and Higher Education
Open Learning using distance-learning tutorial materials and, where appropriate, cassette tapes plus tutorials, by telephone and face to face. Current options are GCSE/A-level French, Beginners/GCSE German, Beginners/GCSE/A-level Spanish, GCSE English, How to Study Effectively, How to Write Essays. GCE A-level English, Sociology. Links with Open College for wide range of courses.

Portsmouth College of Art, Design and Further Education
Centre for the Portsmouth Open Learning Programme, with distance-learning packages for both Return to Study and GCSE/GCE A-level subjects.

Portsmouth: Highbury College of Technology
Flexible/Open Learning Workshops – details from college. Flexistudy for adults – details from college.

Rochester: Mid Kent College – see under Chatham

Southampton Technical College
Flexistudy, using tutorial material produced mainly by the National Extension College, with tutorial support from college by post, telephone or face to face. Options include GCSE or A-level Biology, Chemistry, Computing, Economics, English Literature, French, German, History, Human Biology, Mathematics, Physics, Politics and Government, Spanish, Statistics. Other options may be possible – ask for details from the college.

Southend College of Technology
Open Learning: distance facilities in a wide range of subjects to suit individuals, including those interested in a 'minority' subject. Study materials for use at home plus tutorials at college to suit your circumstances.

Watford: Cassio College
'A very wide range of Open Learning materials is available and MSC grants are available for people who have been unemployed for less than six months as well as those eligible under JTS. Enquiries regarding open learning and short courses to Mrs Sue Baker, Watford 248828.'

Watford College
Open Access Centre with distance-learning packages, use of equipment and tutorial help available to everyone – employed/unemployed, industrial, commercial and private clients, from 9.30 a.m.-8.30 p.m. Monday to Friday, 9.30 a.m.-4.30 p.m. Saturdays by appointment, 46 weeks a year. Areas of training are: Computer-Aided Engineering (13 study programmes, including Computer Programming and Electronics Servicing), IBM PC Business Systems (six study programmes, including Word-processing and Databases), Printing (four study programmes, including Lithography, Flexography, Screen Printing), Automotive Electronics (five study programmes, including Electronic Fuel Injection Systems). Also Open and Distance Learning provision, especially for the Printing, Publishing and Ink Industries (also open to unemployed people). No entry qualifications: candidates can work for BTEC National Certificate on a unit-based system, or in modules of training. Wide range of units and modules for self-study, ranging from Design and Print Planning to Costing and Estimating,and Bookbinding and Print Finishing; plus specialist modules on Silk-Screen Printing and Magazine and Book Publishing. Extensive range of GCSE/ A-level courses, Small Business courses and Self-Management courses – send for Midtech Catalogue.

Welwyn Garden City: De Havilland College
(Also at Borehamwood and Hatfield.) Open Learning provision for most courses in general prospectus and some others; tutorial materials are designed for home study plus college tutorial support. Details from the college.

The following college in this region supplied information about open and distance learning courses in 1987 but no response was received to 1988 enquiries. Readers may nevertheless wish to make individual contact:

Luton: Barnfield College

Central England

Abingdon College
Open Learning with distance-learning materials, including books, tapes and videos plus telephone or face-to-face tutorials at convenient times. Details of available subjects from college: start at any time of year.

Abingdon: The Open College
(See description given in introductory chapter.) Designed to provide vocationally related courses, linked to qualifications in many instances, for people to study in their own time at home. No pre-qualifications are needed to study a course. The Open College will offer courses leading to nationally recognised qualifications and is working closely with the National Council for Vocational Qualifications (NCVQ), a body which is examining and accrediting work-related courses and the value of their qualifications. Students of the national Open College will use home study materials and practical kits, supported by radio and television programmes. The programmes began on Channel 4 in September 1987 and are now also shown on BBC. Future broadcasting is planned on independent TV and local radio. NB: Open College students will work for the examinations of outside organisations, rather than the College's own awards. The address given is the one to which you write for the *Open Book*, which lists all the courses available (see p. 00). You can, of course, study these courses anywhere in the UK.

Bridgenorth and South Shropshire College of Further Education
Centre for the Open College – please contact for full details.

Chesterfield College of Technology and Arts
Open-learning facilities on demand – details from college.

Corby: Trensham College – see under Kettering

Coventry: Henley College
Homestudycourses for Pitmans Shorthand and Typewriting (Beginners and Advanced), Word-Processing. Technical Training Packs: Mathematics,

General and Communication Studies, Electronics and Electronic Principles, Physical Science, Line and Customer Apparatus, Telecoms Systems, Electrical Drawing. Business Development Courses in Tourism (65 units). Computing – Beginners, Advanced, Understanding Computers, Computer-Aided Design. Catering – Royal Institute of Public Health and Hygiene Certificate, Running and Establishing Small Guest Houses. Short courses in, e.g: Office Administration, Purchasing, Personnel (12 subjects altogether). Language packs (10 languages, including Indonesian and Malay). Export courses (languages plus cultural background courses). Catering courses (Basic canteen to executive dining room). Education Engineering (for people writing new training programmes), Public Speaking, Executive Fitness, Technical Authorship. GCSE (16 subjects), GCE A-level (11 subjects). Pre-entry courses. RSA examination courses (12 Stage Two, seven Stage Three).

Dudley College of Technology
Flexistudy distance-learning packages plus tutorial support. Options are: BTEC National, Institute of Bankers, GCSE and A-level Physics, Chemistry, Accounts, Mathematics, Law, Sociology, Geography, Economics, Psychology, Statistics, Government and Politics. GCSE only: Human Biology, English Language. GCE A-level only: English Literature. Fleximaths. RSA Book-Keeping. Open Access Centre which students can attend by appointment during opening hours (12 hours a day, five days a week): uses training packages with tutorial help available if required. Programmes include: Industrial Electronics, Control Engineering, CAD/CAM, Business Computer Applications, Microelectronics, Robotics, CNC Machine-Tool Programming, Word-Processing. Centre for the Open College.

Hinkley College of Further Education
Open Learning using distance-learning packages plus tutorial support.Options are: Understanding Information Technology, Word-Processing/Keyboard Skills, Basic Digital Electronics, Decoders and Combinational Logic Digital Devices, Microprocessor Appreciation in Business, Computer Applications in Business, Supervisory Studies (NEBSS), Book-Keeping for the Small Business, Food-Handling for the Small Business. Fabric Analysis, Design Appreciation and all other materials from the Knitting Industry Open Tech.

Kettering: Trensham College
(Same distance-learning facilities available at Corby, where the contact is Mr P. Hindley: Corby 203252.) Distance Learning Packages include Leadership, Pricing for Profit, This is Marketing, Typing made easy, Decision Making, Time Management, CNC Appreciation, Basic Electrical Skills, Microelectronic Level I and Level II, Report Writing, Your Own Business, Food Handling, Book-Keeping for a Small Business, Computers and Business, Understanding Information Technology, Introduction to Distribution,

Looking After Children. Also Open Learning facilities for Preparatory Psychology, BASIC Programming, GCSE Chemistry, English Literature, Human Biology, Mathematics, English Language, Geography, History, World History, GCE A-level Biology, History, Sociology, English Literature, Mathematics, Geography. Inside Information (Information Technology) can lead to City and Guilds certificate. Centre for the Open College. College spokesperson says: 'In Open Learning, we can offer almost anything the customer requires – our free leaflet shows some of the courses available at both Kettering and Corby.'

Kidderminster College
Flexistudy – details from college. Also Open Office – a new flexible facility available for anyone who would like to learn new skills or update existing ones. Areas of study include Word-Processing, Audiotyping, Typing and Shorthand; each may be followed at all levels.

Leamington Spa: Mid Warwickshire College
Open Learning GCSE in English, Mathematics, Human Biology, Sociology, Child Psychology, Law. A-level in English Literature, Economics, Mathematics. Open BTEC awards in 'Management and Leadership within Small Firms' and 'Working with People'. Open College courses – e.g: Electronics, Book-Keeping and many others. Study packages to use at home, plus tutorial support by post or telephone, or face to face.

Lichfield College
Open Learningprovision in association with North Staffordshire Polytechnic. At present, Lichfield College can only support certain GCE A-level subjects but candidates seeking other subjects are helped to contact the North Staffordshire Polyechnic Open Leaning Unit.

Loughborough Technical College
Open Access New Technology Learning Centre provides individual learning packages, backed up with computer- and video-based training. Options include: Basic Electrcicity; Analogue Electronics; Digital Electronics; Microprocessors; Starting in Information Technology; Computer Literacy (can lead to City and Guilds certificate). Open Learning Basic Maths – no qualifications needed, suitable for people preparing for Skillcentre tests, pre-Nursing, pre-GCSE, etc.

Nottingham: South Nottinghamshire College of Further Education
Open Learning unit with provision for GCSE and GCE A-levels, Management courses, Information Technology courses, Office Skills, Typewriting, Word-Processing Workshops.

Redditch College

Flexastudy system, provides both for intensive full-time study at college, using distance learning materials, and part-time and evening facilities using distance-learning materials, both with tutorial support and use of college facilities. Examination courses available include: Accountancy (several professional institutes), Institute of Chartered Secretaries and Administrators, Institute of Marketing, Institute of Export, Institute of Purchasing and Supply, Institute of Taxation, Overseas Trade, Institute of Personnel Management, Institute of Credit Management. Open Learning: part of the county Open Tech project, with distance-learning packages for students to use at home plus telephone advice service and group study sessions. NB: This college is to be merged in Autumn 1988 with North Worcestershire College, to become North East Worcestershire College. There may be changes as a result of the merger.

Flexastudy: viewpoint

'There's a lot of reading to start off with. Remember, you have to read everything that a lecturer would have researched and put into a lecture. You are given a scheme of work at the beginning, with the topics you have to cover to get through the part you are studying for, and then, within each topic, you are given suggested reading from recommended books. You are also given worksheets which contain printed examination questions, generally of the standard that you are at, and it's suggested that if you feel you understand the topic, you should go ahead and work through the questions.'

[Student, Flexastudy Accountancy course, Redditch College]

'At this college we are prepared to take anybody who has reached the necessary standard to be able to register with a professional body. That is the only requirement in which we need to be satisfied. In any one year, you will find within the system students ranging from 18 up to the mid-50s. We find that the problems which arise in a correspondence course are very much more easily dealt with and comprehensibly dealt with on a face-to-face basis, and it is perhaps illuminating to take one of the major accountancy bodies, the Chartered Institute of Cost and Executive Accountants, where in the last six years of examinations, the pass rate here has not dropped below 9O%. When you compare this with the national average, somewhere in the region of 35%, it speaks volumes for the system.'

[Spokesperson, Flexastudy unit, Redditch College]

Retford: Easton Hall International

Primarily distance-learning courses (some residential element) in Teaching English as a Foreign/Second Language (see 'Retraining' and New Skills Courses').

Stafford College of Further Education
Open College course in Twentieth Century Life. No entry requirements,but this is the kind of open-learning course where you attend college (two evenings a week for the first year, one evening a week for the second). It can lead to a degree course at North Staffordshire Polytechnic. Open Learning Access courses are available in a variety of GCSE, GCE and Business Studies subjects.

Solihull College of Technology
Distributive Industry Open Learning (DIOL) support centre. Open College support centre (offering a full range of facilities and course advice). NEBSS Supervisory Studies by open training and a full range of GCSE/A-level Flexistudy courses.

Stoke-on-Trent
Range of Open Learning courses at GCSE and A-level.

Stoke-on-Trent: North Staffordshire Polytechnic
Open Learning Unit in association with further education colleges, details from Polytechnic.

Stratford-upon-Avon: South Warwickshire College of Further Education
Homestudy distance-learning facilities for GCSE Mathematics, RSA Typing, Stage 1, and Teeline Shorthand.

Tamworth College of Further Education
Distance Learning: All Languages, Distribution, Inn-Keeping, GCSE and A-level subjects. Courses, details from college.

Warley and West Bromwich: Sandwell College
Flexistudy GCE English and Shorthand, with distance-learning packages and tutorial classes at college. Open Tech course in Computer-Aided Engineering – distance-learning materials plus personal computer graphics workstation plus telephone and face-to-face tutorials. Open Learning distance-learning plus tutorial facilities in various subjects, including LCCI Private Secretary's Diploma, Shorthand and Association of Medical Secretaries and Practice Administrators Diploma. The college says: 'Our distance-learning provision has extended considerably but not all details are finalised yet for 1988/9 – the new prospectus will give details.'

Warwick University
Distance Learning MBA: The university states: 'This is a flexible programme, normally completed in four years, though some students may complete in three years while others may take up to eight years; should a student have to discontinue studying, he or she may be eligible for a

Certificate or Diploma. The programme consists of examined courses, taken over three years at the rate of four courses per year, plus a dissertation based on a project agreed between the university and the student. The distance-learning scheme for the course work is administered by Wolsey Hall, Oxford (a leading distance-learning college for over 90 years), students being required to complete approximately three assignments per month; a compulsory eight-day seminar is held each September at the University of Warwick to review topics studied the previous year; course assessment is by examination (sometimes under an 'open-book' system). Applicants should either hold or expect to obtain a first- or second-class honours degree, *or* the final qualification of an acceptable professional body, *or* a Higher National Diploma or equivalent qualification, provided that they are over 27 on their proposed date of entry to the programme, and have a minimum of four years' experience in an executive capacity in industry, commerce or the public sector; some candidates (especially those with non-UK qualifications) may be asked to take the Graduate Management Admission Test.'

Wolverhampton: Bilston Community College
Flexistudy: home study courses, tutorial support available or students may attend occasional classes. Options include the following courses (but similar arrangements may be possible for other subjects), and teaching is generally geared towards GCSE, though work may be undertaken at other levels: American Studies A-level; Britain, Europe and the World 1848-1950; Business Studies; Classical Civilisation GCSE/A-level; Community Studies; Creative Writing; English; English Literature; General Studies GCSE/A-level; Geography, Government and Politics, Greek (Classical) GCSE/A-level; History of Medicine with Social Aspects; Human Biology; Integrated Humanities GCSE; Latin GCSE/A-level; Maths; Religious Studies GCSE (Mark and Christian Responsibility); Religious Studies A-level (two chosen from The Old Testament, The New Testament and Aspects of Religious Belief); Social and Economic History of Britain since 1750; Sociology; Welfare and Society; Study Skills.

Wolverhampton: Wulfrun College
Homestudycourses using specially prepared learning materials plus support from tutors at pre-arranged times (telephone tutorials or face-to-face tuition). Options are: Introductory English, Introductory Mathematics, How to Study, 30-hour course in BASIC, Shorthand, Typewriting. GCSE Accounts, Art, Biology, Commerce, Economics, English Language, English Literature, Geography, Human Biology, History, Law, Mathematics, Sociology, Local History, Religious Education. GCE A-levels in Economics, English Literature, History, Sociology. Open University Preparatory courses in Arts and Social Science.

Homestudy: viewpoints

'I did two O-levels at college last year and I decided I would like to do Maths – well, not that I would like to do it, but that I needed to do it if I was going to do anything else. A lot of employers will ask you for both O-level English and O-level Maths. I did do the Pre O-level Maths course at college, but I decided that with the O-level I would probably fall behind in a classroom full of younger students, who had probably come straight from school. I don't think I would have tackled Maths if there hadn't been this way of doing it, in my own time. At home, I can take all the time I need to get through any specific part that I find difficult.'

[Homestudy student, Wulfrun College of Further Education]

'The beginning of the course is crucial. As a tutor, you've got to be extremely supportive in the early stages, because you want the students to get into the course of study, to become familiar with their materials, and to enjoy the course. Then the aim is to try and keep the students motivated and get them to study at fairly regular intervals, which can be a problem, given that many of them have other commitments apart from studying. All the tutors involved in the Homestudy programme get together regularly to discuss how they are getting on, and share ideas and experiences. We find that one of the advantages is that students work at their own pace and some are able to progress quite rapidly – for instance, some who start in September are sitting an examination the following June. Other students are deferring their entry for another few months or for a year. We can cater very much for an individual student's needs, and if we have just one student who wants to do a particular subject, and one tutor who wants to teach it, that's perfectly possible in a way that it wouldn't be in a classroom situation, where we have to have at least 10 or 12 students for one tutor.'

[Spokesperson, Wulfrun College of Further Education]

The following colleges in this region supplied information in 1987 about their Open-distance-learning courses but no response was recieved to 1988 enquiries. Readers may neverthless want to make individual contact:

Bromsgrove: North Worcestershire College (being amalgamated with Redditch College, so courses may be shared)
Buxton: High Peak College
Derby College of Further Education
Henley-on-Thames: King James's College of Henley
Herefordshire Technical College
Nuneaton: North Warwickshire College of Technology and Art
Stoke-on-Trent Technical College
Sutton College – has been amalgamated with Garrets Green College to form East Birmingham College. No details available yet.
Witney: West Oxfordshire Technical College

Northern England

Altrincham: South Trafford College of Further Education
Flexistudy courses using distance-learning materials at home with tutorial support at college. Options are: English Language and Literature, Foreign Languages, Geography and History, Marketing and Economics, Sociology, Psychology and Child Development, Human Biology, Physics, Art.

Ashington: Northumberland College of Arts and Technology
NEBSS Certificate in Supervisory Studies (for unemployed people), Opening Learning – MSC-sponsored.

Barrow-in-Furness College of Further Education
Open-learning facilities for students who cannot attend conventional classes – include tutorials and practical classes as required. Details from the college.

Blackburn College
Open College facilities, validated by Lancaster University and Lancashire Polytechnic, no formal entry requirements. Unit-based part-time courses, day or evening. Options include Study Techniques, Sociology, Electronics, Microprocessor Systems, Computing, Business Studies, Music, English Literature, Politics, Edwardian Britain, Art, German, Economics, Drama, Accounting, Philosophy, English Language, Economic and Social History, Psychology, Spanish, Women's Studies, Creative Writing, European Studies, Italian, Sociology, Mathematics, Industrial Relations, Classical Studies.Students do have to attend college one session per week for their part-time courses, though they can work at their own pace at home. 'A' units are introductory and 'B' units are widely recognised as A-level equivalents.

Bradford and Ilkley Community College
Open Learning as part of the West Yorkshire Open Learning Federation. Courses at foundation, preliminary, intermediate, advanced and post-experience/higher education levels.

Bridlington: East Yorkshire College of Further Education
College acts as agent: it can offer guidance and obtain and sell Open Learning materials.

Burnley College
Participates in Open Learning scheme, details from college.

Consett: Derwentside Tertiary College
Is part of the Durham Access Centre of North East Open Learning network.

Dewsbury College
Home-Based Study programmes with texts, practical kits, video or computer programmes (students can use them at the college) plus tutorial support, by phone or face-to-face counselling. Options include How to Study, Accounting (GCSE/A-level), Biology (GCSE/A-level), Chemistry (A-level), Economics (A-level), English Language (GCSE), English Literature (GCSE/A-level), History (GCSE/A-level), Physics (A-level), Psychology and Child Development (A/O-level) French (Preliminary/GCSE), German (Preliminary/GCSE), Spanish (Preliminary/GCSE), Maths (GCSE/A-level – Pure, Applied, Pure and Applied), Sociology (GCSE/A-level). SciTech modules for use by laboratory technicians in schools,college or industry. Fabrication Engineering (for mature students with a working kowledge of plate, structural or sheet metal trades), leads to City and Guilds awards. Open Tech: wide range of options. Students are usually employer-sponsored but individuals may purchase study packs. Options include Computing, Construction, Engineering, Health Professions, Management, Supervisory Skills, Maths and Statistics, Science, Service Industries, Training.

Durham: New College Durham
Open Learning collaborative training venture involving New College, Durham, Peterlee College, Consett Technical College and the North East Open Learning Network. Tutorial materials, audio tapes, video tapes, computer programmes and practical kits are supported by college tutorials, workshops and study groups. Wide range of options include Open BTEC courses, Open Learning for Small Businesses, Open Learning for Supervisory Management. Flexistudy using National Extension College materials with college tutorial support, by telephone or face to face.GCSE options include English Language, English Literature, History, Human Biology, Mathematics, Statistics, Social Studies. GCE A-levels include English Literature, History, Sociology.

Gateshead Technical College
Has Open Learning Access Centre. Flexistudy programmes using National Extension College materials with college tutorial support – wide range of GCSE/GCE A-level subjects. Open University leisure packages with tutorial

support. Open Tech study packages for technician, supervisory and management studies, all levels from beginner to advanced.

Halifax: Percival Whitley College of Further Education
Flexistudy for GCSE/A-levels and City and Guilds awards – home study packages and practical kits to use at home, plus telephone and face-to-face tutorials. Open Learning as part of the West Yorkshire Open Learning Federation – no entry requirements, attendance at college when possible for individual students. Options include literacy, numeracy, adult education and courses equivalent to GCSE and A-levels for higher education. Details from college. This college is also a Gateway centre for the Open College.

Lancaster College of Adult Education
Part of the Open College of the North West and can supply a leaflet with details of all the participating colleges.

Leeds: Park Lane College
Distance-learning courses available in a wide range of GCSE, A-level and professional subjects, including English Language, Maths, Biology, Law, Chartered Insurance Institute, Chartered Institute of Bankers course, Association of Accounting Technicians course, Legal Secretaries course, Gateway centre for the Open College.

Manchester University
Distance-learning: Return to Study course, home-based study packages for 10 unit modules, plus postal and telephone contact with a tutor plus five Saturday group meetings. Based on six months' completion period but you can take longer. Also possible to study the course on a 'roll-on, roll-off' basis. Completion earns Preparatory Certificate in Higher Education.

Middlesborough: Longlands College of Further Education
Open Learning packages in all Engineering, Technology, Science and Computing courses, produced by the college itself, and multi-disciplinary material available to HND level. Distance-Learning courses in Process Plant Operation, Quality Control, Fabrication, Welding Inspection and Quality Control, Basic Mathematics. Flexistudy provision – wide range of subject options available. Drop-In centre facilities – wide range of subject options available.

Newcastle-upon-Tyne
'Telelang' Language Laboratory, using self-selected packages, working in the privacy of an individual booth and attending as often as you like. Tutorial help is available. There are 35 languages available at various levels: Afrikaans, Arabic, Chinese (Mandarin and Cantonese), Czech, Danish, Dutch, Finnish, French, Gaelic (Irish and Scottish), German, Greek,

Hebrew, Hindi, Hungarian, Indonesian, Italian, Japanese, Malay, Mongolian, Norwegian, Persian, Polish, Portuguese, Punjabi, Romanian, Russian, Serbo-Croat, Spanish, Swahili, Swedish, Turkish, Urdu and Welsh. Contact Nigel Thomas, Department of Modern Languages, ext. 3791.

Peterlee College

Access Centre under North East Open Learning Network (see Durham, New College Durham, above). Mathematics Open Learning Workshop – all stages, using self-study packages with tutorial help available. Open Learning 'Step by Step' packages on Small Business themes. Open Learning Computing Workshop with packages and tutorial help allowing study to be divided between home and college.

Preston: Lancashire Polytechnic

Distance-learning provision for Analytical Chemistry (ACOL) and Criminology (in conjunction with Open College of the North West). Law degree in development. BTEC unit in Construction available.

Rotherham College of Arts and Technology

'Open Workshop' courses, offering a choice between attending the workshop at a time and pace to suit the learner, or by Flexistudy, with occasional contact with a tutor. Courses available include: Improve Your English, Improve Your Maths, Skills for Returning to Study, Preparatory Course for the Police Entry Test, Preparatory Course for the Mature Nurse Entry test, Job Application and Interview Skills, Setting up Your Own Business, English as a Second Language, Teach Yourself Word-Processing and Typing – together with a wide range of conventional GCSE and A-level courses. The workshop is open Monday-Thursday 10 a.m.-7 p.m. and Fridays 10 a.m.-4 p.m.

Rotherham: Rockingham College

Co-operating in Open College of South Yorkshire to provide open-learning packages for adults who require no previous entry qualifications. Students should be 24-plus to take advantage of this provision. Also Flexistudy courses for GCSE and A-levels, for professional qualifications in such areas as Marketing, and leisure subjects such as Gardening, Dressmaking and Beauty Care. Also Open Tech packages.

Southport College of Art and Technology

Open Learning Guest House Owners' course, with audio-cassette guidance,telephone help line and tutorial back-up (on student's premises if necessary). Customised learning packages to suit individual students' needs, covering every subject at every level, enabling people to learn at their own speed, in their own home (or at place of work), with tutorial support as needed. Also Open College support centre.

Wakefield: Bretton Hall College
Distance-learning packs can be provided for students wishing to take the Mature Matriculation examination.

Warrington: North Cheshire College
Part of the Manchester Open College Federation; provides Access courses (see 'Pre-Entry, Sample and Access Courses').

Wigan: TRACE (Training Research Advisory Consultancy Enterprises Ltd)
A Wigan College of Technology Company. Distance-learning Return to Study course, home-based study packages plus postal and telephone tutorial contact, plus five group meetings on Saturdays. Based on six month completion, but you may take longer if you wish. NB: TRACE produces specialised distance-learning materials, e.g updating courses for Radiographers. If you are a manager or are professionally qualified and want to update, their brochure could produce some useful ideas for you.

The following colleges in this region supplied information in 1987 about their open and distance learning courses but no response was received to 1988 enquiries. Readers may nevertheless wish to make individual contacts:

Blackpool and Fylde College of Further and Higher Education
Leeds: Airedale and Wharfedale College
Leeds: Kitson College of Technology
Sheffield: Granville College
Wakefield District College

Wales and Western England

Barnstaple: North Devon College
Part of the Devon Open Tech initiative and associated with the Open College. Details from the college.

Bath: Norton Radstock College
Flexistudy courses including: How to Study Effectively, Wordpower, Numbers at Work, Fleximaths. Also Open University Community Education courses: The First Years of Life, The Pre School Child, Parents and Teachers, Work Choices, Action Planning for the Unemployed. Flexible Access by arrangement, to certain specialist rooms for self-directed study: these include the pottery, darkroom, computer room, typing room and workshop/woodwork room.

Bristol: Filton Technical College
Flexastudy: approximately 70% of your time at college is spent in guided private study, with regular individual tutorials from qualified staff, who supply schemes of work and learning resources, and assess each student's work. Students can choose to attend morning, afternoon or evening sessions. The Flexastudy sessions are offered two days a week from 9 a.m. to 9.15 p.m. Choices include: BTEC Continuing Education Units in Computer Studies, Working with People, Information Technology for Managers, Improve your Financial Decision Making, Making Sense of Economics, Making Sense of Marketing, Making Sense of Exporting. Also Institute of Industrial Managers' Certificate and Diploma, NEBSS Introductory course in Supervisory Studies. Institute of Management Services Certificate and Diploma, Institute of Transport Administration Graduateship and Corporate Membership, Institute of Administrative Management Certificate, Association of Accounting Technicians Intermediate and Final, Finance Houses Association Part I, Institute of Chartered Secretaries and Administrators, Diploma in Marketing Foundation Course in Overseas Trade. Computer Programming (BASIC, COBOL, PASCAL). GCE Mathematics A-level by Flexastudy. Also 'Freeway' courses in Sociology and Social and Economic History, using study materials of the National Extension College: you decide how, when and where you'll study.

Flexistudy Courses: viewpoint
'There are lots of quite reputable professional institutes, each of whom, in our catchment area, would only come up with five or six students in any given academic year. We're faced with meeting the LEA minimum recruitment number of 12 students before we can offer a course. By grouping all these minority professional institute students together in the one Flexastudy facility, we've overcome our numbers problem. On a typical evening in the past year we would have anything up to 40 or 45 students taking anything up to six or seven different professional institute schemes, supported by three full-time members of staff, who would be circulating round the room giving tutorials. So far, all our learning materials have been produced by our (intensely overworked) staff, but we are planning to buy in correspondence materials for the scheme in one area in the future.'

[Spokesperson, Filton Technical College, Bristol]

Chippenham Technical College
Flexistudy courses for GCSE, various subjects, Computing in BASIC, Archaeology A-level, Hairdressing, Office Skills.

Exeter College
Open Learning: a wide range of packages is offered with tutorial support. Subjects covered include Return to Learn, Study Skills, Numeracy, GCSEs, A-levels, Business and Management, Office Skills, Computing, Electronics and Microelectronics.

Haverfordwest: Pembrokeshire College of Further Education
West Dyfed Small Business Centre offers distance-learning with coursebooks and audio or video cassettes. Telephone and face-to-face tutorials are arranged. All businesses are eligible, from the new bed-and-breakfast house to the developing engineering firm. Subjects include: Starting Your Own Business, Book-Keeping for the Small Business, The Successful Guest House Owner, Getting into Rural Tourism, The Hygienic Food Handler, Hotel Buildings and their Services, Computers in Business, Computer Typing course, Looking After Children. Also a wide range of Construction courses, including Building Regulations Reviewed (for the building contractor), and Contract Management – Financial and Legal Procedures.

Llanelli: Carmarthenshire College of Technology and Art
Distance learning provision for NEBSS Supervisory Studies awards.

Pontypridd: The Polytechnic of Wales
Participates in the Morgannwg Open Learning Project for Mid, South and West Glamorgan. Has produced open-learning materials in Computer-Aided Manufacturing Systems V, for BTEC Units, and is producing them in

Production Planning and Control IV and Computer-Aided Engineering IV, for BTEC Units.

Salisbury College of Technology

Open Learning: Distance-learning packages for GCSE Biology/Environmental Studies, English, English Literature, Human Biology, Local History, Psychology, Sociology and GCE A-level Biology/Botany/Environmental Studies, English, Human Biology, Zoology; Also distance learning for BTEC Continuing Education units.

Taunton: Somerset College of Arts and Technology

Open Learning: wide range of subjects. Details from the college's Open Learning Co-ordinator.

Weymouth College

Open Learning Unit providing self-study packs and tutorial support over a wide range of subjects, and with some courses leading to qualifications such as GCSE, A-levels, City and Guilds and BTEC awards. The unit has an Open Access Computer Room and Preview Room for viewing course materials, as well as providing audio-visual and photocopying facilities. The Unit has databases which give access to records of courses and open learning materials which may not yet be available through the Unit. In addition, the Open Learning Unit has been selected as Dorset's main Open Access Centre for the Open College. Packages currently available include Autocare, Basic Calculation, Circuit Training, Computers in Business, Introduction to Selling, Is Self-Employment Right for You?, Library and Information Skills, Looking After Children, Pub Business, Report Writing, Understanding Information Technology, Women – the Way Ahead.

The following colleges in this region supplied information in 1987 about their open and distance learning courses but no response was received to 1988 enquiries. Readers may nevertheless want to make individual contact:

Teeside: North East Wales Institute
Dolgellau: Coleg Meirionnydd
Llandridnod Wells: Radnor College of Further Education
Weston-super-Mare College of Further Education
Ystrad Mynach College of Further Education

Scotland and Northern Ireland

Clydebank College
Open-learning facilities available - details from college.

Dumfries and Galloway College of Technology
Distance-learning courses with monthly meetings with the course tutor, or telephone tutorials where this is impractical. SCE O-grade Accounts, Arithmetic, Economics, English, History, Mathematics, Sociology. H-grade English. GCE A-level Sociology. Teeline Shorthand. 'Learning by Appointment' system: attendance to use college equipment at negotiated times with monthly tutorials. Computing – 30-hour BASIC, Advanced Structural BASIC. Modern Languages: French, German, Modern Greek, Italian, Portuguese, Russian, Spanish, English as a Foreign Language. Pitman's Shorthand – Beginner, Refresher Course, Speed Building. Typing – Beginner, Speed Development, Audio. Word-Processing. Keyboarding. Open Tech programmes in: Analogue Electronics – Devices; Analogue Electronics – Waveform Generators; Basic Electrical Skills; Computer Numerical Control – Part-Programming, Computer Numerical Control – Machine Tool Applications, Digital Electronics – Basic Digital Electronics; Digital Electronics – Decoders and Combinatorial Logic; Digital Electronics – Digital Devices, Electronics - Introduction, Fault-Finding; Fault-Finding Methods - Process Control, Hydraulics; Microprocessor Applications in Business and Commerce; Introduction to Electronics – Pneumatics; Servicing Video Recorders.

Edinburgh: Napier College
Open Learning courses using study materials in text, audio-visual media and computer software for self-study facilities. Wide range of subjects, starting from the pre-entry level.

Edinburgh: Queen Margaret College
Main delivery centre in Scotland for the distribution of SCOTVEC Open Learning course Start Your Own Business. Tutorial backup here and at Clydebank Technical College and Dumfries and Galloway College of Further Education.

Glasgow: Strathclyde Business School, University of Strathclyde
Distance-larning: MBA postgraduate course.

MBA by Distance Learning: viewpoints
'I had to make a choice – did I want to take the full-time MBA course, which would have meant taking a year out of work, or was I prepared to fit distance learning in with my job? With the way things are developing in my company, giving up work for a year would have been inappropriate. To cover the reading, tutor-marked and other assignments that I have to do on the distance-learning MBA takes up about 10-15 hours a week, but if you are experiencing any difficulties with any part of the course at all, you can phone up the tutor assigned for each course and you will receive guidance and advice. You are left to a great extent to rely on your own devices, but you can meet people whose experience is of consummate value to you when you need access to tutors.'

[Student, Distance Learning MBA, Strathclyde Business School]

'Distance learning solves three problems. It keeps people in their jobs, so that they can keep up to date with what's happening in their company. Then they can give their company instant feedback on ideas that are starting to emerge from the course and inject suggestions for new approaches to company problems that may crop up as they study. And distance learning gives people flexibility. If they are promoted into demanding new jobs, they can stop their studies for a while, and plug back into the system later on, picking up where they left off.'

[Spokesperson, Distance Learning MBA, Strathclyde Business School]

Glasgow University
Department of Scottish Literature. MPhil programme in Scottish Literature, taught over three years by correspondence with one-day and week-long schools. 'Open to suitably qualified graduates, the course provides a comprehensive study of 600 years of literature in English and Scots, and is aimed at schoolteachers and at all those with interest in the subject.'

Inverness College of Further and Higher Education
Open Learning with telephone tutorials in SCOTVEC National Certificate modules: Communications, Learning and Study Skills, Mathematics Grade 2, Cost Control in Catering, Introduction to Economic Analysis, Organisation of Industry, Starting and Running a Small Business, Financial Record Keeping, Health and Safety in the Work Environment, People and Politics, Local Authorities, Central Government, Fundamentals of Technology: Mechanical, Fundamentals of Technology:Electrical, Basic Telecommunications, Communication 1/2, Communication 2/3, Introduction to Computers, Computer Software, Marketing. SCOTVEC Higher National Certificate in Business Studies. City and Guilds 232 Electrical and Electronic

Craft Studies, 236C Electrical Installation. BTEC/SCOTVEC subjects and modules for technical training. City and Guilds 760/2 Advanced Hairdressing.

Newtownabbey Technical College
Open-learning packages are available for many of the subjects and courses listed for this college in the 'Retraining and New Skills Courses' section of *Make A Fresh Start*. Ask for details from the college.

The following colleges in this region supplied information in 1987 about their open and distance learning courses, but no response was recieved to 1988 enquiries. Readers may nevertheless wish to make individual contact:

Armagh College of Further Education
Ayr College
Ballmoney: North Antrim College of Further Education

DEGREE AND ADVANCED COURSES

Higher education and further qualifications full-time and part-time opportunities

Introduction

Here's the section to convince you that universities, polytechnics and colleges need *you*! And no, it's not just that the number of young students available to go to college is diminishing, as the effect of the reduced birthrate that slimmed down our school numbers now threatens college intakes.

The fact is that mature students do rather well for themselves in higher education. That's officical, by the way. The Council for National Academic Awards (which approves degrees offered in polytechnics and other institutes of higher education outside the universities) carried out a research project that showed that students who went into higher education *without* A-levels tended to do better than those *with* A-levels.

Not that that will come as any surprise to the universities. At Warwick, where nearly one in eight students is a mature student, the prospectus states: 'It is noticeable that mature students generally obtain better degree results than younger students, even though in the majority of cases, the mature students did not have qualifications normally acceptable for entrance when they applied for the course.'

CONCESSIONS FOR ADULTS

It's the idea of starting all over again to get the entry requirements for a degree course that puts many people off going to university or polytechnic, even when they have discovered that they can't make any progress without higher education. The same hurdle confronts people who want to change their lives by getting away from home and job for the degree they've always wanted.

So it's good news that so many universities, polytechnics and colleges of higher education now offer concessions in entry requirements to mature students. The minimum age for a 'mature' student, according to the colleges that answered my enquiry, can be anything from 19 (at the University of Keele) to 25 (at Glasgow College of Technology). The concessions are very variable, too, from entry by interview and essay to the acceptance of an Access or Open University course, or offering one A-level instead of the usual two or three. (The Open University itself requires no prior qualifications for its degree courses; anyone over school-leaving age can apply, with or without GCEs, GCSEs, and the rest.)

APEL is the latest bridge into higher education for mature students. The letters stand for 'Assessment of Prior Experiential Learning', which in turn means that you may be accepted for a degree course at a polytechnic or college without any formal qualifications, but on the basis of your work experience and training. A study was carried out by the Learning from Experience Trust and financed by the Council for National Academic Awards. It covered 147 students aged between 22 and 65. Among those interviewed was a 48-year-old who had no formal educational qualifications but was accepted on the basis of her work experience, from clerk to information consultant, for a BA in Information and Library Studies. And there was a 33-year-old who had only O-levels, but was accepted to take a BEng (Honours) degree course because of his experience and technical certificates in motor engineering. APEL promises to open more routes into more courses for people whose work experience and increasing responsibilities may have left them little time to get formal qualifications.

In the 'Pre-entry, Sample and Access Courses' section of this book, I've referred to Access courses which are one alternative to getting conventional entry qualifications for a degree course. In this section, look out for Associate Student facilities, which could be an alternative to taking a degree, if there's only one part of a degree course you really want to study. (Mind you, many people who sample degree course learning through an Associate Student course do get the taste for it, and decide to expand into degree studies.) You'll find a good description of what's involved in being an Associate Student in the Hatfield Polytechnic entry.

I have made a point of asking universities, polytechnics and colleges to tell me about any degree course that they offer on a part-time basis. Demand for part-time degree study facilities has increased very much in recent years and it's interesting to see which higher education establishments are setting out to cater for the people who want to get letters after their name without giving up their jobs in the process.

Throughout the courses section that follows, I've listed the entry concessions offered to mature students by each higher education establishment that responded to my enquiries. Not all of them did – and since they all received two requests for information, it does suggest that any college without an entry probably has no special policy with regard to mature students.

They are more than made up for by the enthusiasm of the majority who *do* give concessions, *do* put on part-time courses (some even during the evenings for people who are at work by day) and *do* use phrases like 'mature students welcomed' or 'mature students encouraged to apply'. The attitude of North Staffs Polytechnic should encourage anyone, and it's nice to see the University of Cambridge pointing out which are the likely colleges for late starters.

WHAT'S IN IT FOR YOU?

Welcomes apart, do you sincerely want to enter higher education? It needs thinking about because of the time it takes: three yearsor sometimes longer for an honours or sandwich degree course, and often between five and eight years part-time.

Either way, you'll be paying for those letters after your name: in loss of earnings if you become a full-time student, or in loss of freedom at evenings and weekends if you study part-time.

But according to the latest Open University study, which covered 5000 OU graduates, 57% claimed that their job performance or career prospects improved as a result of their studies. Eight out of ten said the experience was good for them as individuals, but 7% warned that there were some bad effects on their family life.

About one-third of all graduate traineeships are open to graduates in any subject (or 'of any discipline', which is the phrase often used in prospectuses). Unless you are substantially older than the usual graduate trainee (say in your 40s and 50s rather than 30s or 20s), you could have an advantage over an untried graduate if you can offer work experience and a work reference as well as a degree. You've proved two things: that you can hold down a job, and that you can achieve an academic target.

Apart from the jobs that require the status of graduate for you to be considered, there are others you can train for on a postgraduate course. You get concessions in the length of training or in the exams you have to take because you are a graduate. Examples: shortened graduate training courses in nursing; exemptions from certain professional exams, such as parts of the Institute of Personnel Management course; 'fast stream' training in the police and in banks. There are graduate 'conversion courses' for which you can be considered once you have demonstrated your intellectual potential: for instance, you'll find information technology and hotel and catering management conversion courses mentioned in this section.

Finally, a degree helps you in the promotion stakes. Given two candidates of equal merit, one with a degree and one without, the one with the degree is likely to get the job because he/she has proved to have the staying power to withstand a three-year study course, and the temperament to succeed in competitive exams or assessments. (And staying power is demonstrated even more by those people who take part-time or distance-learning degrees: the most recent Open University survey showed that 44% of its graduates had been promoted as a result of their studies, while another 22% had changed their jobs. About 17% had moved on from the 'shop floor' to achieve managerial status.)

THE PERSONAL FACTOR

At the end of the day, though, it's not enough just to take a degree for job reasons. You can pick a very 'useful' subject, but if it bores you, you are unlikely to do well. The best reason for going after a degree or advanced course is that you really do want to spend your time studying the subject or subjects concerned. You can't think of anything more enjoyable than being freed of the burden of going to a job or looking after a house, and allowed to learn all about music or modern history or biotechnology or whatever your pet subject might be. And when you leaf through the prospectuses with their pictures of groups of people eagerly discussing new ideas, or using the latest technical equipment or choosing books in a huge, sunny library, you wish that you were one of them. You wouldn't mind living on rice and lentils or dressing out of the Oxfam shop in return for three years of freedom to learn.

GRANTS FOR (NEARLY) ALL

People who haven't previously had a grant for education and are self-supporting are entitled to one when they are accepted for a full-time degree or similar course. It's not a lot but it covers your fees and a spartan lifestyle. You get extra if you are over 26 when your course starts and have earned or received in taxable unemployment or supplementary benefits at least £12,000 during the three years before the start of the first academic year of your course. (See 'Costs and Grants' section.)

It's less easy to get a grant for a postgraduate course, though if you are a graduate wanting to make a change, this can be one of the most convenient bridges into a new career that you can find. Some courses of the 'conversion' kind are MSC-sponsored and others attract grants from research councils, but you may have to look for a part-time version of your ideal full-time course so that you can 'work your way through college' as American students do.

As in the earlier sections, students who have gone into higher education when making a fresh start and sometimes those who teach them have contributed their comments to this section. You'll find these personal views on the following pages:

Higher Education in Later Life: University of Kent at Canterbury
Associate Student Route: Hatfield Polytechnic
Part-Time at the Polytechnic: City of Birmingham Polytechnic
Adult Residential College: Ruskin College, Oxford
BEd Home Economics: Trinity and All Saints College, Leeds
Mature Student Routes in Science and Technology: Manchester Polytechnic
Catering and Hotel Management Conversion Course: Queen Margaret College, Edinburgh

Useful free booklets are *Universities Welcome Mature Students*, from UCCA, PO Box 28, Cheltenham, Glos. GL50 1HY; *Mature Students Handbook*, from Manchester Polytechnic, The Registry, All Saints, Manchester, M15 6BH;

and *A Second Chance to Learn*, from Queen Margaret College, 36 Clerwood Terrace, Edinburgh, EH12 8TS. University, polytechnic and college prospectuses are free, and give you masses of information about individual courses.

London and Middlesex

Colleges appearing in this section are listed below by district, except where the location of the college is obvious from its name. This should help you to discover the most accessible college offering the course that you want.

One college of the University of London – Royal Holloway and New Bedford – appears in the Southern and Eastern England region. This is because, when the two colleges merged, the work formerly done on the Regent's Park site in London by the Bedford College contingent was moved to Egham in Surrey, where the combined Royal Holloway and New Bedford College is now situated.

Avery Hill, Dartford, Mile End, Woolwich	Thames Polytechnic
Barking and West Ham	North East London Polytechnic
Barnet, Enfield and Haringey	Middlesex Polytechnic
Bloomsbury	Birkbeck College Central London Polytechnic
Bow and Mile End	Queen Mary College
Camden and Islington	North London Polytechnic
Clerkenwell	City University
Elephant and Castle	London College of Printing
Euston	University College
Holborn	London School of Economics
Isleworth	West London Institute
Twickenham	St Mary's College, Strawberry Hill
Uxbridge	Brunel University
Waterloo	South Bank Polytechnic

Birkbeck College, University of London

The prospectus states: Birkbeck is primarily a College for working people; we specialise in providing degree level and research facilities for students who are,in the words of the College Charter, 'engaged in earning their livelihood during the day-time and are, therefore, only able to study on a part-time evening basis. If you are not working because you have to look after your children or an elderly or infirm relative during the day-time, or if you are retired, please make this clear on your application form'. Mature student concessions are possible at age 23 via interview plus a record of successful study at mature age (e.g. an A-level, extra-mural diploma or OU credit). Sometimes students are offered a place for a year on a probationary basis. Most popular courses among mature students (NB: these are all Part-Time Degrees) are: BA Classics, English, French, German, History, History of Art, Philosophy and Spanish, and BSc Biology, Chemistry, Geography, Geology, Mathematics (including Statistics), Physics and Psychology. New modular BA degrees being offered in Humanities: Philosophy, Politics and History and other combinations.

Brunel University, Uxbridge

Mature student concessions apply at 23. Students selected by interview. The university states: 'Most courses welcome mature students. Particularly popular courses for mature students include Sociology, Psychology and Government. The Mental Nursing option in some Social Science courses also attracts mature entrants'.

Central London Polytechnic

The prospectus says: 'Normally, but not necessarily, mature students seeking special consideration should be over 21'. The polytechnic's letter adds: 'The Business Studies degree course will consider students over the age of 21 years. Most degree courses ... will consider students as mature students as long as they are 25 years or over. Concessions usually take the form of an informal interview with the course leader.' *Part-Time Degrees*: BA/BA (Hons) Social Science; BA/BA (Hons) Business Studies, in association with the City of London Polytechnic and Polytechnic of the South Bank; LLB/LLB (Hons); BA/BA (Hons) Arabic, Chinese, Russian Studies, BSc/BSc (Hons) Chiropody, in conjunction with the London Foot Hospital and Chelsea School of Chiropody; BSc Computing; BA Photography. *Postgraduate Vocational Courses* include: Diploma in Law, full time – conversion course for non-law graduates who wish to read for the Bar. Foundation course in Accountancy, full time – any graduate. Diploma in Conference Interpretation, two terms full time – for candidates with university degree or equivalent, and thorough knowledge of their working language. Diploma in Technical and Specialised Translation, full time – for candidates with degree or equivalent in any two of the five major languages: French, German, Italian, Russian, Spanish. Postgaduate Diploma in Office Technology and Business Administration, full time – for any graduate.

City University

Mature student concessions possible for those aged 23-plus. Each student is treated individually. The Continuing Education department offers a one-year Open Studies course part time, day or evening, for adults wishing to return to HE. 'The Department of Social Sciences and Humanities finds a high number of mature students attracted to Sociology and Philosophy degrees and a fair number to Psychology'. *Postgraduate Vocational Courses*: wide range, but note particularly Diploma in Industrial and Administrative Sciences, part time – for those with a degree or eqivalent in any technical subject, wishing to train in management. MA/Diploma in Arts Administration, MA in Museums and Gallery Administration, MA in Arts Management in Education – for those with experience in the relevant fields seeking further qualification; MA in Librarianship and Arts Administration – for Senior Librarians; – all of these may be studied full time or part time. Diploma in Music Information Technology, full time or part time, for graduates in music/the arts, business studies, computing or engineering, hoping to work in the media, and others with relevant experience. MBA in Finance, Industrial Relations and Personnel Management, Export Management, full time or evenings: MSc in Shipping Trade and Finance, full time or evenings. MSc in Business Systems, Analysis and Design, full time or evenings. Diplomas in Newspaper Journalism, Periodical Journalism, Radio Journalism, International Journalism full time – any degree acceptable, plus commitment to career in journalism. Diploma in Law, full time – any degree acceptable, for those who wish to become barristers but do not have a qualifying law degree. Diploma in Clinical Communication Studies, full time (acceptable for membership of College of Speech Therapists) – any degree considered but graduates in Psychology, Linguistics or other relevant subjects may gain exemptions.

London College of Printing

Mature candidates without conventional qualifications considered for BA (Hons) Photography and BA (Hons) Film and Video. *Postgraduate Vocational Courses*: Diploma in Design and Media Technology, full time – for graduates in Graphic Design or equivalent. Periodical Journalism course for graduates, full time – any degree, or those over 21 with equivalent qualifications considered. Diploma in Radio Journalism, full time – any degree or equivalent qualification. Diploma in Printing and Publishing, full time – any degree.

London School of Economics, University of London

Mature student concessions possible for those aged 22: the normal number of GCE passes is not always required. The prospectus states: 'To have a larger than normal proportion of older students in its population is one of the traditions of the School, and it is glad to consider applications from candidates who have had several years' work experience, or, for example, from married women who wish, after an interval of some years, to return to full-time study.'

Middlesex Polytechnic

Mature student concessions normally start at 21. For entry to the modular degree scheme, mature students aged 21 or over without formal qualifications who can demonstrate capability and motivation to succeed on the courses within the scheme are welcome to apply. For entry to BEd course 'consideration is given to candidates over 21 who lack the formal entry requirements. Such applicants must either undertake a written examination and tests or provide evidence of a sustained interest and study in an appropriate subject or activity. They must also satisfy the requirements for literacy and numeracy (O-level English and Maths or equivalent), or, *for those over 25*, successfully complete polytechnic tests in these areas prior to entry'. Concessions for mature students are on other degree courses broadly similar to above, though more specific requirements are likely to be made for subjects such as engineering. *Part-Time Degrees*: BA (Hons) Textiles/Fashion, BA (Hons) Three-Dimensional Design, BEng (Hons) Electronic Engineering Design and Production (for students with HND/HNC or equivalent), BA/BA (Hons) Combined Studies, BA/BA (Hons) Humanities, BA (Hons) Literature and Philosophy, BA (Hons) Historical Studies, BA (Hons) History of Art, Design and Film, BA (Hons) Contemporary Cultural Studies, BA (Hons) Social Science. BSc/BSc (Hons) Science, Technology and Society, BA (Hons) Studies in Contemporary Writing. BA (Hons) English Literary Studies. *Postgraduate Vocational Courses*: Polytechnic Diploma in Video, full time. Diploma in Personnel Management, full time or part time. Diploma in Marketing, part time. Institute of Chartered Secretaries and Administrators, part time. Diploma of the Market Research Society, part time. Conversion course: Diploma in Craft, Design and Technology Education, full time – for qualified teachers wishing to move to secondary education. Postgraduate Diploma in Microelectronics Technology, part time – for graduates in electronic engineering or physics; exceptionally, graduates in mathematics, computing or chemistry considered. Postgraduate Diploma in Air/Water Pollution Control, part time – for graduates in science or engineering; others considered. Postgraduate Diploma in Fuel Technology, full time or part time – for graduates in science or engineering: others considered. Postgraduate Diploma in Geotechnics, part time – for graduates in civil engineering, geology, mining engineering or related subjects; other candidates considered if employer-sponsored. Postgraduate Diploma in Water Supply and Public Health Engineering, full time – for professional engineers and scientists employed in or affiliated to the water industry. Diploma in Highway and Traffic Engineering, part time – for graduates and others with HE qualifications in civil or municipal engineering or town planning; others considered. Postgraduate Diploma in Computer Graphics, part time – to retrain graduates in engineering, mathematics or computing. Postgraduate Diploma in Social Work, full time.

North East London Polytechnic

The prospectus does not specify age for mature student concession, but says: 'We wish to encourage applications from older people, with or without the normal entry requirements for a course of higher education. In fact, more than three quarters of our full-time and sandwich students are over 21 and more than one third are over 25.' The School for IndependentStudy admits students aged over 21 without formal entry requirements, and states: 'In addition, a small group of students will be admitted who are aged between 18 and 21 and who do not have the usual entry requirements.' *Part-Time Degrees*: BA/BSc (Hons) by Independent Study - BSc (Hons) Life Sciences, BA/BA (Hons) Business Studies, BEng/BEng (Hons) Civil Engineering (day release), BSc Land Administration, LLB (Hons), BSc/BSc (Hons) Mathematics, BA (Hons) Health Studies (for registered nurses and other health professionals, day and evening release), BSc Archaeological Sciences, BSc/BSc (Hons) Psychology. *Postgraduate Vocational Courses*: these include: Diploma in Careers Guidance, full time – any degree acceptable; Diploma in Management (self-managed), open to self-employed as well as employed; MBA part time. Many courses on day-release basis for those already employed in professional/management areas.

North London Polytechnic

Mature student concessions for those aged 21 and over. Those without the standard entry requirement who can offer alternative qualifications or relevant experience may also be considered, and will need to demonstrate (i) evidence of commitment and (ii) evidence of likelihood to benefit. They may do this in written applications or in personal interview. Tutors may require a brief examination of literacy/numeracy. The polytechnic says: 'Older students are very welcome at PNL and emphasises commitment to mature students, second-career trainers and 'second chances'.' *Part-Time Degrees*: New modular degree schemes in Humanities, Science and Social Science allow a flexible approach to part-time day or evening study, with a wide range of subjects. BA/BA (Hons) Combined Studies – specifically for students over 21, special consideration for non-standard qualifications; BSc Architecture; BSC/BSc (Hons) Chemistry; BEd(Hons) – in-service for qualified teachers. *Associate Student Scheme*: Over 50 units available at preliminary, intermediate and final levels (evenings), can lead to a degree. No specific experience needed for preliminary units. Advisory service to help you choose your level of entry. *Postgraduate Vocational Courses*: Diploma in Computing, full time or part time (conversion course for graduates *without* existing qualifications in computing). Diploma in Health Facility Planning, full time – for graduates with planning experience, architects, doctors, nurses, engineers, administrators. Diploma in Labour Studies, full time or part time – for those seeking graduate membership of the Institute of Personnel Management. Diploma in Library and Information Studies, full time or part time – any degree, preferably but not essentially with library experience (PNL can arrange this).

Queen Mary College, University of London

Welcomes applications from mature students, and over 10% of undergraduates are in this category. Many enter with the usual qualifications, but some are admitted on the basis of other evidence of their ability to study: for example, candidates who have been studying with the Open University and have at least two full credits (gained by course work and examination) with at least one above Foundation level. Access courses are also taken into account. Applicants, who should be aged 21 or over at the proposed date of entry can obtain advice about the acceptability of their qualifications. *Postgraduate Vocational Courses*: MSc/Diploma in Information Technology, full time – for graduates with little computing or electronic experience. MSc Chemical Research, full time – graduates with relevant degrees wishing to develop research expertise. MSc Biochemistry and Chemistry Applied to Medicine, full time (in association with London University Medical College) – for Chemistry and Biochemistry graduates who wish to develop interests in clinical applications of science, and Medical or Dental graduates wishing to develop aspects of basic sciences related to other subjects. MSc/Diploma in Astrophysics, full time or evenings. Diplomas in Intellectual Property Law, International Commercial Arbitration Law, Media Law, full time – for graduates in any discipline whose undergraduate course or previous training/experience is such as to qualify them for admission. (Non-graduates may be admitted in appropriate cases.) MSc in Law and Science: Intellectual Property, full time – for graduates in Mathematics, Engineering and the Natural, Medical and Computer Sciences.

St Mary's College, Strawberry Hill

Mature student concessions possible for those aged 21 and over. They must offer qualifications of equivalent value to the normal entry requirements and demonstrate capacity and academic attainment to enable them to manage the course they have chosen. *Postgraduae Vocational Courses*: Postgraduate Certificate in Education, full time – any graduate. Postgraduate Certificate in the Education of Adults (Religious Education), full time – any graduate. Diploma in the Teaching of English as a Second Language, full time or part time – for those with qualified teacher status; teachers without a teaching qualification considered. Diploma in Drama and Theatre Arts, evenings and two weekends - for secondary school teachers of theatre arts courses, those involved in community work and those involved in amateur theatre. Diploma in Heritage Interpretation, full time – any degree entry.

South Bank Polytechnic

Mature student concessions possible for those aged over 21. Selection by many methods. 'Course directors need to be satisfied that the applicant will benefit from the course and is likely to pass. All courses have a number of mature/exceptional entry students.'

Thames Polytechnic
Mature candidates of 21 years and over without usual entry requirements considered if they have other academic qualifications, experience or evidence of ability related to their chosen course. At Avery Hill Campus, BEd (Hons) degree is particularly attractive to mature students. *Part-Time Degrees*: BA (Hons) Architecture, intended for those working in an architect's office; BSc (Hons) Applied Biology; BA (Hons) Business Studies; BSc (Hons) Applied Chemistry; BSc/BSc (Hons) Computing Science; BEng/BEng (Hons) for mature students only, with experience in Civil Engineering and holding a Higher Certificate at a good standard; BEng/BEng (Hons) Electrical and Electronic, for students working in industry; BEng/BEng (Hons) Mechanical, for students working in industry; BA/BA (Hons) Political Economy; BA (Hons) Humanities; BSc/BSc (Hons) Materials Science; BSc Mathematics, Statistics and Computing; BA (Hons) Sociology; BSc Building Surveying; BSc/BSc (Hons) Estate Management; BSc Quantity Surveying. *Associate Student Scheme*: lead to degree entry. *Postgraduate Vocational Courses*: Architecture, full time. Postgraduate Certificate in Education, full time. Postgraduate Diploma in Physics (retraining course for qualified teachers), full time or part time. Diploma in Chemical Analysis, part time – for graduates with a degree in which chemistry has been a major component. Postgraduate Diploma in Scientific and Engineering Computation, part time – for graduates in computing, mathematics, engineering or a physical science. Postgraduate Diploma in Electronic and Molecular Properties of Materials, part time – for graduates in physics, chemistry, materials science, electronic engineering.

University College, University of London
Mature candidates 21 and over given individual consideration. They must satisfy course requirements but in some circumstances may be exempted from the general entrance requirement.

West London Institute
Special entry procedures for candidates who are not less than 21 on 31st December in the year of entry. Normally, evidence of academic ability at the appropriate level is required, as well as the motivation and potential for study. *Part-Time Degrees*: BA/BA (Hons) Humanities, choosing two subjects from American Studies, English, Geography, History, Religious Studies. *Postgraduate Vocational Courses*: Postgraduate Certificate in Education, full time. Bilingual Secretarial, full time – for those with relevant degree and A-level in French or Italian. Personal Assistant, full time – any degree acceptable. Accountancy Conversion course, part time.

The following colleges in this region supplied information in 1987 about their degree and advanced courses but no response was received to 1988 enquiries. Readers may nevertheless wish to make individual contact:

City of London Polytechnic

Ealing College of Higher Education
Goldsmith's College, University of London
Harrow College of Higher Education
Imperial College of Science and Technology
King's College, London, University of London

Southern and Eastern England

Bedford College of Higher Education
Mature students over the age of 21 may apply for courses even though they do not possess specified academic qualifications.Special consideration is given to each individual case. *Part-Time Degrees*: BA (Hons) Combined Studies – open to students aged 21 and over, selected on the basis of individual merit rather than formal qualifications alone. Students with certain relevant qualifications,such as Open University credits, may claim exemption from part of the course. Group 1 options are: Ecological Studies, English, French, History, Human Geography, Outdoor Recreation Studies, Sociology. Minor Group 2 Options are Computer Studies, Drama, Ecological Studies,Romanticism and Realism. You must take two from Group 1 and one from Group 2. *Postgraduate Vocational Courses*: Postgraduate Certificate in Education (Primary) or PE/Dance (Secondary), full time.

Bognor Regis: West Sussex Institute of Higher Education
Entry concessions possible for students over 21. Mature entry test procedure is essay followed by interview. All degree courses attract late starters.

Brighton Polytechnic
Entry concessions possible for students over 21. Each candidate's application considered on individual merits – education, job experience, personal background, etc. BA Social Administration, BA Humanities among the most popular courses. *Part-Time Degrees*: BA (Hons) Humanities. DipHE/BA (Hons) Business Studies. BSc Nursing Studies – practising registered nurses. BEd (Hons) – for serving teachers. *Postgraduate Vocational Courses*: Postgraduate Certificate in Education, full time. MSc/Diploma Information Systems, full time – any first- or second-class honours degree acceptable, but employment experience is an advantage. MSc/Diploma Microprocessor Technology and Applications, full time – any degree in engineering or science acceptable, but usually not *recent* degrees in electronic engineering. MA/Postgraduate Diploma in Printmaking, part time – for graduates in Art and Design. MA Social Policy – for experienced practitioners with relevant first degree and, exceptionally, applicants with relevant experience without

relevant degree qualification, on demonstration of ability to achieve postgraduate level. Mode not specified – ask college. MA/Postgraduate Diploma in Regional History, for applicants with established interest in history and/or related first degree. Mode not specified – ask college.

Brighton: University of Sussex
Entry concessions for mature and/or unqualified candidates. 'The University will consider mature unqualified candidates for all courses in the Arts and Social Studies area, but candidates without the required Science qualifications will have to demonstrate their abilities in this field if they are applying for a course in the Science area. However, the University does offer a four-year course in Physics or Engineering for candidates without qualifications in science.Special Entry Scheme for Mature and/or Unqualified candidates: all selected will be required to complete a supplementary application form and either write an essay of not more than 2000 words based on one of two books nominated by the University, related to their proposed course of study, or they may, on request submit a recent piece of written work. They are also interviewed. Unqualified candidates will be required to sit the University's entrance examination on the same day as the interview; this exam offers a wide choice of questions on general topics. A mathematics test may be given to candidates applying for courses with a specific requirement for O-level Mathematics.'

Cambridge: Cambridgeshire College of Arts and Technology
Entry concessions possible for students over 21 (often advised to do a preliminary course, e.g. an A-level, to prepare them for the advanced study of a degree). All degree and diploma courses welcome mature students. *Part-Time Degrees*: BA/BSc (Hons) Geography with Economics or Sociology. BA (Hons) Humanities/Social Studies (two subjects chosen from: Economics, Sociology, English, History, the Study of Art, European Thought and Literature, Geography, Spanish, French). *Postgraduate Vocational Courses*: Linguist/Secretary, full time. Personal Assistant/Executive Secretary, full time.

Cambridge University
If you have not previously completed a course at a university or similar institution of higher education, and will be 25 years of age or over by 1st October of the year in which you hope to come to Cambridge, you may apply to come as a mature student. The normal matriculation requirements of entry may be relaxed,though candidates will be expected to produce evidence of high academic potential and recent academic study. Some candidates may be asked to take A-levels, and in other cases a written exercise may be set by the College. Before making formal application, you should approach one or more Colleges, enclosing a very brief c.v. and statement of future plans. Most Colleges admit some mature students, but

the greatest numbers are admitted by Lucy Cavendish (women only), St Edmund's House and Wolfson. Mature students should apply on a special yellow form which is obtainable from any College or from the Cambridge Intercollegiate Applications Office (prospectus with details of colleges and courses from CIAO, address in index). Also *Affiliated Students*: – graduates with an approved degree of another University admitted to work for a Cambridge BA in two years instead of the usual three. If you're accepted, look out for the Cambridge University Students Union *Mature Students Briefing*, free booklet devised to help late entrants settle into university life, and make the most of the facilities provided for them.

Canterbury: Christ Church College

Entry concessions possible for students aged 23 on 1st October in the year of admission. Candidates may be accepted with one A-level or equivalent (e.g. an Access course) rather than the usual two A-levels for entry. Degrees which attract late starters are Art, Education, English, Geography, History, Maths, Movement Studies,Music, Radio/Film/TV Studies, Religious Studies,Science and Occupational Therapy (the Occupational Therapy Honours degree is the first in England).*Postgraduate Vocational Courses*: Postgraduate Certificate in Education, full time. Diploma in Teaching English as a Foreign Language, full time.

Canterbury: University of Kent

Entry concessions sympatheticallyconsidered for those aged 23 and over (also minimum age limit for entry to part time degrees). Candidates without standard A-level qualifications asked to produce evidence of mature-age study – written work or alternative qualifications, such as Access or BTEC awards. *Part-Time degrees*: BA (Hons) French, BA (Hons) Humanities (English), BA (Hons) Social Sciences, BA (Hons) Specialised Social Sciences - e.g. Economics, Politics and Government, Industrial Relations, Social Statistics, etc. Students specialise in a subject selected from the range of options within the full time Social Science course (15 options). Also part time Diplomas, including Ecology, Women's Studies, Theology, Local History, English Literature, Archaeology, German, Italian, Social Sciences, Law. *Postgraduate Vocational Courses*: MSC-sponsored Diploma in Computing, full time – for graduates in subjects other than computing.

Higher Education in Later Life: viewpoint

'When people reach their later 20s, 30s, 40s, many of them feel they have somehow missed out on educational oportunities that are still there, and this is a very important part of their motivation. There are also many adults who feel that if only they had that magic piece of paper, their potential would be much better used, either by their present employer, or another employer. Some are nervous when they first come to university, but the chances are that, because they've been around, perhaps travelled abroad

and had some experience of life, they begin to see the relevance of what the teachers are trying to put across, and then everything starts to slot into place. Your mind is that much more receptive if you've had some experience.'
[Spokesperson, University of Kent at Canterbury]

Colchester Institute
No uniform policy towards mature students. 'In general, admission of mature students with unconventional qualiications is left to the discretion of individual course tutors, but it is true to say that most tutors are sympathetic. The overriding considerations are: Will the student be successful on the course? Will they benefit by being on the course? Would they deprive another student of a place who would be more likely to be successful or benefit more?' Late starters particularly attracted by the BA Music and Graduate Diploma in Music. The college says: 'We encourage adult students to apply for courses and course tutors will waive formal entry requirements where a mature student will show that they can benefit from the course. We are increasingly finding that the inclusion of adult students on full-time classes previously largely composed of school leavers creates a more stable learning atmosphere for the youngsters.'

Colchester: The University of Essex
Entry requirements more flexible for students over 21. Selectors look for evidence of ability to undertake degree-level work, adequate preparation interms of study skills and, where first-year courses presuppose it, detailed subject knowledge (principally for science, mathematics and engineering). Open University Foundation courses, Return to Study, Access and similar courses are considered in lieu of A-levels. Applicants for Comparative Studies, Social Sciences and Law degree courses may be asked to take an entrance examination.

Croydon College
Postgraduate Vocational Courses: Diploma for Personal Assistants, full time – any degree. Certificate of Qualification in Social Work, full time – appropriate degree plus one year of social work experience.

Egham: Royal Holloway and Bedford New College, University of London
Mature student concessions apply at 23. Each case is considered on its merits, but mature student applications are welcomed.

Guildford: University of Surrey
A wide range of entry qualifications is acceptable as an alternative to A-levels for applicants aged 21 and over. These include Open University credits, CNAA certificate courses and other courses specially designed to assist mature students to re-start academic study. Surrey University has

links with a number of Access programmes and is currently planning such courses with Chichester and Guildford Colleges of Technology.

Hatfield Polytechnic

Entry concessions possible for students over 21: entry by interview and/or essay. *Associate Student* scheme may also lead into degree course. *Part-Time Degrees*: BSc/BSc (Hons) Mathematics, BSc/BSc (Hons) Applied Biology, BSc/BSc (Hons) Applied Chemistry, BSc/BSc (Hons) Computer Science, BA/BA (Hons) English, BEd, BA/BA (Hons) Contemporary Studies, BA/BA (Hons) Humanities. *Postgraduate Vocational Courses* include Diploma in Careers Education and Guidance, full time – any degree acceptable.

Associate Student Route: viewpoint

'After I'd taken a New Opportunities for Women course, I decided to carry on and become an Associate Student. I was committed to attend college just one morning a week, and chose the course 'Introduction to Sociology'. I followed on with two more courses as an Associate, and at that point I thought I would join the degree course as a proper student. It is a part-time degree, and because I have done course units as an Associate, I was exempted from those and could join the appropriate year.'

'My company gives time off during the working week for staff to take individual Associate student courses. I'm taking Advanced Maths, which fits in with the sort of work I do. This is a subject that is used in my job that I haven't really covered before, where you tend to use computer programs. The course lets you look inside the black box of the computer, which enables you to understand better what's going on and make better decisions.'

'Having taken the Polyprep course, I couldn't wait to get to the Polytechnic to start on the degree course. It takes four years part-time, but I'm at the end of my sixth year, as I've failed twice to do exams which you must pass in order to go forward to the next year. Nevertheless, I have now arrived at the final year. I've passed 11 subjects (22 modules) and now need just two more to get my degree. Yes, it's very tough, but stimulating beyond words.'

[Part-time students, Hatfield Polytechnic]

'Associate Student courses are not special courses; they are constituent parts of all the degrees we run. We originally put forward a policy statement to our Academic Board saying that we were willing to open up all our degrees to mature students – undergraduate or postgraduate courses. The only proviso would be that the students must be counselled beforehand. Obviously, if someone comes along and wants to take a third-year course in pharmacology and they'd never done any, we'd be crazy to accept that student. Students come in for their counselling sessions and can then take from one to three units, either from the same degree, or from different degrees if that helps them, and they share lectures and seminars with normal enrolled degree students. They have to do their course work, but

they don't have to take the examinations unless they want to do so.'
[Spokesperson, Hatfield Polytechnic]

High Wycombe: Buckinghamshire College of Higher Education
Entry concessions possible on BSc Furniture Production, sandwich, BSc Timber Technology and BSc Sociology. Candidates over the age of 21 with relevant industrial experience may be admitted without usual academic qualifications. *Postgraduate Vocational Courses*: Diploma in Timber Studies, full time – conversion course for graduates from other disciplines. Senior Secretarial course full time – any degree acceptable. Bilingual Secretarial course full time – degree in one foreign language. Diploma in European Marketing Management,full time, degree plus oral ability in French, German, Spanish or Italian plus three years' work experience. Diploma in Export Marketing, full time – any degree acceptable.

Kingston Polytechnic
Entry concessions possible for students over 21. The usual method of deciding on concessions is for students to be interviewed: then a decision as to any entry waiver will be made. There are specific problems with waiver of entry requirements where the course also leads to exemption from a professional body examination. *Part-Time Degreees*: BA/BA (Hons) Combined Studies (two fields, chosen from Economics, Geography, History, History of Art, Architecture and Design, History of Ideas, Labour Studies, Literature, Mathematics, Music, Public Sector Policy Studies, Politics and Sociology). No formal entry requirements – course is specifically for mature students 21 and over. Also BEd for serving teachers, part time; BA (Hons) Music Education, part time; BEng/BEng (Hons), part time for HNC entrants; BA/BA (Hons) and BSc/BSc (Hons) Geography part time. *Postgraduate Vocational Courses*: include MSC-sponsored Engineering, full time; Diploma in Marketing, full time - any degree acceptable; Postgraduate Certificate in Education, full time; MSc Information Technology – any degree acceptable, preferably including computing experience.

Luton College of Higher Education
Entry concessions possible for students aged over 21. *Part-Time Degrees*: BSc (Hons) Biology or Geography and Geology. *Postgraduate Vocational Courses*: Diploma for Personal Assistants, full time – any degree acceptable.

Milton Keynes: The Open University
All courses are by distance-learning methods. Not only are there no qualifications required for entry to an OU *undergraduate degree* course – there is no selection as such. Applications are dealt with in order of receipt, i.e. on a 'first come, first served' principle. You, the student decide if you are able to study for a degree. You also decide how many years it will take; if you need to take a year off because of a change of job or house, or home circumstances,

you are free to do so, and resume study when you are ready. Courses are based on the credit system. You build up your record of successful work through full or half credits. If you've successfully completed previous higher-level study, you may gain exemption from up to three credits. An ordinary degree requires six credits; an honours degree eight credits. You have a choice of more than 130 courses from which to build up your credits. They span the Arts, Social Sciences, Mathematics, Science, Technology and Educational Studies. All students have to take a Foundation Course, which assumes no previous knowledge of the subject and provides a broad introduction to a range of subjects and to study skills. After that they can choose courses at any level. Tutition uses correspondence texts, television and radio broadcasts, home experiment kits, tutorial help through 250 study centres spread throughout the UK (telephone tutorials are possible) and summer schools. For people not ready to commit themselves to a full degree course there is an *Associate Student* programme; you can choose to study part of an undergraduate course and if you later want to apply for a degree course place, the work you've done can be assessed and counted towards your OU degree. The University also offers *Higher Degrees* and *Continuing Education* provisions, including the Open Business School. NB: The application period for undergraduate study is from January to the end of September for studies beginning the following year.

Questions people ask about the Open University

'Can I qualify as a doctor through the Open University?'

No – there are no OU first degrees in medicine (nor are there first degrees in dentistry or veterinary science). For these you must attend a conventional university.

'Can I study with the Open University if I go abroad?'

Yes, if you are a member of the British armed forces serving in West Germany or Cyprus, or a dependent of such a person (limited range of courses). Yes, if you are a resident of Brussels or Luxembourg. Yes, if you are a merchant seaman; your course material can be forwarded by the College of the Sea. If you begin your degree studies in the UK, but susequently have to move abroad, you can usually continue your studies if you have a forwarding address in the UK, i.e. someone who'll act as your intermediary and send course materials to you.

'Can I get a grant to take an Open University degree?'

Not very likely. Some local authorities or employers will help with the cost of fees or attending summer school. But the OU itself has a scheme to help people who are unemployed or on a low income with the cost of fees.

'Do I have to be a mature student?'

Depends what you mean by 'mature'. The minimum age limit for entry is 18. There is no upper age limit.

Norwich City College

Students over 21 are given special consideration. For the BA Hospitality Management course, students over 21 may be admitted without formal qualifications if in the view of the college, they have the necessary motivation, potential and knowledge to succeed. (See also 'Retraining and New Skills Courses'.)

Norwich: University of East Anglia

Entry concessions possible for students over 23. They must submit evidence of ability to pursue the course – for instance, professional qualifications obtained by examination or examinations deemed equivalent to A-levels. (Individual schools may have different/additional requirements.) The university says: 'The Schools of English and American Studies, Economic and Social Studies, Development Studies and Environmental Sciences all run courses attractive to mature students, particularly History and Philosophy. Law generally has a few mature students, while the School of Information Systems attracts mature applicants who have a flair for computing but need to obtain formal qualifications.' *Part-Time Degrees*: American Studies, Development Studies, History of Art, Philosophy, Sociology, also part time BEd for serving teachers. Wide range of part time postgraduate degrees. *Postgraduate Vocational Courses*: Apply to the university, but note that a programme of Museum courses is offered in the Sainsbury Centre for Visual Arts and the Audio-Visual centre has occasional openings for graduates wishing to train for work in television.

Portsmouth Polytechnic

Entry concessions possible for students aged 21-plus, varying according to department. Students are usually assessed on ability to add background experience and whether they are able to cope with and successfully complete the course. Social Studies and BA (Hons) English and European Literature are popular with mature students, but most courses have a few late starters.

Reading: Bulmershe College of Higher Education

Entry concessions possible over 21. 'We look for either two GCE A-level passes or for other evidence that you have the necessary motivation, potential and knowledge to succeed. We may ask for an example of your written work before reaching a decision.' Mature students are welcome on the BA and BEd full time degrees. *Part-Time Degrees*: BA/BA (Hons) Combined Studies. Major options are English Literature and Geography and Development Studies. Minor courses are in Art and Art History, Film and Drama, French, History, Modern English Literature, Philosophy, United States Studies and Landscape Studies. *Postgraduate Vocational Courses*: Postgraduate Certificate in Education, full time. (See also 'Retraining and New Skills Courses'.)

Reading University
Entry concessions possible for students over 21 on Arts and Social Sciences courses, over 23 on other courses. Applications are welcomed from students on Access courses. Late starters are generally valued on all full-time degree courses. *Postgraduate Vocational Courses*: Wide range of Master's degrees; also: Postgraduate Certificate in Education, full time; Certificate in Vocational Guidance, full time – candidates with any degree considered. Interesting range of Diploma and Master's courses for graduates from, or with experience of, developing countries.

St Albans: Hertfordshire College of Art and Design
Entry concessions possible for students over 21 – alternatives to A-levels, for example. Candidates may be required to demonstrate their academic ability with a short piece of writing organised as part of an interview. *Part-Time Degrees*: Fine Art. *Postgraduate Vocational Courses*: Diploma in Dramatherapy, full time or part time – for those with an appropriate degree or professional qualification in occupational therapy, psychiatric nursing, social work or drama teaching, plus relevant work experience and developed interest and practice in drama. Diploma in Art Therapy, full time or part time. Candidates must be over 21, with a degree in Art and Design (other disciplines involving art considered), plus professional qualification in occupational therapy, psychiatric nursing, psychiatry, psychotherapy, social work, teaching or clinical psychology plus portfolio of work plus relevant work experience.

Southampton Institute of Higher Education
In association with the La Sainte Union College of Higher Education, the Institute offers a *Part-Time Degree* in Modern Languages and European Studies, including a programme for DipHE. The course incorporates a Foundation Year, from which applicants with the normal entry requirements may be wholly or partially exempted. Mature students who do not possess the usual five GCE passes with two at A-level, including a modern language other than English may apply for exceptional entry to the course. A preparatory course of one year is advised for students without previous knowledge of a modern language or who have reached less than O-level standard. The degree is organised in three-hour modules over morning, afternoon and evening study periods, so it should be possible to devise a study programme, with the help of tutors, to fit in with other commitments at work or home.

Southampton University
Entry concessions possible for students over 21. Normal entry requirements waived but evidence of 'recent serious study' is required. One or two A-level passes, successful completion of an Open University Foundation course or of an appropriate Access course could be acceptable. Departments which

admit significant numbers of mature students include English, Sociology and Social Policy, Social Work Studies, Psychology.

Surbiton: Hillcroft College
Residential college for women. Provides full time and part time CNAA Modular Certificate courses open to unqualified students seeking to reassess their capabilities and plan for a future career or higher education. Those who complete the two year option may be able to enter directly into the second year of a degree course. Those who choose the social work option within the Certificate improve their prospects of a place on the Certificate of Qualification in Social Work course (CQSW). There are also part time Returning to Learning courses, afternoon and evening classes, and one-week residential courses at Easter and in the summer holiday period. Candidates should be at least 21 and there is no upper age limit. Mandatory grants are available for students on full time courses.

Watford College
Entry concessions for mature students possible at any age, says college. Students may be selected on the basis of industrial experience plus interview. BSc (Hons) Printing and Packaging Technology and HND in Printing are attractive to late starters.*Postgraduate Vocational Courses*: Postgraduate Diploma in Advertising, full time – any degree acceptable. Overseas Stream for the Postgraduate Diploma in Advertising, full time – any degree acceptable. Diploma in Publishing, full time – any degree acceptable.

Wimbledon School of Art
Entry concessions possible for students over 21. All are interviewed at first choice stage, some may be accepted with reduced GCE requirements. Significant mature entry to Art Foundation course. *Postgraduate Vocational Courses*: CNAA Diploma in Printmaking for graduates in Art and Design or equivalent; other degree subjects and non-graduates also considered. CNAA Diploma in Higher Education for Theatre Wardrobe, full time, includes costume design as well as costume making. College emphasises that this is an *advanced* course. Selection is by interview. Candidates must submit examples of their work, which must include evidence of ability in sewing.

Winchester: King Alfred's College
Entry concessions possible for students over 21. Candidates may be accepted with only one A-level, or via Access course, Return to Study, essay, Open University credit, certain professional qualifications, etc. *Part-Time Degrees*: BA (Hons) History with English.

The following college in this region supplied information in 1987 about advanced courses, but no response was received in 1988 to enquiries. Readers may nevertheless wish to make individual contact:

Worthing: Northbrook College

Central England

Birmingham: Aston University
Entry concessions possible for mature students aged 23 or over on entry, who have pursued study to a suitable level, even though they may not meet the formal entry requirements for the desired degree.

Birmingham Polytechnic
Entry concessions for mature students, 21 and over. Various routes: Special Admissions Procedure – interview and/or submission of piece of written work; Access course via college of further education; Assciate Student entry (see below). Direct entry to second year of some courses for candidates already holding advanced qualifications: e.g., someone with HND may be admitted directly to second year of a degree. Mature students welcome on all courses. *Part-Time Degrees* BA/BA (Hons) Business Studies. BA/BA (Hons) Economics. BEng Electronic Engineering. BA (Hons) English Language and Literature. BSc Estate Management. BA/BA (Hons) Government. BEng/BEng (Hons) Mechanical Engineering. BEd (Hons) Multicultural Studies (qualified teachers). BSc Nursing (qualified nurses with advanced qualifications).BSc Quantity Surveying. *Associate Student* scheme: incorporates Visiting and Listening Students Programme. You can choose any of over 200 units of study, in areas such as Business Studies, Law, Social Science, Health Science,Art and Design, Primary Education, Built Environment, Computing and Information Studies and Engineering and Science. Associate students attend daytime or evenings, usually for about two hours a week for each unit studied. *Postgraduate Vocational Courses* include: Postgraduate Certificate in Education, full time; Diploma in Industrial Design, full time or part time – for graduates in Art and Design or, exceptionally, Engineering, Architecture, Management or Education; Diploma in the Management of Modern Technology, part time – for graduates in engineering, technology, science or business studies, or with relevant experience; Diploma in Librarianship and Information Studies, full time or part time – any graduate with at least nine months' library or information experience. For science graduates, MSC-sponsored full time conversion courses at postgraduate level in Software Engineering, Microelectronics and Computer Technology and Electronics Manufacture are available.

Part-Time at the Polytechnic: viewpoints

'I was at a disadvantage at school from the start because I only came to Britain from the West Indies when I was ten. I left school at 15 feeling I'd done very little. It was much later in life, after my divorce, when I had children to look after, that I thought of trying to do something that would give me a better position in life and make a future for them. I've started on a Listening Student course, and at the start, when I saw the younger students and they were discussing topics I knew nothing about, I felt very unsure of myself. After a period of time, I realised that as far as the course was concerned, the young students were basically at the same level as I was. They were no better than me and I was no better than them. It gave me security and I felt I was really laying a foundation for the future.'

'I wanted to do something on a Friday morning when I had time to spare, so I just looked in to the Poly to see what was on on a Friday. It turned out to be Comparative Government. It was such a long time since I'd studied (I had taken an HND before) that I just sat and shook for the first quarter of an hour. I couldn't write at all. But I managed to pass Comparative Government in the end, partly because it was continuous assessment and the marks I'd got for my essays were taken into account. Then they asked me if I would like to take the part-time degree in Government. I had two exemptions because of my HND, so I did two years as a part-time student, and then the Polytechnic advisers suggested I went full-time – they found that because I'd only had two years of grant for my HND, I could get another year of grant to finish my degree. I'm now enrolled as a postgraduate student doing research into politics abroad.'

[Students, City of Birmingham Polytechnic]

'It's my experience, having worked with adults now for going on 15 years, that very often their intellectual horizons broaden, and as they broaden, so does their belief in themselves and what they can do. They start by thinking the young 18- and 19-year-olds who've come in with A-levels are so much better and brighter, when in practice what we find is somewhat the reverse. The 18- and 19-year-olds can be intimidated by the self-confidence and the experience and knowledge of the world that the mature student has. There is a dedication and motivation among mature students that I as a teacher find positively exhilarating and very, very rewarding.'

[Spokesperson, City of Birmingham Polytechnic]

Birmingham: Newman and Westhill Colleges

Entry to BEd possible for mature students via special university examinations and/or Access courses. *Postgraduate Vocational Courses*: Postgraduate Certificate in Primary Education, full time.

Coventry Polytechnic

Entry concessions possible for students over 21. 'Often they will simply be interviewed to satisfy course admissions tutors they have the commitment/capacity to cope with the course. They may have to demonstrate aptitude in certain subjects for certain courses, e.g. in Mathematics and English, but this would be decided on an individual basis with the tutor and potential student.' *Associate Student* scheme – may also lead into degree course. *Part-Time Degrees*: BSc Remedial Health Sciences (for professionally qualified occupational therapists, physiotherapists, etc.) DipHE/BA/BA (Hons) Social Studies. DipHE/BA/BA (Hons) Modern Studies. BA/BA (Hons) Applied Economics. *Postgraduate Vocational Courses*: Diploma in Electronic Graphics, full time – for graduates in Art and Design subjects; others considered. Diploma and Certificate in Craft, Design and Technology, full time and part time – conversion course for teachers. Diploma in Engineering Systems, full time and part time – for graduates in engineering, technology or science; others considered. Diploma in Computer-Aided Engineering, full time and part time – gradutes in mechanical or production engineering; others considered. MSC-sponsored Diploma in Robotics – Systems and Applications, full time; for graduates in Mechanical, Electrical, Production, Control or similar Engineering subjects, Physics, Mathematics, Computer Science, or Chartered Engineer, or HNC/HND in Mechanical, Production or Electrical Engineering and two years approved industrial experience. Diploma in Employment Relations, full time – any graduate, holder of Diploma in Technology, HNC/HND with appropriate work experience, professional society qualification; other candidates considered - entry concessions possible for those over 27.

Derby: Derbyshire College of Higher Education

Entry concessions possible for mature students with experience or aptitude for the chosen course. Students may like to note: BA (Hons) Photographic Studies – those lacking normal entry qualifications may be admitted if they show particular aptitude for photographic studies; BA (Hons) Earth and Life Studies; BSc Power Engineering, where special provision is made for mature students; and BEd (Hons), for which mature candidates over 23 who lack the usual qualifications but who have recently studied at an appropriate academic level and show special promise may be allowed to sit a Special Entrance Examination set by the University of Nottingham. All BEd candidates must have GCE O-level or equivalent in both English Language and Mathematics. For the Bachelor of Combined Studies (Hons) candidates may sit the Special Entrance Examination or enrol for the college's Pathway course, part time, which offers direct entry. *Postgraduate Vocational Courses*: Postgraduate Certificate in Education, full time. Graduate Bilingual Secretarial course, full time - for candidates with degrees in French and/or German, or other degrees with O/A-level in the appropriate language.

Keele University

Entry concessions possible for mature students aged 19 or over on 1st October of the year in which they wish to be admitted, who have been away from full-time education for three years, and have in the recent past attended a systematic course of study (Adult Education classes, Further Education course, Open University, Access course, etc.). NB: though candidates for three-year degrees must satisfy *course requirements*, i.e. have passes in any A-level exams or OU/Access credits specified for a particular degree, there are *no course requirements* for any four-year degree course. These begin with a multidisciplinary Foundation Year. About 10% of undergraduates at Keele are mature students.

Loughborough: Co-operative College

See 'Pre-Entry, Sample and Access Courses', which is the section in which the college authorities requested that details of their courses should appear.

Loughborough University

Considers sympathetically applications from mature students aged 21 and over, outside its normal matriculation requirements. Admission may be granted on the basis of individually approved qualifications such as Access courses, or interview and special assignments. *Part-Time Degres*: BA (Hons) English. *Postgraduate Vocational Courses*: MSC-sponsored Information Technology, full time or part time - conversion course for graduates of any discipline. MSC-sponsored Theory and Applications of Computation, full time - conversion course for graduates in disciplines other than computer science. MSC-sponsored Computer Integrated Engineering, full time – aimed at mathematics graduates and others who are mathematically inclined. Postgraduate Diploma/MA/MSc in Library and Information Studies/Information Studies/Archives/Publishing/School Librarianship, full time – for graduates of any discipline, normally with a year's experience of work in a library, documentation centre, records office or the book trade. MSc Recreation Management, full time – open to graduates from industry, recreation, tourism, local government, town and country planning, professional sport, community development and education; preference for those with work experience, but others considered. MSc Polymer Technology, full time or part time – for graduates in science, engineering or an appropriate technology-based discipline. MSc Airport Planning and Management, full time or part time – for graduates in transport, human geography, economics, business and management studies, civil engineering or planning, or other graduates with work experience in airports or other organisations concerned with aviation. MA/MSc Negotiated Studies, full time or part time – appropriate for mature students who have clear ideas about their needs and who are prepared to devote considerable effort to developing a personal syllabus of study. Any first degree is acceptable and mode of attendance is determined by the negotiated syllabus. Postgraduate Diploma/MA Labour

Market Studies, part time, for graduates of any discipline with an interest in the way in which the labour market operates. Postgraduate Diploma/MA Labour Studies, part time – for graduates of any discipline.

Northampton: Nene College
Entry concessions for mature students. Note specially BA/BSc (Hons) Combined Studies (choice of 29 subjects). One quarter of all enrolments are mature students: those without the normal academic requirements, but with equivalent professional qualifications, or OU Credit, or one A-level, or successful completion of an Access course are invited to apply. *Part-Time Degrees*: BSc (Hons) Chemical Science, for holders of BTEC HNC Science (Chemistry) or equivalent. BSc (Hons) Health Science Studies – for members of one of the recognised Professions Supplementary to Medicine, or for Registered Nurses, with at least two years' post-qualification experience. BEd (Hons) for qualified teachers. *Postgraduate Vocational Qualifications*: Postgraduate Certificate in Education, full time. College Diploma for Personal Assistants, full time – graduate in any discipline considered; options in Personnel Management, Marketing, Law.

Oxford: Plater College
This is The Catholic Workers' College. For students aged over 21 (no upper age limit), offering the chance to study for one or two years at university standard. All courses lead to qualifications of the University of Oxford and involve a study of Catholic social teaching.No formal educational qualifications are needed: 'Average intelligence and love of God and neighbour are qualifications enough. Students come from all walks of life – manual and office workers, skilled and unskilled, married and single, laity and religious – and from all parts of the world, although most come from the United Kingdom.' Adult Education Bursaries are payable to cover fees and maintenance. The college has asked that all their courses should be listed: Two-year courses: Oxford University Special Diploma in Social Studies; Oxford University Special Diploma in Social Administration; Plater College Diploma in Theology and Social Studies; Plater College Diploma in Youth and Community Studies. One-year courses: - Plater College Certificate in Social Ethics; Plater College Certificate in Social Studies for Pastoral Ministry.

Oxford Polytechnic
Entry concessions possible for mature students aged 21 and over. Note specially modular degree course available on *full-time*, *part-time* or *mixed-mode* basis: you can vary the amount of time you spend studying. A 'module' is a study unit: there are 800 different modules available. Each module represents between one-quarter and one-third of a term's work for most full-time students. A DipHE can be achieved by studying 20 modules, a degree by studying 28, and an honours degree by studying 30 modules. Most students on modular courses combine the study of two 'Fields' – a field

is a single area of study like psychology or law, food science, catering, publishing, musical studies, microelectronic systems and so on. Full list from polytechnic. Also available: non-modular degrees, including BA (Hons) Planning Studies, for which mature students are encouraged to apply, even though they may not hold the minimum entry qualifications. *Postgraduate Vocational Courses* include: Postgraduate Certificate in Education, full time; Diploma in Urban Planning, full time or part time – for graduates from social science or design disciplines.

Oxford: Ruskin College
A college providing further education for working men and women, which from its foundation has had close links with the trade union movement (many scholarships are offered by individual trade unions and by the Trades Union Congress Educational Trust). The minimum age of entry is 20, the average age of students is normally about 30 and formal entrance qualifications are not required for admissions (preference is given to those who have had little or no full-time education beyond the statutory school-leaving age, though evidence of efforts towards self-education e.g. serious reading, adult education classes, trade union schools, etc. – is an advantage). Students are selected partly on the basis of their record in voluntary work and service to the community, especially through the trade union movement and associated bodies. Adult Education Bursaries are usually available for fees and maintenance. Course choices include: Labour Studies, Literature, Development Studies, History, Social Studies, Applied Social Studies. A four-week residential course in Advanced Trade Union Studies is also available and can be followed by a one-year distance-learning programme. Computer Access and Language Study facilities are available.

Study at an Adult Residential College: viewpoints
'I left school at 16 with three O-levels and went to work in the Health Service, where I stayed for about 13 years, ending up with a job as a technician in a cardiac unit. I was active in a Union branch and became branch secretary, finding that I was a good organiser. I began to realise, though, that there were great gaps in my education and I needed the discipline of being somewhere to study. Just reading by yourself and studying by yourself, you feel there's always something else to take you away from what you're doing. I thought Ruskin College was the kind of place I could function in because I would be studying with people who were older, like myself. I felt I would meet people from a similar background and therefore we'd all be starting from the same point. The hardest part of the selection was having to write an essay – the first one I'd done since 'compositions' at school. The interview wasn't too bad; it was arranged through my union and the college tutor and wasn't too daunting. I've chosen to take Labour Studies – things like labour history, the sociology of work, economics and industrial relations.'

[Student, Ruskin College, Oxford]

'Our selection is based broadly on the applicant's record of activity at work and service to the community, with an emphasis - given our particular background and traditions – to work undertaken in the trade union movement and similar bodies. Courses are designed for adults. Many of the students have forgotten, if they ever mastered, the techniques of structuring arguments and of written expression. That, from our standpoint, is what an educational process means. It's not to buttress prejudices. It's not simply to solidify beliefs that students may have had before they came to Ruskin. It's to give them a whole range of views and thinking that otherwise they may not have confronted. At the end of the course, some are content to go back to their original jobs (though they may seek more responsibility), but many also go on to university or to careers like social work.'

[Spokesperson, Ruskin College, Oxford]

Oxford University

Application and selection procedures for mature students are formally the same as for school-leaver students – but the Admissions Office is happy to advise on your application or to put you in touch with a college tutor in the subject of your choice. (Tel: 0865 270210.)

Stoke-on-Trent: North Staffordshire Polytechnic

Entry concessions for students over 21 on entry. 'Almost 15% of our students are over 21 on enrolment and nearly 5% are over 25 (all types of course)'. Thirty per cent of students at the polytechnic attend in various part-time modes. There is a Mature Students' Association. *Associate Student* scheme: wide range of units available part time, day and evening, may lead to degree entry. BA (Hons) Design – 'Exceptionally, students without the minimum academic qualifications but with evidence of outstanding talent will be admitted.' BA (Hons) History of Design and the Visual Arts – 'We welcome applications from mature students (21 and over) who may in certain cases be admitted to the course without the standard qualifications.' BA (Hons) Economics – 'Mature students (over 21) with minimal formal qualifications who satisfy us that they can cope with the course will be admitted.' BA (Hons) Geography – 'We are pleased to welcome applications from mature students, for whom special conditions apply.' BA (Hons) Literature and History – 'We have a positive attitude towards mature students, who may be admitted to the course without standard qualifications in certain circumstances.' BA (Hons) International Studies – 'In exceptional cases, mature students with minimal formal qualifications will be admitted.' LLB (Hons) – 'If you are a mature student, you can be considered on the basis of work or other experience if, in our opinion, you would benefit from the course.' BA (Hons) Modern Studies – 'We have an active policy of encouraging mature students who may have missed a conventional sixth-form education to apply.' BA (Hons) Sociology – 'We are pleased to recieve applications from mature students for whom special conditions apply.' BSc/BSc (Hons) Computing – 'Mature students lacking formal qualifications are considered on an individual basis.' *Part-Time Degrees*: BA Business Studies. BA (Hons) Economics. BA (Hons) International Studies. BA (Hons) Sociology. LLB (Hons). LLB plus Hons conversion course. *Postgraduate Vocational Courses*: MSc Computing Science, full time – for graduates in any discipline. Postgraduate Diploma in Marketing Management, full time – for graduates in any discipline. Postgraduate Diploma in Management Studies, full time – for graduates in any discipline. Postgraduate Diploma in International Marketing, full time – for language graduates and others with equivalent qualifications. Certificate in Microelectronics Applications for Scientists, part time – for teachers, engineers and industrialists.

Walsall: West Midlands College of Higher Education

Entry concessions possible for mature students over 21 on 31st December in year their course commences. For candidates over 25, internal tests in English Language and Mathematics may be provided, to meet the needs of initial teacher training, through BEd (Hons) *Postgraduate Vocational Course*: Postgraduate Certificate in Education, full time.

Warwick University

Entry concessions possible for mature students 21 and over at the proposed date of entry, who have been unable to complete a normal secondary education.Selectors look for evidence of the candidate's general motivation and indication of appropriate academic ability – e.g., participation in Open Access/evening courses. Candidates are interviewed and may be required to submit written work. *Part-Time Degrees*: Historical Studies, Literary and Cultural Studies, Social Studies, Classical Civilisation, English and American Literature, English and European Literature, European Studies, French Studies, French and European Literature, History. 'Approximately one in every eight undergraduates arriving at the University is a mature student. A steady rise in the number of older students has led to the formation of a Mature Students Society at the University ... It is noticeable that mature students generally obtain better degree results than younger students, even though in the majority of cases the mature students did not have qualifications normally acceptable for entrance when they applied for the course.' (See also 'Open and Distance Learning Courses'.)

Wolverhampton Polytechnic

Entry concessions possible for mature students – those 21 and over by 31 December in the year their course commences. Work experience is taken into account and GCE requirements can be reduced. Students are normally counselled. All degree courses encourage applications from mature students. 'Great stress is placed on the value of past practical experience in admissions procedures. Mature candidates can discuss their specific requirements and personal circumstances directly with course admissions tutors or, in the first instance, with experienced counsellors in the Polytechnic's Advice Centre.' (A professionally staffed playgroup is provided for students with children under five.) The polytechnic currently recognises a total of seven Access courses, run at the following centres: Bilston Community College, Dudley College of Technology, Garrets Green College, Walsall College of Technology, Wulfrun College of Further Education. From 17 September 1988, further Access courses will be available at Sandwell College of Further and Higher Education and Kidderminster College of Further Education. This polytechnic also operates an *Associate Student* scheme and plans to publish an Associate Students Handbook with details of the full range of modules available in September 1988.

The following colleges in this region supplied information in 1987 about their degree and advanced courses, but no response was received to 1988 enquiries. Readers may nevertheless wish to make individual contacts:

Birmingham: Fircroft College
Birmingham University
Leicester University
Loughborough College of Art and Design
Nottingham: Trent Polytechnic
Nottingham University

Northern England

Blackburn College
Part-Time Degrees: Mature students with various entry qualifications can study for Levels One, Two and Three of the LINCS Combined Studies degree. (LINCS = Lancashire Integrated Colleges Scheme. Where necessary, students can study and obtain credits building up into a degree at more than one college – i.e. if you have to move home,and away from the college in Lancashire where you have been studying, you can pick up your course in the new area, at the same level.) Subjects offered in the LINCS Combined Studies degree are Linguistics, History, Organisation Studies, Psychology, Economics, Maths, Computing, Law, Politics, English.

Bolton Institute of Higher Education
Entry concessions possible for students aged 21 or over (e.g. reduced GCE requirements after interview). Mature students are particularly attracted to the BA (Hons) Humanities and BSc (Hons) Psychology degrees, both available either full time or part time. *Associate Student* scheme for entry to the BA (Hons) Humanities, part time. *Part-Time Degrees*: In addition to the two mentioned: BA Business Studies; BSc Mathematics; BEd (Hons) – for qualified teachers. *Postgraduate Vocational Courses* include Postgraduate Certificate in Education.

Bradford and Ilkley Community College
Entry concessions possible for students over 21. BA Art and Design – exceptional entry can be given if an applicant shows marked creative promise but does not possess the formal entry qualifications. DipHE/BA (Hons) Community Studies – over-21s admitted if their qualifications may be considered; evidence of work with children and/or ability to speak a second community language would be an advantage. DipHE/BEd (Hons) Home Economics for Secondary Education – possible concessions, as for previous Education degree. *Part-Time Degrees*: BEd (Hons) for qualified teachers. BEd (Hons) Organisation Studies. *Postgraduate Vocational Courses* include Postgraduate Certificate in Education (Primary), Postgraduate Certificate in Education (Secondary), Home Economics. Professional Diploma in Education (Special Education), part time.

Bradford University

Entry concessions possible for students of 21 and over. University-supplied literature on courses at the Management Centre – e.g. Honours degrees in: Business Studies; Managerial Sciences; Management Studies and French; and Management Studies and Science. Other degree courses may offer concessions. *Part-Time Degrees*: DipHE/BA (Hons) Social Studies. *Postgraduate Vocational Courses* include a part-time MBA programme. Like the full-time MBA, this is designed for good honours graduates who ideally have had at least three years' business experience. Diploma in Computing, full time – a conversion course for people qualified in a field other than computing who seek a formal qualification in computing in order to obtain jobs. Diploma/ MSc in Computing, full time and part time. For the Postgraduate Diploma, applicants must hold at least the equivalent of a British pass or ordinary degree in any scientific or engineering discipline or in economics or business studies. For the MSc, applicants must hold at least a British second-class honours degree in any scientific or engineering discipline or in business studies or economics. (See also 'Pre-Entry, Sample and Access Courses' section for details of Foundation Year preliminary course, enabling candidates without conventional qualifications to convert to engineering.)

Doncaster: Humberside College – see under Hull

Durham: New College Durham

Entry concessions possible for students aged over 21. BA (Hons) Travel and Tourism, in association with Newcastle Polytechnic. *Part-Time Degrees*: BEd (Hons) for qualified teachers. BA (Hons) Criminal Justice Studies (in association with Newcastle Polytechnic).

Gateshead Technical College

Postgraduate Vocational Course MA Conservation of Fine Art, full time – any graduate considered.

Grimsby: Humberside College – see under Hull

Huddersfield Polytechnic

The college wishes to encourage applications from mature entrants. No set level of qualification (or lack of qualification) for mature students – each case considered individually. Mature students are defined as 21 or over at the time of admission. The following degree entries indicate that mature candidates are expected to apply: BSc (Hons) Behavioural Sciences – 'Mature students may be exempted [from usual requirements] and are encouraged to apply.' BA/BA (Hons) Computing in Business – 'Mature students who do not meet the entry requirements may be admitted if they can show evidence acceptable to the polytechnic of their suitability for the course.' BA/BA (Hons) Humanities – as previous degree. BSC (Hons) Human Ecology –

applications are welcomed from mature students. BSc (Hons) Transport and Distribution – 'special arrangements can be made for mature students, from whom applications are encouraged.' *Part-Time Degrees*: BA/BA (Hons) Social Welfare Administration – for holders of the Certificate of Qualification in Social Work (CQSW); others considered. BEd (Hons) – for serving teachers in further education establishments. BEd (Hons) – for serving teachers in schools and further education. BA/BA (Hons) Humanities. BA (Hons) Business Studies. BSC (Hons) Textile Technology. *Postgraduate Vocational Qualifications* include Postgraduate Certificate in Education (Further Education), full time.

Hull: Humberside College of Higher Education
Campuses also in Doncaster, Grimsby and Scunthorpe.
Entry concessions possible for mature students – see individual courses. BA (Hons) Architecture – mature students especially welcome. BA (Hons) Fine Art – applicants with less than the minimum requirements admitted when there is clear evidence of exceptional merit. BA (Hons) Graphic Design – some entry requirements waived for mature students. BSc (Hons) Fishery Studies – candidates with maritime, fishing or other industrial qualifications, plus evidence of suitable industrial experience and academic potential admitted without usual academic qualifications. BSc/BSc (Hons) Industrial Food Technology – over-21s may be granted concessions in entry requirements if they satisfy college they have the necessary motivation, potential and knowledge to succeed. BA (Hons) Social Science – over-21s without usual qualifications considered. DipHE, full time Hull, part time Grimsby - over-21s without usual qualifications considered; can lead to entry to third year of BA (Hons) Business Studies, BA (Hons) Combined Studies, BA (Hons) Social Science, full time. *Part-Time Degrees*: see college statement at the end of this entry. Certificate/DipHE/BA/BA (Hons) and Certificate/ DipHE/BSc/BSc (Hons), as appropriate, in Applied Biology, Business Studies (also at Grimsby), Combined Sciences, Combined Studies (also at Grimsby and Scunthorpe), Humanities (also at Scunthorpe), Office Systems Management, Social Studies (also at Scunthorpe), Visual Studies. BEd (for qualified teachers) also at Doncaster and Scunthorpe. BSc Engineering. Postgraduate Vocational Courses include: Postgraduate Diploma in Food Technology, full time - any graduate considered. Postgraduate Diploma in Fishery Harbour Operations and Management, full time – any graduate considered. Postgraduate Diploma in Port Operations and Management, full time – any graduate considered. Postgraduate Certificate in Education, full time – any graduate considered. Postgraduate Diploma in Refrigeration and Air Conditioning, full time – any graduate in engineering discipline. The college says: 'Evening-only attendance, with occasional Saturday Day Schools. Mixed-mode attendance available in some areas. No specific entry requirements for over-21s. Courses to Honours Degree level, with intermediate qualifications available, in Applied Biology, Applied Social Science,

Business Information Systems, Business Studies, Documentary Studies, Humanities, Office Systems Management,Visual Studies or Combined Studies. All are run in Hull, with selected courses at Grimsby.'

Lancaster: St Martin's College

Entry concessions for mature students on BEd Primary Teaching. Alternatives to A-levels include OU Foundation Credit or Open College awards. Mature students should normally be under 50 years of age. BA Youth Studies (recognised JNC Youth Work qualification). Experience of working with young people is most important. A wide range of formal qualifications can be accepted – ask college. *Postgraduate Vocational Courses*: Postgraduate Certificate in Education (Primary and Secondary teaching), full time. Postgraduate Diploma in Youth Work – degree-equivalent training accepted. Department of Education and Science Special Initiatives: 2-year courses for Maths and Physics Teaching. Degree-equivalent courses and/or industrial experience acceptable – ask the college for details.

Lancaster University

Entry concessions possible for students aged 21 and over. Very welcoming – has special free *Guide for Mature Students* – ask for a copy. For entry to degree courses, there are numerous alternatives to A-levels: BTEC and similar awards at certain specified levels, and a wide range of professional qualifications – for example, Registered General Nurse, Registered Mental Nurse, Institute of Chartered Secretaries and Administrators, Institute of Linguists grade II, police promotion examinations, with further study experience, etc., and Open University. Lancaster University, jointly with Lancashire Polytechnic, validates a wide range of courses of the Open College Federation of the North West as alternatives to A-levels for adults. These are offered at colleges of further and adult education in Nelson and Colne, Accrington, Blackburn, Burnley, Preston, Blackpool, Leyland, Wigan, Kirby, Southport, Oldham, Morecambe and Lancaster. Degrees attracting mature students: potentially all courses but, in practice, the social sciences – Psychology, Social Work, etc. *Postgraduate Vocational Courses* include Postgraduate Diploma in Social Work, Postgraduate Diploma in Business Administration – any degree acceptable.

Leeds Polytechnic

Welcomes applications from mature students, aged 21-plus without normal entry qualifications, who are considered on merit. BSc/BSc (Hons) Environmental Health - entry for mature students without normal entry requirements is possible. BA (Hons) Architecture – mature students without qualifications are assessed on portfolio and at interview. BA (Hons) Landscape Architecture – regulations as preceeding degree. BA (Hons) Fine Art, Graphic Design or Three-Dimensional Design (Furniture, Industrial Design or Interior Design) – exceptionally gifted studens without normal qualifications may be admitted. BA (Hons) Food and Accommodation Management – mature students may be admitted. BSc (Hons) Information Science – 'The School actively encourages mature students without formal qualifications to apply.' *Part-Time Courses*: BA/BA (Hons) Management and Administration. BEd/BEd (Hons) for qualified teachers. BSc (Hons) Nursing Studies for registered nurses.Certificate/DipHE/BA/BA (Hons) Combined Studies. LLB/LLB (Hons) Law. BA/BA (Hons) Librarianship. BSc Production Engineering. BA (Hons) Social Policy and Administration. *Postgraduate Vocational Courses*: Graduate Conversion course in Accounting, full time – any graduate considered. Postgraduate Diploma in Personnel Management,full time – any graduate considered. Postgraduate Certificate in Education, full time - any graduate considered. Postgraduate Diploma in Dietetics, full time – any graduate in science who has read human physiology and biochemistry to an approved standard. HCIMA graduate conversion course, full time – any graduate. Polytechnic Diploma in Hotel, Catering and Institutional Management, full time – any graduate. Postgraduate Diploma in Health Education/Health Promotion, full time – any graduate. Postgraduate Diploma in Information Administration for Linguists, full time – graduates in French, German, Italian or Spanish. Postgraduate Diploma in Information Administration, full time – any graduate. Law – Common Profesional Examination for non-law graduates, full time. Postgraduate Diploma in European Community Law and Integration, full time – graduates in Law, Economics, Business Studies, Political Science, Modern Languages. Postgraduate Diploma in Librarianship and Information work, full time – any graduate with a year's approved library/ similar acceptable experience. Postgraduate CQSW social work, full time – graduates in social sciences/other approved degree plus relevant experience. Business Automation Analysis /Electrical Engineering conversion courses for arts graduates. Part-time prospectus available.

Leeds: Trinity and All Saints College

Entry concessions possible for students aged 21-plus. JMB Mature Matriculation process used (see description under Liverpool University). All BA/BEd degrees attract mature students,but the Home Economics BEd is particularly popular. Honours degrees of the University of Leeds awarded in BA/BSc Planning and Administration, BA/BSc Public Media. BEd (Primary or Secondary). *Part-Time Degrees*: In-service BEd (Primary or Secondary) for qualified teachers.

Home Economics BEd: viewpoint

'A government grant has enabled the college to equip spacious and attractive new premises for Secondary Education, and this means more opportunities for the growing number of mature students who wish to train for a career in teaching. For such would-be students, the combination of Home Economics with Secondary Education is particularly attractive.

We recognise that many mature students will not have the same qualifications as students coming straight from school, but mature students do bring to their studies other skills. Alternative means of entry to the course are available, and qualifications such as BTEC may be acceptable for entry, so it is worth writing to us to find out.

The Home Economics component includes units on health education, textiles, social studies, consumer studies, design in the home, nutrition and food science and technology.

The Education component develops the knowledge and skills needed to become a secondary school teacher and includes regular and frequent contacts with pupils in schools. The course encourages mature students to bring their own experience to their studies and eventually into the classroom.

Job prospects are very good. Indeed, since 1985, everyone graduating with a BEd in Home Economics has obtained employment and many of our former students have found that progress can be rapid.'

Liverpool Institute of Higher Education

'The Institute wishes to positively promote enquiries and applications from mature students.' An explanatory booklet has been produced by the Joint Matriculation Board, Manchester: *A University Degree: A Second Chance at 21-plus* (see under Liverpool University for admissions procedure) and can be obtained from this Institute as well as any of the participating universities (see address list).

Liverpool University

Students over 21 who are not matriculated in the usual way may opt for the Mature Entry Scheme of the Joint Matriculation Board. Candidates using this procedure may be interviewed following their application to the university and given conditional offers of places, subject to their passing a 'package' of tests to be set by the university. These may include: a mature matriculation interview; a general test of comprehension and essay-writing; a test or tests set by the department they wish to enter. All undergraduate courses consider mature entrants, but departmental tests vary with the character of the subject and the level of demand from students. NB: This JMB Mature Entry scheme also applies to the universities of Birmingham, Leeds, Manchester and Sheffield and to colleges affiliated to the five constituent universities.

Manchester Polytechnic

(NB: An excellent *Mature Students Handbook* is available free from The Registry, Manchester Polytechnic, All Saints, Manchester M15 6BH.) Entry concessions possible for students aged 21 and over. In general, admissions tutors must be satisfied you can cope with the course, and normally you should have done some preparatory study (Access course, Open College,

Gateway, Threshold, Polymaths – see 'Pre-Entry, Sample and Access Courses', BA (Hons) Applied Community Studies – applications welcomed from mature students. BEd (Hons) – mature students invited to apply and may be considered under exceptional entry arrangements. BSc/BSc (Hons) Environmental Management – mature students lacking normal requirements should contact the departments for discussion. BSc Speech Pathology and Therapy – applications from mature candidates always welcome. BA/BA (Hons) English Studies or Historical Studies – special consideration given to unqualified mature students. BA/BA (Hons) Humanities/Social Studies – special consideration given to unqualified mature students. BA/BA (Hons) Economics – entry requirements may be waived for over-21s who can show evidence of continued study since leaving school. *Part-Time Degrees* – prospectus being reprinted at time of enquiry, but the following are known to be on offer: BA (Hons)/BSc/BSc (Hons) Business Studies. BA/BA (Hons)Humanities/Social Studies. BA(Hons) Public Administration. BA (Hons) Social Science. BEng/BEng (Hons) Electrical and Electronic Engineering/Mechanical Engineering/Engineering. BSc/BSc(Hons) Applied Biological Sciences. BSc (Hons) Combined Studies (Science and Technology subjects). BSc (Hons) Polymer Science and Technology. BSc (Hons) Psychology. LLB (Hons). *Postgraduate Vocational Courses* include: Postgraduate Diploma in Personnel Management, full time – any graduate. Accountancy Foundation course, full time – any graduate. Law – Common Professional Examination, full time – any non-law graduate. Postgraduate Diploma in Hotel and Catering Administration, full time – any graduate. Polytechnic Diploma in Tourism, full time – any graduate. Polytechnic Diploma in Clothing Technology, full time – any graduate. Postgraduate Diploma in Librarianship, full time – any graduate with at least six months' experience in librarianship/other approved experience. Postgraduate Certificate in Education, full time.

Mature Student Routes in Science and Technology: viewpoints

'I started out in a job in industry where I had to do Chemistry and that involved taking the TEC (now BTEC) part-time college course. Then I was made redundant, so I went through the telephone directory and just phoned people up till somebody gave me an interview for another job. I asked them to send me to college and they said, yes, I could do the Higher National Certificate in Chemistry. Then, round about Christmas, the firm started going under and I asked Manchester Polytechnic if I could transfer from the HNC to the degree course. They said to stay on at work if I could and keep doing the HNC because, if I did, I'd get the necessary industrial experience for the sandwich degree, and I could do it in two years – which is what I did.'

'People don't expect middle-aged Mums like me to want day release, but when I got a job in a hospital laboratory, I applied to come to the polytechnic. It was only after a lot of persuasion that I managed to get on this medical laboratory technology course (I think they'd originally wanted somebody who'd just be an extra pair of hands at the hospital). Now that I've got the chance I can't afford to fall behind with the course. That means working my diary out very carefully, because at times I'm 'on call' at work, and there are things like visiting my children's school on various occasions, which have all got to be fitted in. Unlike young students, I don't feel I can take time off work to catch up if I get behind with homework, so I have to be organised.'

[Students, Faculty of Science and Engineering, Manchester Polytechnic]

'In virtually all our CNAA degree courses, we have a clause which allows the admission of students without the standard entry qualifications as prescribed in the prospectus. This may range, for example, from leaving school with very modest attainments but having a period of relatively mature experience in industry – which we deem equivalent experiential learning, as it's called - or again, there may be a gap in the education record, which we feel has been made up in other ways.'

[Spokesperson, Faculty of Science and Engineering, Manchester Polytechnic]

Manchester: UMIST (University of Manchester Institute of Science and Technology)

Entry concessions possible for students aged 21 and over. Mature Matriculation entry: could be by interview or directed reading programme and written examination. Students also accepted via Access courses and all two-year courses leading to Diplomas and Certificates offered by the following Residential Colleges: Fircroft (Birmingham), Coleg Harlech (Wales), Hillcroft (Surrey), Newbattle Abbey (Scotland), Northern (Barnsley), Plater (Oxford), Ruskin (Oxford). BSc (Hons) Chemistry, Industrial Chemistry,Chemical Physics, Polymer Chemistry and Analytical Chemistry – applications from mature candidates considered via JMB Mature Matriculation scheme. You *must*, however, have some scientific background. Mature Matriculation scheme. BSc Ophthalmic Optics, consideration given to mature students and others with different educational backgrounds.*Postgraduate Vocational Courses*: MSC-sponsored Postgraduate Diploma in Computation for non-computing graduates, full time – Postgraduate Diploma in Management Sciences, part time – any graduate. Postgraduate Diploma in Technical Science, full time – various options, but the Polymer Science option is open to science and engineering graduates with no previous training in polymers.

Manchester University

Entry concessions possible for students aged over 21. Selection by interview, possibly involving the submission of an essay or essays, or taking an examination. Preparatory courses available (see 'Pre-Entry, Sample and Access Courses'). *Part-Time Degrees*: Comparative Religion; Economic and

Social Studies; Education; Environmental Studies; History; History of Art; Literary Studies; Nursing Education; Nursing Studies; Theology and Religious Studies. Also conversion courses, both at graduate and under-graduate level. For details, contact the Office of Continuing Education and Training at the university.

Middlesbrough: Teesside Polytechnic
Mature students (over 21) are exempted from minimum qualifications if, in the opinion of the course officers, they would be capable of completing the course without formal qualifications. Entry to BA Humanities, full time and part time, and BSc Social Studies, full time, via Access/Gateway courses. *Part-Time Degrees*: Humanities, with a wide range of courses in the areas of Literature, History, Politics, French and Sociology, which may be studied either as single subjects or in combination.

Newcastle-upon-Tyne Polytechnic
Mature students may be admitted without the usual minimum qualifications at the Polytechnic's discretion. NB: a Higher Education Foundation course is offered at Newcastle-upon-Tyne College of Arts and Technology, Gateshead Technical College, Derwentside Technical College, Peterlee College and North Tyneside College of Further Education on a part-time basis for candidates over 20. The Polytechnic also runs an *Associate Student* scheme for over-21s to take units from degree/diploma/certificate courses, part time. (See also 'Pre-Entry, Sample and Access Courses'.) BA (Hons) Design for Industry – mature candidates with relevant experience considered. BA (Hons)Media Production - over-21s and those of marked creative promise without minimum qualifications considered. BA (Hons) Travel and Tourism - mature applicants welcome and fully considered. BA (Hons) Business Studies – over- 21s considered without minimum entry requirements; aptitude tests may be given. BSc (Hons) Mathematics – mature students and those with non-standard qualifications considered. BSc/BSc (Hons) Computing for Industry - over-21s considered without minimum entry requirements. BA Secretarial Studies – over-21s considered without minimum entry requirements. BSc (Hons) Sociology – mature students without formal entry qualifications welcomed. BSc (Hons) Applied Consumer Sciences – over-21s considered without minimum entry requirements. BEng/BEng (Hons) – mature applicants welcome, including those with non-standard qualifications. BA/BA Hons. English and History – mature candidates are specially and sympathetically considered. BA (Hons) Geography, mature candidates without formal qualifications welcomed. BA (Hons) Information and Library Studies- mature students are always welcome. BA (Hons) Economics – over-21s encouraged to apply, even without minimum entry qualifications. BA (Hons) Government and Public Policy – older candidates who do not possess the formal qualifications outlined will be welcomed. LLB (Hons), mature students may submit

applications for consideration. *Part-Time Degrees*: BA/BA (Hons) Business Studies. BA Applied Computing. BSc (Hons)Health Studies – for registered nurses, paramedical professionals, NHS administrators, etc. BSc Applied Chemistry. BEng Engineering Technology. BSc/BSc (Hons) Physical Electronics. BEd/BEd (Hons) for qualified teachers. BA/BA (Hons) English and History. LLB/LLB (Hons) Law. Projected BA (Hons) Criminal Justice Studies. *Postgraduate Vocational Courses* include: Postgraduate Certificate in Education, full time. Postgraduate Diploma in Library and Information Studies – for any graduate, full time. Postgraduate Diploma in Optoelectronics, full time - for graduates in physics, electronic engineering or similar. Postgraduate Diploma in Computer-Assisted Manufacture, full time – for graduates in engineering, science or similar. Postgraduate Diploma in Offshore Materials and Corrosion Engineering, full time – for graduates in Applied Science (Physical or Chemical) or Engineering, or similar.Postgraduate Diploma in Secretarial/Bilingual Secretarial Administration, full time - any graduate for the former, graduates in French, German or Spanish for the latter. Postgraduate Diploma in Marketing Studies, full time – for any graduate. Postgraduate Diploma in Business Information Technology, full time. NB: Part-time prospectus available.

Ormskirk: Edge Hill College of Higher Education
Entry concessions possible for mature students aged 21 and over; applicants are considered by the Special Admissions Committee of Lancaster University, but would normally be expected to have undertaken recent academic study at an appropriate level and might be asked to undertake an assignment related to their chosen course. 'Each year, some 100 older students of widely varying ages enter the College's undergraduate courses; indeed a few of them have reached the pinnacle of success by achieving a first-class honours degree, and most of them achieve degrees of a good honours standard.' *Part-Time Degrees*: DipHE/BA (Hons) Applied Social Science, English, Geography, History, Urban Policy and Race Relations. DipHE/BSc/BSc (Hons) Geography. Courses are credit-based with a wide choice of options. Part-time students may move on to a full-time course by arrangement.

Preston: Lancashire Polytechnic
Entry concessions widespread for students aged 21 or over. May be admitted by virtue of prior experience, ability to cope with and benefit from the course, advanced standing from previous learning plus disadvantage criteria. Credit Transfer possible, particularly to 25-subject Combined Studies Programme. Open College entry via local colleges. Access courses and Foundation courses (see 'Pre-Entry, Sample and Access Courses'). Mature students Particularly attracted to Social Sciences, Humanities, Business Studies, Science, Technology, Law and Languages courses (Combined Studies modular scheme). *Associate Student* scheme: part time, choice

of study units from hundreds in most subject areas within the polytechnic. *Part-Time Degrees* include: BMus (London); BA (Hons) Business Studies; LLB Law; BSc Physics; BSc Quantity Surveying; BSc/BSc (Hons) and DipHE/BA/BA (Hons) Combined Studies, 19 subject choices. Some first-year subjects from Combined Studies programme available in local further education colleges (enquire at Polytechnic). *Postgraduate Vocational Courses* – various, including: research by thesis, Social Work Diploma, Journalism, Bilingual Secretaries' course. Prospectus not supplied, so enquire at the polytechnic.

Salford College of Technology
Part-Time Degree: BSc Environmental Health (in association with Manchester Polytechnic). *Postgraduate Vocational Courses*: Graduate Executive Secretaries Personal Assistant's Diploma, full time – for any graduate. Graduate Bilingual Executive Secretaries Diploma, full time – for graduates in French, German or Spanish.

Salford University
Entry concessions possible for students aged 21 or over at the start of the degree programme. Wide varity of concessions: reduced GCE requirements for candidates who demonstrate ability and potential. Interview plus written work plus other exam qualifications plus work experience may be considered. Access course candidates accepted, particularly from courses available in the region. Mature students are particularly welcome on courses in Business and Management, Information Technology, Sociology and Social Sciences, but will also be considered for courses in Science and Engineering subjects. *Part-Time Degrees*: BA Politics and Contemporary History. BSc Sociology. BSc Applied Physics with Electronics.

Sunderland Polytechnic
Entry concessions possible for students aged 21 and over. BA (Hons) Fine Art – mature students without normal qualifications accepted if polytechnic is satisfied they can complete and benefit from the course. BA (Hons) 3D Design in Glass with Ceramics – entry requirements as for BA (Hons) Fine Art, above. BEd (Hons) – students must have O-level/GCSE English and Maths; mature students welcome. Similar regulations for entry to BEd (Hons) Education and Business Studies. BEd Mathematics, Physics, Business Studies and Craft, Design Technology – entry requirements: O-level/GCSE English and Maths and HND/HNC in relevant subject. Students over 25 may be allowed to sit special tests in English and Maths. Also, subject to validation: BEd (Hons) Technology, PGCE in Physics, intercalated Teachers Certificate within the Joint Scheme of Science Degrees and BEng degrees; BA (Hons) Sports Studies; in special circumstances, a mature student without formal qualifications will be accepted. BEng/BEng (Hons) Mechanical Engineering, Digital Systems Engineering and Civil Engineering –

mature students with relevant experience considered without the usual formal qualifications. Electrical and Electronic Engineering: some formal qualifications in Electrical Engineering required, even for mature students. BA/BA (Hons) Business Studies – applications considered from mature studentswithoutminimum qualifications. BA/BA (Hons) Combined Studies (Arts) – mature students particularly welcome and entry requirements waived in certain circumstances. BA/BA (Hons) Economics – applications invited from mature students without normal entry qualifications. BA/BA (Hons) Social Science, applications invited from mature students without minimum entry qualifications. BA/BA (Hons) English Studies. BA/BA (Hons) Communication Studies – applications considered from mature students without minimum qualifications. BA/BA (Hons) Business Computing and Business Computing with Languages, mature students without minimum academic qualifications may be admitted. BSc/BSc (Hons): Applied Biology, Applied Geology, Applied Physics, Combined Studies in Science, Materials Science, Chemical and Pharmaceutical Analysis – students must demonstrate competence in English Language; other requirements for entry may be ascertained from the Admissions Office. Mathematics for Information Processing – in special circumstances, mature students welcome. BSc (Hons) Pharmacy, BSc (Hons) Pharmacology, Diploma/MSC Clinical Pharmacy. *Part-Time Degrees*: Certificate/Diploma/ BA/BA (Hons) Combined Studies (Arts). BSc/BSc (Hons) Materials Science. BSc in Science Subjects. BA (Hons) Fine Art. BA Artist/Designer/Craftsman. (See also 'Retraining and New Skills Courses'.) *Postgraduate Vocational Courses*: Wide range – enquire at polytechnic.

Wakefield: Bretton Hall College of Higher Education

Entry concessions for students aged over 21, via JMB Mature Matriculation scheme (see under Liverpool University for details). 'It should be stressed that the college welcomes adults as mature students on degree courses ... the Mature Student Qualifying Examination as mentioned above is based on an intelligent awareness of the contemporary world and a capacity to present ideas and opinions in clear written English. To help adults suceed in this examination, both day and evening preparation courses are provided by the college.' (The college is noted for its Performance Arts courses and has hosted the National Student Drama Festival on more than one occasion.) BEd (Hons) Early Years (3-8 years) and BEd (Hons) Primary/Middle (5-8 years and 8-13 years), with specialisms in Art, English, Environmental Studies or Music. BA (Hons)Art and Design (Visual Arts and Textile Arts). BA (Hons) Dance. BA (Hons) Drama. BA (Hons) English. BA (Hons) Music. *Postgraduate Vocational Courses*: Postgraduate Certificate in Education, full time – any graduate, various options.

York: College of Ripon and York St John

Mature student concessions unspecified, but there is part time provision.

Part-Time Degrees DipHE/BA/BSc, wide range of options. *Postgraduate Vocational Courses* Postgraduate Certificate in Education, full time – any graduate.

The following colleges in this region supplied information in 1987 about their degree and advanced courses, but no response was recieved to 1988 enquiries. Readers may nevertheless wish to make individual contact:

Barnsley: Northern College
Blackpool and Fylde College
Liverpool Polytechnic
York University

Wales and Western England

Bath College of Higher Education
Entry concessions possible for students aged over 21. BA (Hons) Music – individual and sympathetic consideration given to mature candidates over 21 years of age and exceptional candidates who do not possess the normal entrance qualifications. Successful completion of the Access course offered by City of Bath College of Further Education qualifies candidates for admission to the following: BEd (Hons) full time; BSc (Hons) Home Economics, full time; BA (Hons) Music, full time; BA (Hons) Combined Studies full time; DipHE, full time. Mature candidates are also admitted to the following Art and Design courses on the strength of their portfolio submission: BA (Hons) Fine Art (Painting or Sculpture), full time; BA (Hons) Graphic Design, full time; BA (Hons) Three-Dimensional Design (Ceramics), full time; Foundation course in Art and Design, full time or part time. *Postgraduate Vocational Courses*: Postgraduate Certificate in Education for Primary Teaching (candidates with degrees in subject areas relevant to the primary school curriculum), full time. Postgraduate Certificate in Education for Secondary Age Range: options are Home Economics, Music, Rural and Environmental Science, full time – special entry requirements.

Bath University
Some concessions for mature students; applicants should write to the relevant Admissions Tutor (see prospectus).

Cardiff: University College of Cardiff
This new college has been formed by the merger of University College Cardiff and the University of Wales Institute of Science and Technology. Entry concessions for students aged 21 or over with good general educational background; also reduced entry qualifications for mature candidates. Interview essential. Students aged 23 or over. *Part-Time Degrees*: LLB (Law).

Cardiff: South Glamorgan Institute of Higher Education
Entry concessions possible for students aged 21 or over on CNAA courses, or aged 23 or over on University of Wales degree courses. These may include reduced GCE requirements, admission by interview and submission of case to University of Wales for approval. The Institute lists the

following degrees as attracting mature students: BA (Hons) Fine Art; BA (Hons) Ceramics; BA (Hons) Industrial Design; BA (Hons) Interior Design; BA (Hons) Art Education Studies; BEd (Hons); BA (Hons) Human Movement Studies; BSc (Hons) Dietetics.; BSc (Hons) Speech Therapy; BSc (Hons) Applied Life Sciences; BA Tourism. *Postgraduate Vocational Courses* include: MA Fine Art; MA Ceramics; Postgraduate Certificate in Education (various options), full time; Graduate Entry to Journalism, full time (mainly for those sponsored by the newspaper industry; some places available for non-sponsored students). Bilingual and non-linguistic secretarial courses.

Cheltenham: College of St Paul and St Mary
Entry concessions for students aged 21 and over on 31 December of the year of entry. They still need O-level English and Mathematics, but those over 25 may be able to take an alternative test for Mathematics. Special Access course mainly for members of ethnic minorities (see 'Pre-Entry, Sample and Access Courses'), leading to the BEd (Hons) degree. Mature students are also attracted to part-time degrees and to the BA (Hons) Combined Studies and BSc (Hons) Geography/Geology courses. *Part-Time Degrees*: BA (Hons) Combined Studies - options English and History, English and Geography, English and Religious Studies Geography and History, History and Religious Studies; BSc (Hons) Geography and Geology; BEd (Hons) of Bristol University for serving teachers. *Postgraduate Vocational Courses* include: Postgraduate Certificate in Education, full time – any graduate. Conversion course, full time, for secondary teachers wishing to teach in primary schools.

Exeter University
Entry concessions possible for students aged 23 and over. Concessions depend on recommendation by department, based on interview, and taking account of academic background and experience. The prospectus states: 'applications are welcomed from those who for a variety of reasons may not have had the opportunity of embarking upon University eduation when they left school but are now interested in doing so.' Mature applicants are welcomed for all degree courses, but they find Social Studies to be among the most attractive.*Postgraduate Vocational Courses* include two new two-year degrees for students who *either* have already completed two years of a degree course in Physics, Mathematics or Engineering or are HND-holders with relevant professional experience, *or* mature students with degrees or professional qualifications including one year's relevant main subject study,with at least four years' professional experience.

Lampeter: St David's University College
Entry concessions for students over 21 at the time of admission – the need for formal GCE qualifications may be waived. Mature applicants are normally called for interview and occasionally asked to submit written work.Wide

range of BA (Hons) degree choices and BD of the University of Wales.

Plymouth Polytechnic
Applications welcomed from mature students for all courses, no minimum age limit specified. 'a place will be offered if we feel someone will benefit from and complete satisfactorily the particular course.' *Part-Time Degrees*: DipHE/BSc/BSc (Hons) Combined Honours – Science, Social Science, Science and Social Science. BSc Applicable Mathematics. *Postgraduate Vocational Courses* include: MSc Intelligent Systems, full time or block – any honours degree acceptable provided candidates have a strong interest in artificial intelligence and some knowledge of computers; Doctor of Clinical Psychology, full time or part time – good honours degree in Psychology needed. Postgraduate Diploma/MSc Applied Fish Biology, full time or part time – for honours graduates in biology or a joint honours/modular degree with biology forming the major part (includes option in Fish Farming).

Pontypridd: Polytechnic of Wales
Entry concessions possible for mature students (age unspecified) if the polytechnic is satisfied they will benefit from the course and have the necessary motivation, potential and knowledge to complete it successfully. *Part-Time Degrees*: BEng/BEng (Hons) Civil Engineering; BSc/BSc (Hons) Chemistry; BSc/BSc (Hons) Computer Studies; BA/BA (Hons) Humanities; LLB/LLB (Hons); BA (Hons) Police Studies – majority of students will be serving police officers. *Postgraduate Vocational Courses* include: Common Professional Examination in Law, full time - for graduates in non-Law degrees. Polytechnic Diploma in Craft, Design and Technology, part time – for practising teachers. Postgraduate Diploma in Computer Science part time – for any graduate. MSc Education Management, part time.

Poole: Dorset Institute of Higher Education
Most full-time courses are open to those mature students without formal qualifications who can present evidence that convinces admissions staff that they have the capacity and ability to succeed in and benefit from the course. Choices include: BA (Hons) Business Studies; BA (Hons) Combined Studies; BSc (Hons) Engineering Business Development; BA (Hons) Financial Services; BSc (Hons) Food and Catering Management; BA (Hons) Hospitality Management; BSc (Hons) Information Systems Management; BA (Hons) Media Production; BA (Hons) Tourism Studies. *Part-Time degrees*: BEng Computer-Aided Engineering; BA/BA (Hons) Business Studies.

Swansea: University College
Entry concessions possible for students aged 21 or over. They are required to attend for interview with the chosen department and the department's recommendation is considered by a special committee. The College looks for a genuine commitment and ability to pursue a course of study; this can be

demonstrated in a variety of ways – e.g. by pursuing an Open University course, successes in GCE, or attendance at the College's own Extra-Mural Department.

Weymouth College

Postgraduate Vocational Courses Diploma in the Conservation of Stonework, full time – for graduates in any subject.

The following colleges in the Wales and West region supplied information in 1987 about their degree and advanced courses, but no response has been received to 1988 enquiries. Readers may nevertheless wish to make individual contact:

Harlech College (Coleg Harlech)
Plymouth: College of St Mark and St John
Swansea: West Glamorgan Institute of Higher Education
Totnes: Dartington College of Arts

Scotland and Northern Ireland

Belfast: Stranmillis College
Mature students accepted for BEd courses on offer; appropriately qualified mature students who wish to take Craft, Design and Technology as the main academic subject may be permitted to enter the second year of the degree course. *Postgraduate Vocational Courses* include: Postgraduate Certificate in Education,full time – any graduate considered; Graduate Certificate in Education (Honours Psychology option) full time – for intending educational psychologists who wish to proceed to the MSc in Development and Educational Psychology of Queen's University.

Coleraine: University of Ulster
Entry concessions possible for students aged at least 21 at the date of entry to a course.

Dundee: Duncan of Jordanstone College
Entry concessions possible for students aged 23 and over. Up to 10% of admissions may be without any formal qualifications for the first year course in Art and Design: however, applicants must present outstanding portfolios of art and/or design work, appear for interview and convince the committee of an ability to complete the course satisfactorily, including written assignments. BA (Hons) Fine Art attracts most mature students.

Dundee University
Entry concessions possible for students aged 21 or over at the time of entry to the university. The minimum level of attainment expected will be the equivalent of two A-levels or three SCE Highers, or an approved national certificate or diploma. In some faculties, candidates can qualify with Open University credits or by attending the University's Return to Study course. *Part-Time Degrees*: 'Some degree courses in the Faculties of Arts and Social Sciences and of Science and Engineering can be attended by part-time students; details are available on request from the Admissions Officer.'

Edinburgh College of Art
Entry concessions possible for students aged 23 or over. The college's

assessment of the standard and promise indicated by the portfolio of work is of great importance in arriving at the final selection of candidates. *Postgraduate Vocational Courses*: MArch, full time or part time; MSc Architectural Conservation, full time or part time; MSc Urban Design, full time or part time; Postgraduate Diploma in Art and Design, Painting, Printmaking or Sculpture, full time; Postgraduate Diploma in Town and Country Planning, full time or part time – recognised by the Royal Town Planning Institute; Postgraduate Diploma in Housing, full time – recognised by the Institute of Housing; Postgraduate Diploma in Architecture, full time; Postgraduate Diploma in Urban Design, full time – recognised by the Royal Institute of British Architects; Postgraduate Diploma in Architectural Conservation, full time.

Edinburgh: Heriot-Watt University
Entry concessions possible for students aged 21 or over. *Part-Time Degrees*: BA Business Studies; BSc General.*Postgraduate Vocational Courses* include: Diploma in Accounting, full time – conversion course for graduates wishing to enter a professional accounting studentship; MSc/Diploma conversion course in Digital Techniques for Information Technology, full time – for graduates in mathematically based subjects. Diploma in Optoelectronics, full time - conversion course for science graduates. The latter two courses are supported by MSC studentships. In conjunction with the MSC, the university runs Management Extension Programmes providing retraining and fresh work experience placements for unemployed managers, and Graduate Gateway Programmes providing management training and trainee placements for recent graduates in any discipline.

Edinburgh: Napier Polytechnic of Edinburgh
The polytechnic states: 'Minimum entry requirements for all full- and part-time degrees or HND courses are normally two SCE Higher Exam passes or two GCE A-level passes, but mature applicants (over 21) can occasionally gain some exemption on the basis of relevant recent work experience. These requirements do not apply to the Open Learning Centre. (See 'Open and Distance Learning Courses'.) This polytechnic supplied information in a form that does not lend itself very readily to the style of *Make A Fresh Start*, and readers may like to refer to the actual prospectus. However, a special mention should be made of *Part-Time Degrees* in Applied Economics, Business Studies, Life Sciences, and of the fact that 'multi-mode' attendance is allowed for Quantity Surveying. *Postgraduate Vocational Qualifications*: again, the material supplied by the polytechnic does not lend itself very readily to assessment in the terms of this book, but the subjects of Accounting, Careers Guidance, European Marketing and Languages, Industrial Management, Personnel Management, Secretarial Studies, Software Technology and Systems Analysis and Design would seem promising for any graduate seeking a vocational course. There is also

mention of a Postgraduate Diploma in Software Technology lasting 33 weeks, 'designed to retrain people with programming skills. A degree is usually required, but exemption may be given to applicants with recent, relevant skill of a similar standard.'

Edinburgh: Queen Margaret College
Entry concessions possible for students over 21, who are warmly welcomed. Send for booklet *'A Second Chance to Learn*. Note especially: BSc Dietetics (preliminary study of Chemistry advised); BA Nursing Studies – the college says, 'we find that older and more experienced students also tend to be determined and adaptable, and our mature students have had a strong record of success on the course; BSc Occupational Therapy, now 30% of entrants are over 21, but the course is a strenuous one, and those over the age of 40 have sometimes found it excessively so; BSc Physiotherapy; BSc Speech Pathology and Therapy; BA Communication Studies – in recent years the majority of entrants have been away from school for some time, with a significant proportion being in their late 20s or 30s'. BSc Food Studies; BA Applied Consumer Studies, with Retailing and Home Economics options. *Postgraduate Vocational Courses*: HCIMA conversion course in hotel, catering and institutional management for those with non-catering degrees – new graduates and graduates wishing to retrain equally welcome.

Catering and Hotel Management Conversion Course
'I had been working in libraries for seven or eight years, but I felt a bit stifled. I wanted to choose a course where I might be able to forge ahead and one day run my own establishment. We had a spell in the first term in the kitchens on the production side, organising meals and banquets and that I hadn't encountered before; it was enormously interesting and good experience, even though what we are learning to do is not being trained as chefs but see the pressures on the chef. A great change from librarianship? Well, yes, but certain things are in common: dealing with people, getting on with them, sociability of approach and so on. I hope I may begin as an assistant trainee manager. That's a sort of manager's dogsbody – a jack of all trades who can take over in any supervisory or management function if someone's off duty.'

[Student, HCIMA conversion course, Queen Margaret College]

Edinbrugh University
Entry concessions possible for students aged over 21 by 1 October in the year in which they begin their degree course. The normal minimum level of attainment will be recent passes at the Higher Grade in three subjects or GCE A-levels in two subjects. Alternatives are two full credits at OU Foundation level, or diplomas such as those from Newbattle Abbey College (adult residential college diplomas). There is also Exceptional Admissions Procedure for students without the normal type of examination pass but

with some evidence of appropriate achievement in a related professional field, or other evidence of intellectual promise. Candidates complete a special application form and, if considered for the Procedure, spend a day at the university where they tackle two tests of academic aptitude, write two essays (one on a general topic, one on a topic relating to the individual's area of interest), and undergo an interview. *Part-Time Degrees*: Faculty of Arts, MA (General); Faculty of Divinity, BD, BD (Hons); BA Religious Studies and MA Religious Studies; Faculty of Music, BMus/BMus (Hons); Faculty of Social Sciences, BSc (Social Sciences).

Glasgow College

Entry concessions possible for students aged 25 and over (entry by interview). *Part-Time Degrees*: BEng (Hons) for candidates with HNC/HND; BA Social Sciences (Economics, Politics, Psychology, Sociology, Geography, History). *Postgraduate Vocational Courses* include: Diploma in Personnel Management, full time – any graduate considered. Diploma in Systems Analysis and Design, full time – mainly for graduates in science or business studies.

Glasgow: University of Strathclyde

Entry concessions possible for students aged 21 and over. Competitive entry standard or General Entrance requirement may be relaxed (less likely in science and engineering). The Faculty of Arts and Social Studies and the Strathclyde Business School run tests for admission for their BA degree courses. The test consists of an unseen essay on a general topic, aptitude tests and interview. There are also preliminary courses (see 'Pre-Entry, Sample and Access Courses'). *Part-Time Degrees*: BA Certificate/Pass degree programme in Economics, English Studies, French, Geography, German, History, Italian, Politics, Psychology, Russian, Sociology, Spanish, Women's Studies; you must take at least two subjects plus other selected classes or three full subjects to obtain a BA Pass degree. *Postgraduate Vocational Courses* include: Legal Practice, Accounting and Finance, Librarianship, Personnel Management etc. (See also 'Open and Distance Learning Courses' for details of MBA.)

Paisley College of Technology

Entry concessions possible for mature students (age unspecified) 'who, though lacking conventional entrance qualifications, have over the years shown an interest in their educational advancement and an aptitude for academic study.' *Postgraduate Vocational Courses*: Postgraduate Diploma in Information Technology, full time conversion course – any graduate considered (with introductory courses for those whose degrees did not include courses in Maths, Physics and Programming); Postgraduate Diploma in Computer-Aided Engineering, full time or part time through Module Credit accumulation – for engineering and science graduates or those with equivalent experience in a relevant industry.

St Andrews University

Entry concessions possible for students aged 21 and over by October of year of entry. The general entrance requirement may be waived, but current evidence of ability to perform well in public examinations is required.

The following colleges in this region supplied information in 1987 about their degree and advanced courses, but no response was received to 1988 enquiries. Readers may nevertheless wish to make individual contact:

Aberdeen: Robert Gordon's Institute of Technology
Aberdeen University
Belfast: Queen's University
Dalkeith: Newbattle Abbey College
Glasgow: Queen's College
Glasgow University
Hamilton: Bell College of Technology
Stirling University

GENERAL INFORMATION

Costs and grants, sources of information and useful addresses

Cost and Grants

Dipping into the financial side of retraining is like trying to drive from Plymouth to Perth without a map. You might get to your objective by following up likely-looking signs, or you might lose yourself completely. Grants and awards are hedged about with so many conditions and regulations that it's living dangerously even to attempt to give figures. Yet there's nothing more irritating than to find a course that really appeals to you, and then find you have no idea of what it might cost because a book doesn't mention the delicate subject of money.

I'm therefore going to live dangerously in this section of the book: quoting the information I've gathered from material sent to me by both educational establishments and government departments – and knowing full well that all the figures could change because of some new regulation within a week of this book appearing in the shops. On the other hand, I feel it's better to know whether something's likely to cost you £20 or £200 or £2000 - and to get some idea, too, of whether you might get any grant.

College prospectuses can only give you an approximate idea of charges because they have to be printed before fees are agreed for the year they are covering. Therefore in giving 'sample fees' and 'typical awards' in this last section of the book, I must emphasise that they're only a guide. Rates of grant and benefit alter every year too. The ones I have quoted are those I found in1988 prospectuses, but, as I said, use them just as a guide to give some idea of what's on offer and what it might cost.

The Department of Health and Social Security can supply you with the latest leaflets on benefits. The Department of Education and Science can supply you with the latest booklets on grants. Your Jobcentre will have details of any training allowances payable for full-time courses, and colleges themselves can tell you how much might be offered on a full-time European Social Fund course.

In matters of finance, you lose nothing by asking. The worst thing that can happen is that people will say, 'No, sorry, nothing is available that suits your situation.' The best is that they might discover that, say, by slightly altering the hours of your attendance at college, you can move yourself into the category covered by the 21-hour rule regulation (explained in the second half of this section, headed 'Grants and Concessions'); or that because you were born in Little Wychwood, you're eligible for a special award only open to residents of that town who are over 30 and retraining. This kind of offer can sometimes be found tucked away at the back of prospectuses. Check the index in each prospectus for 'awards', 'scholarships', 'bursaries'.

Meanwhile, some sample costs. Please remember that costs usually increase a little each year, so you're unlikely to find yourself paying the same at the end of a three-year course as you did at the beginning!

ACCESS AND SIMILAR PRE-DEGREE COURSES

Most local authorities will consider giving discretionary grants to cover the costs of full-time Access courses. In some cases, they will also give students a maintenance allowance. However, when the courses are part-time, you may have to pay fees. For example, the Fresh Start part-time course at the West London Institute of Higher Education (two evenings a week for one year) costs £72 and there is an additional assessment fee of £15.

The ILEA Access course guide for 1988-89 points out that students on part-time Access courses who are not eligible for grants are eligible for substantially reduced fees. They could pay as little as £3 if they are in receipt of unemployment or DHSS benefits or are getting the state retirement pension.

ADULT RESIDENTIAL COLLEGE

Bursaries are normally available to cover tuition and maintenance. Whichever of the adult residential colleges you want to attend, you should make enquiries about bursaries by writing to the Awards Officer, Adult Education Bursaries, c/o Ruskin College, Oxford OX1 2HE.

ASSOCIATE STUDENTSHIP

This is a unit-based learning scheme. Coventry Polytechnic quoted £18 for a year's study of one hour a week per unit. North Staffordshire Polytechnic quoted £37.80 for a year's study of one unit up to two hours per week. Pensioners and registered unemployed people may have their fees waived.

GCE A-LEVELS

Evening A-level courses at Cambridgeshire College of Arts and Technology are charged at £27 a year for one evening a week or £53 a year for two evenings a week.

WIDER OPPORTUNITIES

MSC-sponsored course, normally free.

BTEC NATIONAL DIPLOMA

Some authorities may give a small discretionary grant to help with fees. Brunel Technical College in Bristol quoted £370 a year for the two-year BTEC

National Diploma in Hotel, Catering and Institutional Operations, plus BTEC Registration fee. National Certificates are often on a part-time day release basis for students permitted by their employers to have time off to study for qualifications. Often the employers will pay fees. For anyone who has to finance themselves, taking the BTEC National Certificate in Science (Pharmaceutical Science) as an example, fees at Cambridge College of Arts and Technology would be £107 a year for one day a week for the first year, and £120 a year for one day a week for the second year, plus BTEC Registration fee.

BTEC HIGHER NATIONAL DIPLOMA

Courses usually attract mandatory grant, just like degree courses. But if you have already had a grant for an HND, a degree or a similar-level course, you may have to pay your own way. For the BTEC HND in Computer Studies offered at the West London Institute of Higher Education, the fee would be £565 a year for the two-year full-time course, plus the BTEC Registration fee. If you took a part-time BTEC HNC in Business Studies at Sunderland Polytechnic, it would cost you £107.20 for each year of the two-year course, which involves one day a week at the Polytechnic plus one residential weekend, and the usual BTEC Registration fee would be payable. (At the time of writing, prospectuses are quoting this at £48, in case you've been wondering).

PROFESSIONAL INSTITUTE MEMBERSHIP

Fees vary, but St. Helen's College School of Management Studies quotes £145 a year for preparation for the Institute of Personnel Management Stage I examinations by evening and distance-learning methods. Cambridgeshire College of Arts and Technology quotes £165 a year for preparation for the Royal Institution of Chartered Surveyors' Diploma in Surveying, offered by day release (one day and one evening) over five terms.

BRITISH AIRWAYS APPROVED BASIC AIRLINE COURSE

Distance-learning £64.50. Five-day intensive tutored course £178.25.

CIVIL AVIATION AUTHORITY APPROVED COURSES

At Brunel Technical College, Bristol, the two and one-third years Aircraft Maintenance Engineering Licence course, covering Airframes and Engines and approved by the CAA, costs £370 a year for the first year and £560 a year subsequently.

TOUR MANAGEMENT TRAINING (EUROPE)

Thirty three-hour lectures, evenings and occasional Saturdays, leading to City and Guilds Certificate, £205.

DEGREES – EVENING

Birkbeck College (University of London) quoted two scales of fees. The first is for students who are personally responsible for meeting the cost of their fees. This would be approximately £280 a year. Students whose fees are paid by sponsoring bodies, such as local education authorities or employers, would be charged £417 a year. This applies to all BA and BSc degrees, but the amount of attendance required could vary from two evenings a week to four evenings a week over four years.

DEGREES – PART-TIME

It's unusual to be offered any help from the local education authority with fees on a part-time degree course, as it's assumed you'll be working and earning while you study. As an example of costs, the University of Stirling charges £220 for the first year of the estimated five years it will take to complete the General degree of BA or BSc on a part-time basis, sharing lectures and seminars with full-time students.

DEGREES – FULL-TIME

These usually attract mandatory grant, though if you've already had a grant for an HND, degree or equivalent course, you will probably have to self-finance. The Polytechnic of Central London quotes £556 a year for the usual three-year full-time degree course, though again I have to warn that fees are likely to go up each year. If you are going to have to live away from home, make careful enquiries about costs.

As an example, if you took your degree at a residential university, where the great majority of students live on the campus, then in 1987 you would typically have been charged £1235 for 30 weeks in halls which provide meals, or about £655 in self-catering halls over the same 30 weeks. As a rough guide, the total living expenses of most students amounted to some £2600, and overseas students who had to spend vacations at their university were advised to allow not less than £3100 for each year's living costs (plus fees).

DEGREES/DIPLOMAS – POSTGRADUATE

Grants are hard to get, but ask the university or polytechnic where you want to study if there is an official grant-awarding body to which you can apply, or if there are any bursaries available. Fees are again very variable, but the University of Bradford quoted £1730 for a year's full-time postgraduate study in all Boards of Studies except for the MSc in Pharmacology, quoted at £2162. For the part-time MBA course, extending over 36 months and involving mainly evening attendance, with some short block-release periods, the fee quoted was £930 for the first year, £692 in the second year and £584 in the third year.

SMALL BUSINESS COURSES

Bracknell College quoted £35 per six-hour seminar on Financial Control, Basic Accounting, Book-keeping, Computers in Business or Taxation, but emphasised that these seminars could be free to people who have been in business less than 12 months. The seminars for people who are thinking of starting a business cost £25 each and cover fields like Marketing and Legal Requirements. MSC grants to cover the cost may be available.

RESIDENTIAL BUSINESS COURSES

St. Helen's College quoted £220 for a three-day Effective Salesmanship course and £120 for a three-day Retail Food Management course. Most students are likely to be paid for by their employers, though individuals who want to work in fields for which the College's School of Management Studies provides residential courses may also apply.

GRANTS AND CONCESSIONS

Many of the courses in this book are free to unemployed people or anyone receiving DHSS benefits. To give you examples, courses that are headed Restart or Replan or are MSC-sponsored are likely to be free, and they may attract a training allowance that is more than an individual's normal benefit if full-time. Wider Opportunities and New Opportunities courses may be free, but you must ask the organisers: don't count on it, because both the MSC and individual colleges use these titles for courses provided for people who want information about new directions they can take.

Some colleges like to devise their own titles for schemes that cater for local unemployed people. Thus Hinckley College of Further Education calls its free scheme an 'Alternative Programme'. It's open to anyone eligible under the 21-hour rule.

WHAT IS THE 21-HOUR RULE?

The 21-hour rule states that unemployed people can study/attend training courses for not more than 21 hours a week while continuing to receive benefits. The courses do not have to be job-related: if you want to take a part-time degree in English Literature or learn to play the guitar and you can find a course of suitable hours, you are still eligible. On the other hand, lots of colleges are putting on special job-related courses, often leading to City and Guilds or other highly regarded job qualifications, that fit conveniently into the 21-hour rule regulations.

Claimants of all ages must:

(a) have completed a period of three months availability for work;
(b) be receiving unemployment benefit, income support or family credit *before* commencing their course;
(c) be available for employment – i.e., willing to take a suitable full-time job if one is offered.

There are a number of additional regulations/concessions: for instance, single parents with a dependent child living with them, or severely disabled people who are regarded as unlikely to get employment within the next 12, months do not have to be available for employment in order to get benefits while studying under the 21-hour rule. For exact details, contact your local DHSS office or ask the College Counselling Service.

NB: Most colleges offer a range of ways of studying particular subjects – part-time day, part-time evening, distance learning and so on – so that you can satisfy the DHSS that you will genuinely be 'available for work' if a job is offered. Make sure you can show the DHSS you have found a way to continue any study/training programme you start under the 21-hour rule, should you be offered a job. In many areas, particularly areas noted for high unemployment, special 21-hour programmes have been set up with provision for people to build on to any qualification they get over a number of years. This helps people who take seasonal work when it happens to be offered, for they are still able to go back to studying when their job ends and they're unemployed again.

AND THE 12-HOUR RULE

The 12-hour rule applies during the three-months 'qualifying' period, i.e. the three months of availability for work that have to elapse before people (usually school-leavers) become eligible to study under the 21-hour rule. Apart from the difference in hours at college, the rules are the same, and you can get in quite a substantial amount of study in 12 hours. For instance, you can do one whole day of work with day-release students, where a space on a course allows you to 'infill', or you can have two or three sessions of a part-time degree course.

LEA GRANTS

The LEA is your Local Education Authority, and that means the one governing the place where you were educated, not the place where you happen to be living now. They provide grants that are *mandatory* and others that are *discretionary*.

To be considered for a *mandatory* grant you have to be accepted on a 'designated course' (more about that presently) and not previously have had a grant. To be considered for a *discretionary* grant, you have to meet your local LEA's specific requirements.

'Discretionary', as you can see, means what it says. The grant is at the discretion of the local education authority and whether you get it depends on how much money they have to spend, how many people are applying for it and how much they think you deserve financial help compared with everyone else applying, so it's a bit like being on a housing waiting list. Your suitability for the course and the prospects of work at the end of it are likely to be taken into account.

Don't let the uncertainty of discretionary awards discourage you. After I had been telling people for years that LEA didn't give discretionary grants for

A-levels because, after all, they could be taken at evening classes or by distance learning, one Leicestershire student wrote triumphantly to tell me that she had a mature student's discretionary grant to take three A-levels full-time. Access course students are often sympathetically received if they apply for discretionary grants. A special effort is made to take into account any factors that may have made it difficult for a student to acquire conventional qualifications at the conventional time: students from ethnic minority groups for whom English is a second language, and who might therefore not have known enough English to do themselves justice at school, are one example.

'Mandatory' means that if you are accepted for a designated course, you will get a grant provided you meet the residence requirements and educational requirements, and have not already had a mandatory grant or used up part of one. It's means-tested, which, for adult students (26 or over) means that instead of taking into account your parents' income, they will take into account that of your husband or wife if you have one.

DESIGNATED COURSES

So what is this 'designated course' that I've just mentioned.

A designated course is one that appears in a list issued by the Department of Education and Science and available at local education authority offices. As this book goes to press it is being revised. But basically, a designated course is a full-time or sandwich first-degree course; a full-time or sandwich higher national diploma course; or a high-level professional course, such as Graduateship in Music at one of the famous music colleges. If you look in college prospectuses, they will usually tell you the good news if a course attracts mandatory grant. If they don't say so, start your own investigations.

HOW MUCH?

Rates of mandatory grant are revised each year but as I write the rates quoted are:

free tuition
maintenance (London)£2,246
maintenance (outside London) £1,901
maintenance (living at home) £1,480

There are extra allowances if you are 26 or over before the beginning of the course and have worked for at least three years, earning at least £12,000 in total. The Older Students' Allowance is £215 a year, rising to £740 for students aged 29 or over. Extra payments may be made if you have dependents. *Changes in the amounts for maintenance come into force at the beginning of September each year*. A free booklet; *'Grants to Students'* is available free from the Department of Education and Science, Room 2/11, Elizabeth House, York Road, London SE1 7PH. For Scotland, write to the Scottish Education department, Awards Branch, Haymarket House, Clifton Terrace, Edinburgh EH12 5DT.

MSC TRAINING ALLOWANCES

At one time there were lots of courses under a scheme known as 'TOPS' – the training opportunities scheme. *This has now been discontinued.* Most MSC-sponsored courses are offered under the 21-hour rule.

But some MSC-sponsored courses are still offered full-time. If you are accepted on one of these, you must normally be unemployed or willing to give up your job to take the course in question, have been away from full-time education for at least two years, and be at least 19. You would get any benefits to which you were entitled plus from £10 to £12 per week extra, and allowances for living away from home (if required) and for the care of dependent children.

DHSS BURSARIES

The Department of Health and Social Security may offer bursaries to students accepted on occupational therapy, orthoptics, physiotherapy, radiography, dental hygiene and dental therapy training courses, at roughly the same rates and with the same regulations as for degree course. Details are available from the DHSS, North Fylde Central Office, Norcross, Blackpool, FY5 3TA.

EUROPEAN SOCIAL FUND

Our membership of the EEC means that we are entitled to a share of the funds made available for retraining some categories of unemployed people or women 'returners'. The actual regulations are so complicated that colleges submitting courses for ESF sponsorship usually have at least one person who is an expert on them, and woe betide any college which loses its expert. However, if the description 'ESF-sponsored' appears in front of a course, it normally means that it is free, with travel costs paid where necessary and *possibly* a training allowance.

ANY OTHER POSSIBILITIES?

Ex-service personnel may be able to obtain financial help with retraining. Charities sometimes have funds available to help people train for new careers – for instance, MENCAP funded the first students on the Further Education and Training of Mentally Handicapped People scheme. Grants or bursaries may be available from groups concerned with special interests – for example, the Arts Council offers various bursaries for students in the music, art, film-making and similar fields. You should find that the college you apply to has knowledge of opportunities of this kind: they tend to keep records of organisations which have helped to fund students in the past. Scholarships and bursaries may be 'closed' – that is to say, open only to people who have attended certain schools,or belonged to certain trades unions, or are the sons or daughters of people in particular occupations. When you're looking through prospectuses, always look up scholarships. The talent that wins you an extra £100 a year to spend on train fares could well have nothing to do with your course (e.g., you may get a music bursary though you're a chemistry student), but it's none the less valuable for that.

Sometimes there are special awards to attract people to particular courses: for instance, the University of Salford has competitive scholarships for women who want to study engineering, and there are 'enhanced' DES grants for people retraining in the shortage teaching areas of maths, physics, and craft, design and technology. Many libraries keep the reference books *'Charities Digest'*, published by the Family Welfare Association, and *'Directory of Grant-Making Trusts'*, published by the Charities Aid Foundation. You may find a philanthropic organisation offering an award for which you are eligible – it might only be a small sum, but if it covers your books it'll be a great help.

People threatened by redundancy may find that their professional association or trade union has funds for helping people who are retraining. The MSC has Career Development Loans, offered, in association with banks, to people living (or intending to train) in Aberdeen, Bristol/Bath, Greater Manchester or Reading/Slough. The three-year pilot scheme has been running since April 1986 and is being extended nationally.

Some students have told me they financed their own studies with the help of bank overdrafts or loans. There are some formal schemes, such as the Midland Bank's loan scheme for certain business studies and accountancy courses, and the National Wetminster Bank's scheme to help medical students with the cost of necessary books. If your bank doesn't offer any kind of loan scheme for study, they may be able to advise you on government finance sources, such as the Enterprise Allowance scheme for people setting up new small businesses.

In conclusion, the Citizens Advice Bureau (address of the nearest one in your local phone directory) can usually advise on grants, allowances, awards and concessions. When the person on the spot doesn't know, then, given time, authorities will be contacted who *will* know if there are any sources of funds you haven't tried for a scholarship or a bursary. When you think you have found out as much as you can for yourself, double-check with the CAB. Because their information service is so regularly updated, they are often the first to know of new awards or concessions being made available nationally or for special groups.

Information Sources

Throughout *Make A Fresh Start*, whenever it's seemed useful, I have directed readers to books, but listing *all* possible sources of extra information each time might have been confusing. Therefore I have compiled this list of information sources that you can tap into to extend your knowledge in the areas that tie in with your own plans.

SOURCES OF IDEAS

Always ask the library if they have *the latest edition* of a book: it's really important in the education and careers field, where changes can be rapid.

Careers A-Z(Collins). Quick-reference, easy-to-read paperback based on answers to Daily Telegraph Careers Information Service readers; hence concise explanations of job content, course choices and acronyms like AGCAS, BTEC, COIC.

Equal Opportunities(Penguin). Careers guide which grew out of *'Careers for Girls'*, so very strong on opportunities for women, and on 'late start' opportunities and age limits. Good, clear job descriptions – valuable if you don't know what a quantity surveyor or legal executive might do all day.

Careers Encyclopaedia(Cassell). Close-packed pages of detailed information on every conceivable job from archivist to zoo-keeper. Strongly recommended for useful forecasts of demand in occupations (you can avoid jobs likely to be overtaken by technology). Also helps you track down courses, naming colleges.

Careers In ... series (Kogan Page). Separate careers booklets on every occupation you might have considered, from Alternative Medicine to Careers in Crafts (two of my favourites as they include unusual occupations). Very useful preliminary reading when you're trying to decide between retraining courses.

Working In ... series (COIC). Separate, illustrated, magazine-style booklets on occupational areas, rather than separate jobs – for instance: *Work with Animals, Farms and Forests, The Boating Industry*. Personal case-histories are augmented by very good information source lists.

SOURCES OF COURSES

Residential Short Courses (National Institute of Adult Continuing Education). Lists weekend and one-week study courses that could let you sample a new skill before you commit yourself to training for it – cookery, furniture restoration, bookbinding, photography, foreign languages, writing etc. Two issues a year (summer and winter courses), £1.15 including postage, from NIACE, 19b De Montfort Street, Leicester LE1 7GE.

A survey of Access courses in England (University of Lancaster). Will explain access concept in detail and help you decide if it is the right route for you to take – and where.

Educational Credit Transfer Gives details of concessions in entry requirements or course content allowed by certain universities, polytechnics and professional organisations to mature students of diferent kinds. Compiled from the ECCTIS database at the Open University. (Try your library; if they don't have a copy, ask them to redirect you to the Educational Guidance Service, or, if there isn't one, to the Careers Service Office.)

Second Chances (COIC). Excellent source book of factual information on everything from YTS scheme to courses for retired people; includes personal development courses, leisure courses and learning through radio and TV as well as all the sorts of career change course listed here.

Directory of Further Education (CRAC/Hobsons). Extensive coverage of courses in local authority sector nationwide. Very useful for anyone who wants to track down a particular subject, be it fashion writing or sports studies, and who's willing to go to where the course is offered. Includes some independent colleges.

Directory of Independent Training and Tutorial Organisations (Careers Consultants). Extensive coverage of courses in the private sector, including unusual options like training to be a butler, male model or aromatherapist. Ideal for people looking for courses to match specific needs – 'crash' courses, distance learning, residential training, etc.

University Entrance – The Official Guide (Sheed and Ward). Will tell you where you can take a university degree in anything from Acountancy to Avionics or Victorian Studies to Virology. Mainly for young applicants but useful reference also for mature entrants. Cross-refer to *The Student Book* and *Degree Course Offers* (see below).

Polytechnic Courses Handbook (Committee of Directors of Polytechnics). Lists full-time, sandwich degree, HND and other advanced courses in polytechnics. Use with free *Directory of First Degree and Higher Diploma Courses* (includes *part-time* courses) available from the Council for National Academic Awards, 344 Gray's Inn Road, London, WC1X 8BP and *Survey of Polytechnic Degree Courses*(Careers Consultants). The latter has useful information about attitudes to mature students, ratio of male to female students, what sorts of jobs with which employers past graduates have achieved.

The Student Book (Papermac). Lively university, polytechnic, college descriptions to give you the 'feel' of individual institutions. Highlights courses for which a college is noted, good on social life and on factors that you might find important – e.g., do most students go home at weekends?

Degree Course Offers (Careers Consultants). Another guide primarily aimed at young candidates, but this year with comments about attitudes to mature students. It always has useful comments from authorities, e.g: Psychology, Bristol – Nursing qualifications are acceptable as well as A-levels or equivalent qualiications; Manchester Polytechnic – All suitable applicants are sent a questionnaire and asked to write an essay on their choice of psychology. Selection is based on their answers; Nottingham (and others) – preference is given to local applicants. An innovation this year is to include examples of questions likely to be asked at interview.

British Qualifications (Kogan Page). The book to check if you want to establish which qualifications are recognised nationally. Covers all fields of work including conventional ones like accountancy and engineering as well as the more off-beat activities like musical instrument-making and timber technology.

Working for Yourself (Kogan Page). Full of facts and ideas for self-employment or setting up in business. Not quite the same as *Going Freelance* (Muller), which concentrates on sidelines and ways of earning at home. Together, both very good for people trying to decide *how* to switch from employment to self-employment. Use in conjunction with *Down to Business* (COIC), which is a simple, step-by-step guide to all the tasks you'll be taking on when you decide to go it alone. *Action for Jobs*, free from your local Jobcentre, lists all the schemes set up to help would-be entrepreneurs, including the Enterprise Allowance (that's the one where you get £40 a week for 52 weeks if you meet the MSC's regulations). NB: You'll stand a better chance if you read the books first, and an even better one if you take a short course!

The Yearbook of Recruitment and Employment Services 1987 (Longman). Another big reference book listing all the independent employment agencies in the UK, classified as to location and the types of job(s) each one handles. If you want to talk over the job prospects you might have after taking a course that appeals to you, you could do worse than call in on a placement agency (not at a rush time, like lunch-hour) and get their views.

EDUCATIONAL GUIDANCE SERVICES

For personal, face-to-face advice, local authorities are increasingly making the effort to fund Educational Guidance Services. The extent to which they operate and the times at which they are able to open will really depend on how much money is available in your local authority's kitty, but ask at the public library if your area has an EGS – they'll know the address. Don't forget the help available from Jobcentres and the increasing number of Jobclubs and if you are in any doubt, get an authoritative view of any course from the appropriate trade union or professional institute. Again, the librarian in the reference section of your local public library will be able to help you find the right organisation and the right address.

Addresses

LONDON AND MIDDLESEX

Academy of Travel Management (formerly British Airways College of Marketing), International House, Ealing Broadway Centre, The High Street, London W5 5BD

Birkbeck College, University of London, Malet Street, London WC1E 7HX

British Isles Study Programme, 150 Conway Crescent, Perivale, Greenford, Middx UB6 6JE

Brunel University, Uxbridge, Middx UB8 3PH

Camden Training Centre, 57 Pratt Street, London NW1 0DP

Central London Polytechnic, 309 Regent Street, London W1R 8AL

Chelsea School of Art, Manresa Road, London SW3 6LS

City and East London College, Pitfield Street, London N1 6BX

Central London Adult Education Institute (formerly the City Lit), Stukeley Street, Drury Lane, London WC2B 5LJ

City University, Northampton Square, London EC1V 0HB

College for the Distributive Trades, 30 Leicester Square, London WC2H 7LE

Cordwainers Technical College, Mare Street, Hackney, London E8 3RE

London College of Fashion, John Princes Street, London W1M 9HE

London College of Printing, Elephant and Castle, London SE1 6SB

London School of Education and Political Science, Houghton Street, London WC2 2AE

Merton Institute of Adult Education, Whatley Avenue, London SW20 9NS

Middlesex Polytechnic, 114 Chase Side, London N14 5PN

Morley College, 61 Westminster Bridge Road, London SE1 7HT

Newham Community College (amalgamation of East Ham and West Ham Colleges), Welfare Road, Stratford, London E15 4HT

North East London Polytechnic, Longbridge Road, Dagenham, Essex, RM8 2AS

North London Polytechnic, Holloway, London N7 8DB

Paddington College, 25 Paddington Green, London W2 1NB

Pitman Central College, 154 Southampton Row, London WC1B 5AX

Queen Mary College, University of London, Mile End Road, London E1 4NS

Richmond Adult and Community College, Clifton Road Centre, Clifton Road, Twickenham TW1 4LT

Royal Holloway and Bedford New College, University of London, Egham Hill, Egham, Surrey TW20 0EX

St Mary's College, Strawberry Hill, Twickenham, Middx TW1 4SX

South Bank Polytechnic, Borough Road, London SE1 0AA

South East London College, Breakspeare Road, Lewisham Way, London SE4 1UT

South London College, Knights Hill, London SE27 0TX

South West London College, Tooting Broadway, London SW17 0TQ

Thames Polytechnic, Wellington Street, London SE18 6PF

Tour Management Training Centre, 85 St George's Square Mews, London SW1V 3RZ

University of London, Senate House, Malet Street, London WC1

University College, University of London Gower Street, London WC1E 6BT

Uxbridge Technical College, Park Road, Uxbridge, Middx UB8 1NQ

Vauxhall College of Building and Further Education, Belmore Street, Wandsworth Road, London SW8 2JY

West London Institute of Higher Education, 300 St Margaret's Road, Twickenham, Middx TW1 1PT

Westminster College, Battersea Park Road, London SW11 4JR

Willesden College of Technology, Denzil Road, London NW10 2XD

The following colleges in the region supplied information in 1987 but did not confirm it in 1988:

Brixton College, 50 Brixton Hill, London SW2 1QS
City of London Polytechnic, 31 Jewry Street, London EC3N 2EY
Ealing College of Higher Education, St Mary's Road, Ealing W5 5RF
Goldsmiths' College, Lewisham Way, New Cross, London SE14 6NW
Hackney College, 89-115 Mare Street, London E8 4RG
Hammersmith and West London College, Gliddon Road, Barons Court, London W14 9BL
Harrow College of Higher Education, Watford Road, Northwick Park, Harrow HA1 3TP
Imperial College of Science and Technology, South Kensington, London SW7 2AZ
Kings College London, Strand, London WC2 2LS
Kingsway College, Sidmouth Street, Gray's Inn Road, London WC1H 8JB
Tottenham College of Technology, High Road, Tottenham N15 4RU

SOUTHERN AND EASTERN ENGLAND

Aylesbury College, Oxford Road, Aylesbury, Bucks HP21 8PD

Basildon College of Further Education, Nethermayne, Basildon, Essex SS16 5NN

Basingstoke Technical College, Worthing Road, Basingstoke, Hants RG21 1TN

Bedford College of Higher Education, Polhill Avenue, Bedford MK41 9EA

Bracknell College, Church Road, Bracknell, Berkshire RG12 1DJ

Brighton Polytechnic, Moulescoomb, Brighton, East Sussex BN2 4AT

Brighton: University of Sussex, Sussex House, Falmer, Brighton BN1 9QN

Bromley College of Technology, Rookery Lane, Bromley Common, Kent BR2 8HE

Cambridge College of Further Education, Newmarket Road, Cambridge CB5 8EG

Cambridge University, Cambridge Intercollegiate Applications Office, Kellet Lodge, Tennis Court Road, Cambridge CB2 1QJ

Cambridgeshire College of Arts and Technology, East Road, Cambridge CB1 1PT

Canterbury: Christ Church College, North Holmes Road, Canterbury CT1 1QU

Canterbury College of Art – see Kent College of Art

Canterbury College of Technology, New Dover Road, Canterbury, Kent CT1 3AJ

Canterbury: University of Kent at Canterbury, Canterbury, Kent CT2 7NX

Chatham: Mid Kent College of Further and Higher Education, Horsted, Maidstone Road, Chatham, Kent ME5 9QU

Chichester College of Technology, Westgate Fields, Chichester, West Sussex PO19 1SB

Chichester: West Dean College, (indepentent college), Chichester, West Sussex

Chichester: West Sussex Institute of Higher Education, College Lane, Chichester, West Sussex, PO19 4PE

Colchester Institute, Sheepen Road, Colchester, Essex CO3 3JL

Colchester: The University of Essex, Wivenhoe Park, Colchester CO43 3SQ

Crawley College of Technology, College Road, Crawley, West Sussex RH10 1NR

Croydon College, Fairfield, Croydon CR9 1DX

Eastleigh College of Further Education, Chestnut Avenue, Eastleigh, Hants SO5 5HT

Egham: Royal Holloway and Bedford New College, Egham Hill, Egham, Surrey TW20 0EX

Epsom: North East Surrey College of Technology, Reigate Road, Epsom, Ewell, Surrey KT17 3DS

Guildford College of Technology, Stoke Park, Guildford GU1 1EZ

Guildford: University of Surrey, Guildford, Surrey GU2 5XH

Hatfield Polytechnic, PO Box lO9, Hatfield, Herts

Havering Technical College, Ardleigh Green Road, Hornchurch, Essex RM11 2LL

Hemel Hempstead: Dacorum College, Marlowes, Hemel Hempstead, Herts HP1 1HD

High Wycombe: Buckinghamshire College of Higher Education, Queen Alexandra Road, High Wycombe, Bucks HP11 2JZ

Ipswich: Suffolk College of Higher and Further Education, Rope Walk, Ipswich, Suffolk IP4 1LT

Kent College of Art and Design (Amalgamation of Canterbury College of Art, Maidstone College of Art and Medway College of Design), New Dover Road, Canterbury, Kent CT1 3AN

Kingston Polytechnic, Penrhyn Road, Kingston Hill, Kingston-upon-Thames, Surrey KT2 7LB

King's Lynn: Norfolk College of Arts and Technology, Tennyson Avenue, King's Lynn, Norfolk PE30 2QW

Luton College of Higher Education, Park Square, Luton, Beds LU1 3JU

Milton Keynes: The Open University, Walton Hall, Milton Keynes, MK7 6AA

Morden: Merton College, Morden Park, London Road, Morden, Surrey SM4 5QX

Mendlesham: RTT Training Services Ltd (independent college), Mendlesham Training Centre, Norwich Road, Mendlesham, Stowmarket, Suffolk IP14 5ND

Newbury College, Oxford Road, Newbury, Berkshire RG13 1PQ

Norwich City College of Further and Higher Education, Ipswich Road, Norwich NR2 2LJ

Norwich: The University of East Anglia, Norwich NR4 7JT

Portsmouth College of Art, Design and Further Education, Winston Churchill Avenue, Portsmouth PO1 2DJ

Portsmouth Health Authority: Portsmouth and District School of Nursing, Queen Alexandra Hospital, Cosham, Portsmouth PO6 3LY

Portsmouth: Highbury College of Technology, Cosham, Portsmouth PO6 2SA

Portsmouth Polytechnic, Museum Road, Portsmouth PO1 2QQ

Reading: Bulmershe College of Higher Education, Woodlands, Earley, Reading, Berks RG6 1HY

Reading University, Whiteknights, Reading, Berkshire RG6 8AH

St Albans College of Further Education, 29 Hatfield Road, St Albans, Herts AL1 3RJ

St Albans: Hertfordshire College of Art and Design, Hatfield Road, St Albans, Herts

St Albans: Hertfordshire College of Building, Hatfield Road, St Albans, Herts

Slough: Langley College of Further Education, Station Road, Langley, Slough, Berkshire SL3 8BY

Southampton Institute of Higher Education, East Park Terrace, Southampton SO9 4WW

Southampton Technical College, St Mary Street, Southampton SO9 4WX

Southampton University, Southampton SO9 5NH

Southend College of Technology, Caernarvon Road, Southend-on-Sea, Essex SS2 6LS

Stevenage College, Monkswood Way, Stevenage, Herts SG1 1LA

Surbiton: Hillcroft Adult College, Surbiton, Surrey KT6 6DF

Sutton College of Liberal Arts, St Nicholas Way, Sutton, Surrey SM1 1EA

Watford College, Watford, Herts WD1 2NN

Watford: Cassio College, Langley Road, Watford, Herts WD1 3RH

Welwyn Garden City: De Havilland College, The Campus, Welwyn Garden City, Herts AL8 6AH

Wimbledon School of Art, Merton Hall Road, Wimbledon SW19 4QA

Winchester: King Alfred's Collge, Sparkford Road, Winchester, Hants SO22 4NR

The following colleges in the region supplied information in 1987 but did not confirm it in 1988:

Brighton College of Technology, Pelham Street, Brighton, East Sussex BN1 4FA
Chelmsford: Essex Institute of Higher Education, Victoria Road South, Chelmsford, Essex CM1 1LL
Farnborough College of Technology, Boundary Road, Farnborough, Hants GU14 6SB
Folkestone: South Kent College of Technology (also at Ashford and Dover), The Grange, Shornecliffe Road, Folkestone, Kent
Luton: Barnfield College, New Bedford Road, Luton, Beds LU3 2AX
Orpington College of Further Education, The Walnuts, High Street, Orpington, Kent
Thurrock Technical College, Woodview, Grays, Essex RM16 4YR
Waltham Forest College, Forest Road, London E17 4JB
Winchester School of Art, Park Avenue, Winchester, Hants SO23 8DL
Worthing: Northbrook College of Design and Technology, Broadwater Road, Worthing, West Sussex BN14 8HJ

CENTRAL ENGLAND

Abingdon College of Further Education, Northcourt Road, Abingdon, Oxfordshire OX14 1NA

Abingdon: The Open College, Freepost, PO Box 35, Abingdon, OX14 3BR

Birmingham: The University of Aston, Gosta Green, Birmingham B4 7ET

Birmingham: Bournville College of Art, Birmingham Polytechnic, Bournville, Birmingham B30 1JX

Birmingham Polytechnic, Perry Barr, Birmingham B42 2SU

Birmingham: Matthew Boulton Technical College, Sherlock Street, Birmingham B5 7DB

Birmingham: Newman and Westhill Colleges, Genners Lane, Bartley Green, Birmingham BT32 3NR

Bridgnorth and South Shropshire College of Further Education, Stourbridge Road, Bridgenorth, Shropshire WV15 6AL

Chesterfield College of Technology and Arts, Infirmary Road, Chesterfield, Derbyshire S41 7NG

Coventry: Henley College, Henley Road, Bell Green, Coventry CV2 1ED

Coventry Polytechnic, Priory Street, Coventry CV1 5FB

Coventry Technical College, Butts, Coventry CV1 3GD

Derby College of Further Education, Wilmorton, Derby DE2 8UG

Derbyshire College of Higher Education, Kedleston Road, Derby DE3 1GB

Dudley College of Technology, The Broadway, Dudley, West Midlands DY1 4AS

Hinckley College of Further Education, London Road, Hinckley, Leicestershire LE10 1HQ

Keele University, Staffs ST5 4BG

Kettering: Trensham College, St Mary's Road, Kettering, Northamptonshire NN15 7BS

Kidderminster College, Hoo Road, Kidderminster, Worcestershire DY10 1LX

Leamington Spa: Mid Warwickshire College of Further Education, Warwick New Road, Leamington Spa, Warwickshire CV32 5JE

Lichfield College, Cherry Orchard, Lichfield, Staffs WS14 9AN

Loughborough Co-operative College, Stanford Hall, Loughborough, Leicestershire LE12 5QR

Loughborough Technical College, Radmoor, Loughborough, Leicestershire LE1 3BT

Loughborough University of Technology, Loughborough, Leciestershire LE11 3TU

Newcastle-under-Lyme College, Liverpool Road, Newcastle-under-Lyme, Staffs ST5 2DF

Newark Technical College, Chauntry Park, Newark, Nottinghamshire NG24 1PB

Northampton: Nene College, Moulton Park, Northampton NN2 7AL

Nottingham: South Nottinghamshire College of Further Education, Greythorne Drive, West Bridgford, Nottingham NG2 7GA

Oxford: Plater College, Pullens Lane, Headington, Oxford OX3 0DT

Oxford Polytechnic, Gypsy Lane, Headington, Oxford OX3 0BP

Oxford: Ruskin College, Walton Street, Oxford OX1 2HE

Oxford University, Oxford Colleges Admissions Offices, University Offices, Wellington Square, Oxford OX1 2JD

Redditch College, Peakman Street, Redditch, Worcs B98 8DW

Retford: Eaton Hall International, Retford, Nottinghamshire DN22 0PR

Shrewsbury College of Arts and Technology, London Road, Shrewsbury, Shropshire SY2 6PR

Solihull College of Technology, Blossomfield Road, Solihull, West Midlands B91 1SB

Stafford College of Further Education, Earl Street, Stafford, ST16 2QR

Stoke-on-Trent Technical College, Moorland Road, Burslem, Stoke-on-Trent, Staffs ST6 1JJ

Stoke-on-Trent: Cauldon College of Further and Higher Education, Stoke Road, Shelton, Stoke-on-Trent, Staffs ST4 2DG

Stoke-on-Trent: North Staffordshire Polytechnic, College Road, Stoke-on-Trent, Staffs ST4 2DE

Stourbridge College of Technology and Art, Hagley Road, Stourbridge, West Midlands DY9 1LY

Stratford-upon-Avon: South Warwickshire College of Further Education, The Willows, Alcester Road, Stratford-upon-Avon, Warwickshire CV37 9QR

Sutton Coldfield College of Further Education, Lichfield Road, Sutton Coldfield, West Midlands B74 2NW

Tamworth College of Further Education, Upper Guingate, Tamworth B79 8AE

Thame: Rycotewood College, Priest End, Thame, Oxfordshire OX9 2AF

Walsall: West Midlands College of Higher Education, Gorway, Walsall, West Midlands WS10 0PE

Warley: Sandwell College (amalgamation of Warley College of Commerce and West Bromwich College of Technology), Woden Road South, Wednesbury, West Midlands WS10 0PE

Warwick University, Coventry CV4 7AL

Wellingborough College, Church Street, Wellingborough, Northants NN8 4PD

Wolverhampton: Bilston Community College, Westfield Road, Wolverhampton, West Midlands WV14 6ER

Wolverhampton Polytechnic, Molineux Street, Wolverhampton WV1 1SB

Wolverhampton: Wulfrun College of Further Education, Paget Road, Wolverhampton, West Midlands WV6 0DU

The following colleges in the region supplied information in 1987 but did not confirm it in 1988:

Banbury: North Oxfordshire Technical College, Broughton Road, Banbury, Oxfordshire OX16 9QA
Birmingham College of Food and Domestic Arts, Summer Row, Birmingham B3 1JB
Birmingham: Fircroft College, 1018 Bristol Road, Selly Oak, Birmingham B29 6LH
Birmingham University, PO Box 363, Birmingham B15 2TT
Bromsgrove: North Worcestershire College, Bromsgrove Worcestershire B60 1PQ
Buxton: High Peak College of Further Education, Harpur Hill, Buxton, Derbyshire SK17 9JZ
Henley-on-Thames: King James's College of Henley, Henley-on-Thames RG9 1TZ
Henley-on-Thames: South Oxfordshire Technical College, Deanfield Avenue, Henley-on-Thames, Oxfordshire RG9 1UH
Herefordshire Technical College, Folly Lane, Hereford HR1 1LT
Leicester: Coalville Technical College, Bridge Road, Coalville, Leicester LE6 2QR
Leicester Polytechnic, PO Box 143, Leicester LE1 9BH
Leicester: The University, Leicester LE1 7RH
Lincolnshire College of Art, Lindum Road, Lincoln LN2 1NP
Loughborough College of Art and Design, Radmoor, Leicestershire
Nottingham: Basford Hall College of Further Education, Stockhill Lane, Notttingham NG6 0NB
Nottingham: Trent Polytechnic, Burton Street, Nottingham NG1 4BU
Nottingham University, University Park, Nottingham NG7 2RD
Nuneaton: North Warwickshire College of Technology and Art, Hinckley Road, Nuneaton, Warwickshire CV11 6BH
Telford College of Arts and Technology, Haybridge Road, Wellington, Telford, Shropshire TF1 2NP
Witney: West Oxfordshire Technical College, Holloway Road, Witney, Oxfordshire OX8 7EE

NORTHERN ENGLAND

Altrincham: South Trafford College of Further Education, Manchester Road, West Timperley, Altrincham, Cheshire WA14 5PQ

Ashington: Northumberland Technical College, College Road, Ashington, Northumberland NE26 9RG

Ashton-under-Lyme: Tameside College of Technology, Beaufort Road, Ashton-under-Lyme, Tameside, Greater Manchester OL6 6NX

Barrow-in-Furness College of Further Education, Howard Street, Barrow-in-Furness, Cumbria LA14 1NB

Blackburn College, Fielden Street, Blackburn BB2 1LH

Bolton Institute of Higher Education, Deane Road, Bolton BL3 5AB

Bradford and Ilkley Community College, Great Horton Road, Bradford, West Yorkshire BD6 1AY

Bradford University, Bradford, West Yorkshire BD7 1DP

Bridlington: East Yorkshire College of Further Education, West Street, Bridlington, North Humberside YO15 3EA

Burnley College, Shorey Bank, Ormerod Road, Burnley BB11 2RX

Consett: Derwentside Tertiary College, Park Road, Consett, DH8 5EE

Dewsbury College, Halifax Road, Dewsbury, West Yorkshire WF13 2AS

Durham: New College, Framwellgate Moor Centre, Durham DH1 5ES

Durham University, Old Shire Hall, Durham DH 3HP

Gateshead Technical College, Durham Road, Gateshead, Tyne and Wear NE9 5BN

Halifax: Percival Whitley College of Further Education, Francis Street, Halifax, West Yorkshire HX1 3UZ

Huddersfield Polytechnic, Queensgate, Huddersfield, West Yorkshire HD1 3DH

Humberside College of Higher Education, Cottingham Road, Hull, North Humberside HU6 7RT

Lancaster College of Adult Education, St Leonard's House, St Leonardgate, Lancaster LA1 1NN

Lancaster: St Martin's College, Lancaster LA1 3JD

Lancaster University, Lancaster LA1 4YW

Leeds: Jocob Kramer College, Vernon Street, Leeds LS2 8PH

Leeds: Park Lance College of Further Education, Park Lane, Leeds LS3 1AA

Leeds Polytechnic, Adult Training Unit, 22 Queen Square, Leeds LS2 8AF

Leeds: Trinity and All Saints College, Brownberrie Lane, Horsforth, Leeds LS18 5HD

Liverpool Institute of Higher Education, PO Box 6, Stand Park Road, Liverpool L16 9JD

Liverpool: South Mersey College, Childwall Abbey Road, Liverpool L16 0JP

Liverpool Polytechnic, 7O Mount Pleasant, Liverpool L3 5UX

Liverpool University, PO Box 147, Liverpool L69 3BX

Manchester Polytechnic, All Saints, Manchester M13 9PL

Manchester University, Extra-Mural Department, Oxford Road, Manchester M13 3PL

Manchester: University of Manchester Institute of Science and Technology (UMIST), PO Box 88, Sackville Street, Manchester M60 1QD

South Manchester Community College, Barlow Moor Road, West Didsbury, Manchester M20 8PQ

Manchester: Withington Centre for Community Education, 3 Mauldeth Road, Withington, Manchester M20 9NE

Middlesbrough: Longlands College of Further Education, Douglas Street, Middlesborough, Cleveland TS3 2JW

Middlesbrough: Teesside Polytechnic, Brough Road, Middlesbrough, Cleveland TS1 3BA

Newcastle-upon-Tyne Polytechnic, Ellison Building, Ellison Place, Newcastle-upon-Tyne NE1 8ST

Ormskirk: Edge Hill College of Higher Education, St Helen's Road, Ormskirk, Lancs L39 4QP

Peterlee College, Peterlee, Co. Durham SR8 1NU

Preston: Lancashire Polytechnic, Preston PR1 2TQ

Rotherham College of Arts and Technology, Eastwood Lane, Rotherham, South Yorkshire S65 1EG

Rotherham: Rockingham College of Further Education, West Street, Wath-upon-Dearne, Rotherham, South Yorkshire S63 6PX

St Helen's College, School of Management Studies, Water Street, St Helen's, Merseyside WA10 1PZ

Salford College of Technology, Frederick Road, Salford, Lancs M6 6PU

Salford University, Salford M5 4WT

Sheffield Polytechnic, Pond Street, Sheffield, S1 1WB

Sheffield: Rother Valley College of Further Education, Doe Quarry Lane, Dinnington, Sheffield S31 7NH

Sheffield: Shirecliffe College, Shirecliffe Road, Sheffield S5 8XZ

Shipley College, Exhibition Road, Shipley, West Yorkshire BD18 3JW

Southport College of Arts and Technology, Mornington Road, Southport, Merseyside PR9 0TT

Sunderland Polytechnic, Langham Tower, Ryhope Road, Sunderland SR2 7EE

Wakefield: Bretton Hall College, West Bretton, Wakefield, West Yorkshire WF4 4LG

Warrington: North Cheshire College, Padgate Campus, Fearnhead, Warrington WA2 0DB

Wigan College of Technology (TRACE Ltd), Parsons Walk, Wigan, Lancs WN1 1RR

York: College of Ripon and York St John, Lord Mayor's Walk, York YO3 7EX

The following colleges in the region supplied information in 1987 but did not confirm it in 1988:

Barnsley College of Technology, Church Street, Barnsley, South Yorkshire S7 2AX
Barnsley: East Barnsley Community Education Unit, Community Education Centre, Barnsley Road, Wombwell, Barnsley, South Yorkshire S73 8HT
Barnsley: Northern College, Wentworth Castle, Stainbrough, Barnsley, South Yorkshire S75 3ET
Blackpool and Fylde College of Further and Higher Education, Ashfield Road, Bispham, Blackpool, Lancs FY2 0HB
Darlington College of Technology, Cleveland Avenue, Darlington, DL3 7BB
Doncaster Metropolitan Institute of Higher Education, Waterdale, Doncaster DN1 3EX
Don Valley Institute of Further Education, Beechfield School, Chequer Road, Doncaster, South Yorkshire, DN1 2AF
Grimsby College of Technology, Nuns Corner, Grimsby, South Humberside DN34 5BQ
Hartlepool College of Further Education, Stockton Street, Hartlepool, Cleveland TS25 7NT
Huddersfield Technical College, New North Road, Huddersfield, HD1 3DH

Leeds: Airedale and Wharfedale College of Further Education, Calverley Lane, Horsforth, Leeds, West Yorkshire
Leeds: Kitson College of Technology, Cookridge Street, Leeds LS2
Leeds University, Leeds L89 9JT
Liverpool: Sandown College (three centres) – details from Mabel Fletcher Centre, Sandown Road, Liverpool L15 4JB
Nelson and Colne College, Scotland Road, Nelson BB9 7YT
Newcastle College of Arts and Technology, Maple Terrace, Newcastle-upon-Tyne NE4 7SA
Newcastle University, 6 Kensington Terrace, Newcastle-upon-Tyne NE1 7RU
Sheffield: Granville College, Granville Road, Sheffield S2 2RL
Sheffield: The University of Sheffield, Western Bank, Sheffield S10 2TN
South Shields: South Tyneside College, St George's Avenue, South Shields, Tyne and Wear NE34 6ET
Stockport College of Technology, Wellington Road South, Stockport, Cheshire SK1 3UQ
Sunderland: Monkwearmouth College of Further Education, Swan Street, Sunderland, Tyne and Wear SR51 lEB
Wakefield District College, Margaret Street, Wakefield, West Yorkshire WF1 2DH
York College of Arts and Technology, Dringhouses, York YO2 1UA
York: Pocklington Institute of Further Education, Kilnwick Road, Pocklington, York YO4 2LL
York University, Heslington, York YO1 5DD

Wales and Western England

Aberystwyth: Ceredigion College of Further Education, Llanbardan Colleges, Llanbardan Fawr, Dyfed SY23 2BP

Barnstaple: North Devon College, Old Sticklepath Hill, Barnstaple, Devon EX31 2BQ

Bath College of Higher Education, Newton Park, Bath, Avon BA2 9BN

Bath: Norton Radstock Technical College, South Hill Park, Radstock, Bath, Avon BR3 3AW

Bath University, Claverton Down, Bath BA2 7AY

Bridgewater College, Bath Road, Bridgwater, Somerset TA6 4PZ

Bristol: Brunel Technical College, Ashley Down, Bristol BS7 9BU

Bristol: Filton Technical College, Filton Avenue, Filton, Bristol BS12 7AT

Bristol Polytechnic, Coldharbour Lane, Frenchay, Bristol BS16 1QY

Cardiff: South Glamorgan Institute of Higher Education, Western Avenue, Llandaff, Cardiff CF5 2YB

Cardiff: The University College of Wales, PO Box 78, Cathay's Park, Cardiff CF1 1XL

Cardiff: University of Wales Institute of Science and Technology (merging with above), PO Box 78, Cathay's Park, Cardiff CF1 1XL

Cheltenham: College of St Paul and St Mary, The Park, Cheltenham, Glos GL50 2RH

Chippenham Technical College, Cocklebury Road, Chippenham, Wilts SN15 3QD

Dolegellu: Meirionnydd College (Coleg Meirionnydd), Dolgellau, Gwynedd LL40 2YF

Exeter College, Hele Road, Exeter, Devon

Exeter University, Northcote House, The Queen's Drive, Exeter EX4 4QJ

Haverfordwest: West Dyfed Small Business Centre – Pembrokeshire College of Further Education, off Dew Street, Haverfordwest, Dyfed SA61 1SZ

Lampeter: St David's University College, Lampeter, Dyfed, SA48 7ED

Llanelli: Carmarthenshire College of Technology and Art, Llanelli Campus, Alban Road, Llanelli SA15 1NG

Plymouth Polytechnic, Drake Circus, Plymouth, Devon PL4 8AA

Pontypridd: Polytechnic of Wales, Llantwit Road, Treforest, Pontypridd, Mid Glamorgan CF37 1DL

Poole: Dorset Institute of Higher Education, Wallisdowne Road, Poole, Dorset

Salisbury College of Technology, Southampton Road, Salisbury, Wilts SP1 2LW

Street: Strode College, Church Road, Street, Somerset BA16 0AB

Swansea: Gorseinon College of Further Education, Belgrave Road, Gorseinon, Swansea, West Glamorgan SA4 2RF

Swansea: University College of Swansea, Singleton Park, Swansea, West Glamorgan SA2

Taunton: Somerset College of Arts and Technology, Wellington Road, Taunton, Somerset TA1 5AX

Tiverton: East Devon College of Further Education, Bolham Road, Tiverton, Devon EX16 6SH

Weymouth College, Cranford Avenue, Weymouth, Dorset DT4 7LQ

The following colleges in this region supplied information in 1987 but did not confirm it in 1988:

Bath Technical College, Avon Street, Bath, Avon BA1 1UP

Cardiff: Rumney College of Technology, Trowbridge Road, Rumney, Cardiff CF3 8XN
Connagh's Quay: North East Wales Institute of Higher Education, Deeside, Connagh's Quay, Clwyd CH5 4BR
Gloucester: Gloucestershire College of Arts and Technology, Oxstalls Lane, Gloucester GL2 9HW
Harlech College (Coleg Harlech), Harlech, Gwynedd LL46 2PU Llandrindod Wells: Radnor College of Further Education, Llandrindod Wells, Powys LD1 5ES
Plymouth: College of St Mark and St John, Plymouth, Devon PL6 8DH
Swansea: West Glamorgan Institute of Higher Education, Mount Pleasant, Swansea, SA1 6ED
Totnes: Dartington College of Arts, Totnes, Devon TQ9 6EJ
Weston-super-Mare College, Knightstone Road, Weston-super-Mare, Avon BS23 2AL
Ystrad Mynach College of Further Education, Twyn Road, Ystrad Mynach, Hengoed, Mid Glamorgan CF8 7XR

Scotland and Northern Ireland

Belfast College of Technology, College Square East, Belfast BT1 6DJ

Belfast: Stranmills College, Stranmills Road, Belfast BT9 5DY

Clydebank College, Kilbowie Road, Clydebank, Dunbartonshire, G81 2AA

Coleraine: University of Ulster, Cromore Road, Coleraine, Co. Londonderry BT52 1SA

Dumfries and Galloway College of Technology, Heathall, Dumfries DG1 3QZ

Duncan of Jordanstone College, Perth Road, Dundee DD1 4HT

Dundee University, Tower Building, Nethergate, Dundee DD1 4HN

Edinburgh: Heriot-Watt University, Riccarton, Edinburgh EH14 4AS

Edinburgh: Napier College, Collinton Road, Edinburgh EH10 5DT

Edinburgh: Queen Margaret College, 36 Clerwood Terrace, Edinburgh EH12 8TS

Edinburgh College of Art, Lauriston Place, Edinburgh EH3 9DF

Edinburgh University, Old College, South Bridge, Edinburgh EH8 9YL

Glasgow College, Cowcaddens Road, Glasgow G4 0BA

Glasgow University, Glasgow G12 8QQ

Glasgow: The University of Strathclyde (Scottish Business School), 16 Richmond Street, Strathclyde, Glasgow G1 1XW

Inverness College of Further and Higher Education, 3 Longman Road, Longman South, Inverness IV1 1SA

Lisburn College of Further Education, Castle Street, Lisburn, Co. Antrim BT27 4SU

Newcastle College of Further Education, Donard Street, Newcastle, Co. Down BT33 0AP

Newry/Kilkeel Continuing Education Programme, Downshire Road, Newry, Co. Down BT34 1EE

Newtownabbey Technical College, Shore Road, Newtownabbey, Co. Antrim BT37 9RS

Paisley College of Technology, High Street, Paisley, Renfrewshire PA1 2BE

St Andrews University, College Gate, St Andrews, Fife KY16 9AJ

The following colleges in the region supplied information in 1987 but did not confirm it in 1988:

Aberdeen University, University Office, Regent Walk, Aberdeen AB9 1FX
Aberdeen College of Commerce, Holburn Street, Aberdeen AB9 7YT
Aberdeen: Robert Gordon's Institute of Technology, Schoolhill, Aberdeen AB9 1FR
Armagh College of Further Education, Lonsdale Street, Lismally Lane, Co. Armagh
Ayr College, Dam Park, Ayr KA8 0EU
Ballymoney: North Antrim College of Further Education, 2 Coleraine Road, Ballymoney, Co. Antrim
Belfast College of Business Studies, Brunswick Street, Belfast BT2 7GX
Belfast: Queen's University, Belfast BT17 1NN
Cumbernauld Technical College, Town Centre, Cumbernauld G67 1HU
Dalkeith: Newbattle Abbey College, Dalkeith, Midlothian EH22 3LL
Down College of Further Education, Market Street, Downpatrick, Co Down BT30 6ND
Edinburgh: Telford College of Further Education, Crewe Toll, Edinburgh EH2 2NZ
Glasgow: The Queen's College, 1 Park Drive, Glasgow G3 6LP
Glasgow: Springburn College, 110 Flemington Street, Glasgow, G21 4BX
Hamilton: Bell College of Technology, Almeda Street, Hamilton, Lanarkshire ML3 0JB
Larne College of Further Education, 32-34 Pound Street, Larne, Co. Antrim BT40 1SQ
Limavady Technical College, Limavaddy, Co. Londonderry BT49 0EX
Lurgan College of Further Education, Kitchen Hill, Lurgan, Co. Armagh BT66 6AZ
Stirling University, Stirling K9 4LA